Music Therapy Supervision

of related interest

Receptive Methods in Music Therapy
Techniques and Clinical Applications for Music Therapy
Clinicians, Educators and Students
Denise Grocke and Tony Wigram
ISBN 978 1 84310 413 1
eISBN 978 1 84642 585 1

Music Therapy Assessment
Theory, Research, and Application
Edited by Stine Lindahl Jacobsen, Eric G. Waldon, and Gustavo Gattino
Foreword by Barbara L. Wheeler
ISBN 978 1 78592 295 4
eISBN 978 1 78450 602 5

MUSIC THERAPY SUPERVISION

Diverse Perspectives on its Cultures and Practices

EDITED BY

Catherine Warner and Ann Sloboda

Jessica Kingsley Publishers
London and Philadelphia

First published in Great Britain in 2025 by Jessica Kingsley Publishers
An imprint of John Murray Press

2

A CIP catalogue record for this title is available from the
British Library and the Library of Congress

ISBN 978 1 78775 923 7
eISBN 978 1 78775 924 4

Printed and bound in the United States by Integrated Books International

Jessica Kingsley Publishers' policy is to use papers that are natural,
renewable and recyclable products and made from wood grown in
sustainable forests. The logging and manufacturing processes are expected
to conform to the environmental regulations of the country of origin.

Jessica Kingsley Publishers
Carmelite House
50 Victoria Embankment
London EC4Y 0DZ

www.jkp.com

John Murray Press
Part of Hodder & Stoughton Ltd
An Hachette Company

The authorised representative in the EEA is Hachette Ireland,
8 Castlecourt Centre, Castleknock Road, Castleknock, Dublin 15, D15 YF6A, Ireland.

This book is dedicated to all supervisees and supervisors of the future.

Contents

Introduction

Supervision is central to therapy; the dialogue between the therapist who wishes to explore their work, and the supervisor. There are surprisingly few books dedicated to the practice of supervision in the creative therapies, and fewer still that focus on the specific modality of music therapy. It is over 15 years since Helen Odell-Miller and Eleanor Richards edited the influential *Supervision in Music Therapy* for Routledge, which explains partly why this new book was commissioned by Elen Griffith of Jessica Kingsley Publishers. Since 2009, many new influences have been brought to bear in music therapy. Together with Michele Forinash's two rich editions of *Music Therapy Supervision* (Forinash 2001, 2019), based in the USA but international in reach, and the revised *Supervision in the Helping Professions* (Hawkins & Shohet 2012), the texts cover a broad range of approaches, good practice and contemporary cultural concerns, and the reader is encouraged to rediscover them while engaging with this text.

It will be clear that many of the invited contributors here refer to the Covid-19 pandemic, as they were writing either during it or in the months that followed the easing of restrictions. The pandemic delayed the book's completion yet gave the opportunity for contemporary reflection on how supervision practice and culture has changed. While we have dedicated the third section of the book to that focus, it is also referenced and reflected on in other chapters. All contributors are music therapists or dramatherapists.

In this book, we aim to balance the supervisee and supervisor's voices; an original idea of Ann's. We wanted to share our experiences of being both supervisees and supervisors. Rather than promoting the idea of the supervisor being all powerful and that the learning is all one way, here, contributors emphasise shared learning processes. We wanted to introduce new voices and to learn from lived experience. Sometimes the supervisee or supervisor is hidden through anonymity, but in many chapters, supervisees identify themselves and talk about their experiences in dialogue with their supervisors. At times this dialogue reflects symmetry within the supervision process. Contributors have offered a range of retrospective accounts, contemporary practices, distinct traditions, innovations, challenges to supervision and experiences of transprofessional supervision in honest, reflexive detail. Some chapters have used a recorded conversation as the basis of the text.

In terms of the editors' professional relationship, when Catherine trained in 1993, Ann was both her placement supervisor and tutor. We are both heads of training; at the University of the West of England (UWE) and the Guildhall School of Music & Drama (GSMD) respectively. Catherine has developed a supervision training module for music therapists at UWE.

This means we have the privilege to hear about a very wide and rich range of current music therapy thinking and practice through trainee experience on placement, offer supervision regularly, and are in a helpful position of being able to encourage the range of voices we include here.

With so many diverse perspectives, it was challenging to find a shape to the book. However, we have decided to follow a developmental schema: the first part focuses on trainee supervision both from the perspective of supervisor and supervisee; the second and third parts introduce new practices and address the sustainability of supervision in different circumstances as a working therapist; the book ends with a fourth part written by contributors who have substantial supervisory experience to draw on.

Collaboration comes about in diverse ways here; through dialogue, through review or through autoethnography to explore creative supervision practices, the discipline of practice, the meaning of supervisory experiences, and the meaning of a life of being a supervisor. There are retrospective accounts, detailed explanations of processes that are handed down as oral tradition, approaches that involve cross-modal and cross-disciplinary practice, and approaches that consider lifespan, memory, trauma and prolonged lived experience.

The contribution across cultures is particularly welcome, including insights into working in São Paulo during the pandemic (Chapter 9). Creative processes within supervision at that time are illustrated with photographs and overlap with other creative arts supervision practice. The contribution of dramatherapy thinking is important.

Music therapy is both quite straightforward to understand (building a relationship between people through music) and yet, as microanalysis of session detail reveals, involves processes of astonishing complexity. The music therapist, through every encounter and every supervision experience, builds knowledge and understanding of these processes that can become implicit and tacit. In some ways, this tacit knowledge can be taken for granted and become invisible to and even 'forgotten' by the therapist. We have often noticed how unconfident people seem to be about their capacity to supervise initially, a view which can be countered through supervision training. Given a space to explore supervision, trainee supervisors discover how much they can draw on within themselves: creatively, empathically and as thinkers. This initial uncertainty is perhaps to do with the traditional 'expert' construction of music therapy supervision, a view that is regularly challenged in this book.

The first part of the book concerns the experience of training supervision.

In Chapter 1, Luke Annesley and Andy Lale begin with a retrospective dialogue about Luke's placement experience with Andy, and how it informed the next 15 years of his music therapy practice. Inspired by Luke's series of podcasts for the British Association for Music Therapy, *Music Therapy Conversations*, Andy and Luke address the commitment of both supervisee and supervisor in facing up to issues of power and vulnerability in acute mental health settings from the outset of supervision, and the importance of this in a formative training placement.

In Chapter 2, Anna Macken openly discusses how she faced the fears brought up when she started placement supervision for the first time and in a new setting. Drawing on creative reading and supervisory texts, her reflexive account also includes reflections from her first supervisees.

In Chapter 3, Nicky Haire introduces a chapter co-created between her as training supervisor and trainees in a group from Queen Margaret University in Scotland. Using an autoethnographically informed approach, which requires critically engaging with self-experience, Nicky and colleagues explain and reflect on the role of improvised music in the training supervision experience, and how this can be sustained when supervision can only take place online.

The second part of the book focuses on diverse cultural aspects of the practice of supervision.

In Chapter 4, Davina Vencatasamy and Michaela Da Cruz address racial aspects of supervision that have felt difficult to broach, including feeling unable to bring concerns around race to the supervisor's attention, and feeling silenced or not sufficiently heard. Through dialogue as peers, they argue for the benefits of using affinity groups as a form of peer supervision, reflecting on how and why these may be a helpful choice for therapists of colour.

In Chapter 5, Oksana Zharinova-Sanderson and Simon Procter explore the oral tradition of Nordoff and Robbins group supervision practice through a case study of training group supervision, vividly outlining the processes and craft of the practice. They bring a spotlight to the skill and judgement needed moment to moment during the supervision process, and an exploration of the importance of courage in supervision.

In Chapter 6, music therapist supervisee Sophie Riga de Spinoza and dramatherapist supervisor Mandy Carr make use of the Seven-Eyed Model of supervision developed by Hawkins and Shohet. They consider creativity in relation to current neuroscience, and using images of their creative supervision process, they illustrate how they addressed aspects of their supervisory relationship through a medium of three-dimensional sculpture and object work.

In Chapter 7, Catherine Warner, Adam Kishtainy and Abigail Williams discuss the origins and future applications of the Ahonen method of group supervision. This makes use of free musical improvisation as a core process to help uncover what lies beneath the surface of music therapy practice examples. Adam discusses the influence of the Balint model of supervision and Abigail explains how it can be developed across other creative modalities.

Part 3 of the book focuses on the use of online supervision practice during the Covid-19 pandemic.

In Chapter 8, music therapy supervisor Maria Radoje and music therapy supervisee Sally Pestell revisit a pre-pandemic publication of theirs about online supervision. They reflect on both how their experience of their working during the pandemic period was changed and how this affected their online supervision at the time.

In Chapter 9, music therapy supervisor Gustavo Gattino and the members of an online supervision group of music therapists working with children in São Paulo discuss how the themes arising from their supervision experience sustained their work, helped address burnout and brought about new decisions to change their practice for the better.

In Chapter 10, Joy Rickwood, Hilary Storer and Catherine Warner explain how they adapted a workshop on the Ahonen supervision method for an online conference, enabling a large-scale embodied group supervision experience involving more than 80 people.

The concluding section of the book involves long-term supervisory narratives and theoretical exploration, with experienced music therapy supervisors, several of whom have engaged in further training as therapists and supervisors.

In Chapter 11, music therapist and psychoanalyst Ann Sloboda and associate professor of music therapy Hilary Moss look back at Hilary's early career supervision with Ann and how it developed her practice.

In Chapter 12, music therapist Robin Wiltshire, from the perspective of a trained psychodynamic supervisor and group analyst in training, presents a theoretical exploration of symmetry in the supervisory relationship, sometimes known as *parallel process* in supervision, based on his work with people with learning disabilities.

In Chapter 13, palliative care music therapist Jane Lings presents her supervisory work with a palliative care medical consultant and their discovery of the value of interdisciplinary supervision of this nature.

In Chapter 14, psychoanalyst and music therapist Julie Sutton reflects and theorises on the idea of being a 'grandparent' supervisor, exploring this through several vignettes.

We hope that this diverse offering of dialogic explorations will inspire the next generation of creative therapy supervisors as much as it has us.

Catherine Warner and Ann Sloboda
January 2024

REFERENCES

Forinash, M. (ed.) (2001) *Music Therapy Supervision*. Gilsum, NH: Barcelona Publishers.

Forinash, M. (ed.) (2019) *Music Therapy Supervision* (second edition). Gilsum, NH: Barcelona Publishers.

Hawkins, P. & Shohet, R. (2012) *Supervision in the Helping Professions* (fourth edition). Maidenhead: McGraw-Hill Education.

Odell-Miller, H. & Richards, E. (eds) (2009) *Supervision of Music Therapy: A Theoretical and Practical Handbook*. London: Routledge.

PART 1

TRAINING SUPERVISION

CHAPTER 1

'The First Cut is the Deepest'

A Conversation Between a Music Therapist and Their First Training Supervisor, 15 Years On

LUKE ANNESLEY AND ANDY LALE

INTRODUCTION BY LUKE ANNESLEY

The idea for this chapter was inspired by the work of Felicity (Fliss) Biacsi. In 2019–20, I supervised Fliss's master's research into music therapists' reflections on their first supervisory experiences in training (Biacsi 2020). I myself had a very positive clinical supervision experience when I was a trainee at the Guildhall School of Music and Drama, embarking on clinical practice for the first time, which continues to influence me today. In supervising Fliss's fascinating research, I found myself reflecting on this. The invitation to contribute a chapter to this book seemed an interesting opportunity to explore it further. Looking over the transcript, not only do I find it interesting to read Andy Lale's insights about our work together, and about supervision in general, but also to observe supervisor–supervisee dynamics being played out on the page. For example, at one point I ask Andy about his first experiences of supervision, but then quickly bring the subject back to myself: I'm the supervisee, after all! In this conversation we revisited some of the key concepts which came up in supervision during my placement with Andy in 2007, such as the importance of centring the client, the potential for the client to make astute observations about the therapist, and the need for reflexivity, to understand our own motivations for training. It's also about the importance of supervision as a two-way process, where, as with therapy, there can be challenge in both directions.

DIALOGUE

Luke: What do you remember about supervising me back in 2006–07?

Andy: I remember you being quite a mature student, both in age and in attitude, quite a serious trainee, and a very accomplished musician. But also having this real interest in psychoanalysis as well, having thought about that a bit already. You were up for examining the psychodynamics of the relationship with the patient, and in those more interesting Kleinian concepts which are quite challenging – things like 'hate is older than love'. We had loads of conversations about the concepts, as well as the technique of music therapy. I can't swear to this, but I might have asked you to play less at times. That was possible.

Luke: You certainly advised me against getting carried away, musically. In fact, I wrote an article, which was published in the *British Journal of Music Therapy* (Annesley 2019), in which I gave an example of your supervision where the client I was working with said, 'You make it sound good', and I probably at the time thought, 'Yes I do!', having found some pretty harmonies to support their improvisation. This was pulled apart, not only by you, but by my clinical seminar leader as well, following on from your supervision. You both warned me about taking the focus away from the client, and perhaps about the allure of positive transference. That was a useful moment. In the article, I explored whether there might be other ways of looking at it, for example that I was musically engaging the client. I was looking at the idea that you don't have to choose between a 'music-centred' and a psychodynamic stance.

Andy: Yes, and I think that's a point well made. I was surprised by one of the senior members of staff where I work, who had been Nordoff Robbins trained, writing a psychosis pathway policy, and stating that 'music therapy could prepare the patient for psychodynamic work', which implied that he was thinking about psychodynamics purely in terms of verbal psychotherapy. This was ignoring a reality, a very important aspect of the unconscious, that themes can be directly presented and negotiated, transmitted and projected, through the musical exchange, as well as underneath the words, through affect, in the verbal discourse. It really surprised me.

Luke: Coming back to our work together, did you have a particular stance towards supervision at that time which you could describe?

Andy: I was with you as a supervisor for quite a long time, I think about six months. We started in January 2007. I'd always had an interest in psychotherapy, right from the word go.

I remember being a 16-year-old kid doing some washing up in the back of a chip shop and trying not to get cut by the large knives, which I had left in the dirty sink water. I remember looking at these big knives and thinking about suicide, in relation to my brother's suicide attempts. I was looking into this dishwasher, and the dangerous knives, thinking about suicide at 16, and wondering, 'Do I want to be a musician, or do I want to be a shrink?' That was the term I used, because it was colloquial language I used with my brother at the time, and I think it's really interesting that I've really tried to synthesise those two things in my life journey, for my own goals.

Even though I hadn't been to the Tavistock Institute in London at that point, and got my psychodynamic stance fully screwed down, I think that, right from the start of training, I was interested in mental health; adult mental health, specifically. I didn't find myself that interested in working with children or older adults with physical conditions. The adult mental health population seemed to me to have the potential for psychological change, and this was of profound interest to me. When you improvise, you can share unconscious material, which can get underneath what a verbal discourse can provide. I was especially interested in that in relation to psychosis.

Luke: I was also very interested in psychodynamic processes, and how they might be playing out through the music. Early on, you said something to me about the 'emptiness' of working in adult mental health. I felt you were disillusioning me quite quickly at that early stage. I probably arrived with a lot of music and was thinking, 'This is going to be exciting', as a keen trainee working with my very first client, or about to. Does that ring a bell?

Andy: It might be true, but I don't remember saying it. People remember different things, don't they? It's interesting, though, because it fits with the possibility that you might have been playing too much or too 'nicely', making it sound 'musical'. On the other hand, I don't think we should deliberately be making our music sound horrible, adopting a fake idea that somehow this is going to better represent the patient's music. I think that's missing the point. You can, however, play from your countertransference, if you're aware of it, which might be in stark contrast to how the patient is presenting in terms of overt affect. If the patient is making a lot of aggressive music, for example, you might feel really disturbed and sad, as part of that projective process. They're not aware of what they're pushing into you consciously, or what you're feeling. Playing from your processed conscious collation of countertransference, against a barrage of sound, can bring the patient into a different experience of themselves. As one gets to grips with this concept, over time, you don't need to say the words relating to this feeling state explicitly, so no verbal defences come up in response to this way of relating, and the music can change into something much more melancholic, and hopefully reflexive. That's part of what I was driving at, perhaps.

Luke: It makes me wonder about whether that was a deliberate pedagogical technique. I guess you adapt to different supervisees. It might be quite common for a supervisee, particularly a first-year trainee, to arrive with lots of hope and enthusiasm. And I'm not suggesting that you were trying to squash that...

Andy: I think you might be! [laughs]

Luke: Well, no, I think it was more like a bucket of cold water, like saying, 'Wake up, wake up.' That's how I experienced it, encouragement to wake up to what's actually happening. I had all of my hopes and dreams about what it was going to be like to be practising music therapy, and this was presenting me with a mirror image, perhaps.

Andy: Sure. And I think that speaks to this term, emptiness, the bucket of cold water being that, yes, you might want to play your best jazz chops, but somebody else may well be in a very different place. Also, I think it's easy to set yourself up to fail; paradoxically, by being musically good, it's possible to be therapeutically bad, by reinforcing the patient's low self-worth. There's so much in that idea of emptiness. There's the power imbalance of somebody who can obviously play very well, and then a patient with a very fragile ego. For example, I had a patient who didn't allow me even to play one note, because if I did, it was proof of my 'genius', and therefore, by implication, proof that their music was 'useless'. There was this horrible power imbalance. And then, actually, sometimes the music can seem to go really well, because you're putting a lot in and being supportive and harmonising things. You might go away with a lot of optimism about the next session and then, surprise, surprise, the patient doesn't come because they're mortally afraid of having to compete with the previous performance. Maybe one has to allow oneself to become empty, in order to allow the patient in, and then really understand what they're bringing, and respond to that.

Luke: That reminds me of something else that happened in supervision. We were listening to some improvisation I was doing with this particular patient, and you noticed that I wasn't really attuning to what they were doing. Then, when I did respond, they stopped. And you said afterwards, 'That was interesting, because I was wondering why you weren't attuning, and then as soon as you did, and they stopped, I realised why. And it was because even the slightest response was too much for them.' And I think you may even have used the term *fragile ego*, or perhaps some metaphor about how the client feels really tiny, in themselves. Do you feel as a supervisor, you were attempting to instil particular ideas? I'm speaking more generally now as well. Did you, and do you, see it as your job to encourage a certain stance?

Andy: I'd only been in post seven years at that point, which doesn't feel that long any more. My guess is that I was still clinging to the academic principle of offering up both sides of an argument and so really attempting not to put forward some sort of political doctrine about how things should be, partly because I was aware that I didn't know everything. But I think that the more supervising I've done, the more clinical work I've done subsequently, the more research I've done, the more life experience I've had, I have become more militant about what seems to work and what doesn't. And, well, why aren't we doing more of what does work? I've become more political, I think, as I've got older. There is this thing about psychoanalytic concepts being simply ideas rather than observable phenomena and fundamental to the human psyche, and therefore real in a systemic sense. But I don't think I saw myself as having an agenda at that point. I think I was just trying to make a basic distinction between a music therapy improvisation and a free jazz improvisation, that the goals are different and the players are different.

Luke: But I'm also thinking of the assumptions that you're making, coming from a certain perspective; for example, using psychoanalytic language to talk about the work, using psychoanalytic ideas to make sense of things that are happening in music therapy, which I guess not all supervisors do.

Andy: Well, I suppose what we're talking about is whether I was encouraging a psychodynamic stance, which has become my method of clinically relating, in order to work with the ill part of the patient. From this stance, you wouldn't start the session by asking the patient how they were, you would just take your seat, and look interested, and let the patient take it from there. And obviously, you're sitting in a room full of instruments, so the implication is that they're there to be used. But also, what's very interesting is when the patient doesn't feel this, or assumes they're not allowed, then that's all very useful, isn't it, and might get you into verbal work. But just as likely the patient will go, 'Oh, wow, the drums!' and bash the hell out of them as if you weren't there.

Luke: That's an interesting example to me, because it makes me think of my subsequent work with children and young people. All of my post-qualifying work has been with children and young people, and yet I feel that your influence as a supervisor is very much there, along with other supervisors.

Andy: 'The First Cut Is the Deepest.' Is that what we're exploring? That sounds like a title!

Luke: It does! But, you know, with a colon after it, and a really long subtitle. I have some thoughts regarding that particular example, that you don't say, 'How are you?' to the client at the beginning of the session. When you're working in a school, and you go to collect a child from class, say, an 11-year-old, 'How are you?' might be just a way of saying, 'Hello'. With a child, sometimes I would say it, when it feels weird not to. I was talking to some trainees the other day, about therapeutic stance. And I think one of them brought up an idea about what happens when a child says, 'How do you play this instrument?' Do you sort of nod and go, 'That's interesting, I wonder how you play it', and retain your 'psychodynamic stance', but in some kind of caricature? Or, do you say, 'This is a beater, you can hit it like this, and it makes a sound'? How much help does someone need, depending on their age and life experience? My advice to the trainees was, 'Don't be weird.' Or do you feel it's okay to be weird sometimes?

Andy: Well, what's behind that statement? I mean, I agree with it, that you're not going to get anywhere without a therapeutic fit. You need to build an alliance, so that the patient feels that they have epistemic trust, that they feel safe, and want to come back. The things that build that alliance, I think, are vital. But also, the ability to understand the traumatic aspects in the patient's presentation is largely a matter of countertransference. So, you might feel 'weird', and you might appear weird, when you're processing feelings that have come in and you're not yet ready to make an expression to the patient. You might feel the rush to say, 'Hey, how's it going this week?' You're very overinvolved at that point. Aren't you desperately trying to save the patient, client or pupil from anxiety? You might want to think about that, on an individual basis. There are no absolutes in this and I agree that we all find practical solutions for the environment that we find ourselves in and the client group and so on.

Luke: I've certainly had moments where I felt that I didn't rescue them soon enough from their anxiety. I'm thinking about one particular time, where a young person couldn't say or do anything for the whole session, after which they disengaged. I felt quite dreadful, that I really should have stepped in and said, 'Look, this doesn't feel good. Let's go back today. That's fine. You don't have to be here,' providing some reassurance a lot sooner.

Andy: I'm sure you would have had your reasons for doing that. I think that's interesting, about saving somebody from their anxiety, because I've been thinking about the role of empathy in our work. The patient needs to feel that you are empathically connected. That's very different from being a blank screen. You can be empathically connected without saying anything, because you're considering your countertransference. When you say, 'It doesn't feel good,' you're admitting that actually, both of you feel terrible. That's where I would step in, to say, 'I can only imagine that you're feeling terrible, because there is this real sense of unease that I'm picking up.'

Luke: I noticed that you said, 'You must have had your reasons for doing that.' And I felt, 'Ouch!' because actually I don't think there was any reasoning going on at all. I think I was trapped with them in that moment. Now I'm thinking that there might be a temptation in this conversation for me to confess all of my failures as a therapist to my first supervisor, so...

Andy: I will if you will!

Luke: Well, it definitely felt like dropping the ball, and I like to think we've all done that, because I certainly have.

Andy: I make mistakes all the time. But most mistakes are really interesting. Honestly, they are! Yes, however it is a real shame when those mistakes contribute to the patient not coming back. It's often difficult to tell whether it's a breakdown of trust which can happen when the patient doesn't feel understood and valued, or other factors out of my control. I had somebody recently who came off their antipsychotics, was great for six months, and then plummeted into a relapse, and it was really weird the way it happened. I don't think I picked up the signs soon enough, and they ended up disengaging, which is disappointing because up until that point we'd got such a long way. But at the same time, I don't think that's the end of the work with the patient. I bet they will come back because they're aware of this pattern. They can't bear the intimacy. You get too close, and they try to destroy the relationship. I'm just making it clear that it's not the case, that they haven't destroyed the relationship, that I'm still here. This hopefully means that at some point they'll dare to return. So yes, we do things wrong. I think we can't help but recapitulate the original trauma as a first trial identification. We are drawn into it, but it's how we recover from it. It's what we what we learn while we're down there, what we bring back to the surface, that becomes material that you can share and work through.

Luke: There you go, you've just done for me what I didn't do for the client.

Andy: Well, yes, supervision is easy, isn't it? Doing the work is hard. Telling somebody where they've gone wrong is not 'cheap and nasty', but it's a lot easier than being in there making the mistakes and learning from them.

Luke: I once wrote a blog post entitled, 'Your supervisor is always wrong' (Annesley 2016). I was quite proud of the title. I often say this to supervisees, that what I'm telling them is quite likely to turn out to be wrong. It's more about the process of us thinking about this together. It's hindsight. Whenever you suggest somebody do something, you're really suggesting what they could have done before, because you don't know what's going to happen next time. I found it reassuring to think about it in that way, because often, my supervisor's voice is in my head during the session, and I have to quieten it. This makes me wonder about your experiences of supervision. Actually, maybe your own training supervision.

Andy: I've always found clinical supervision terrifying. There's a certain amount of worry and expectation that happens before I present my work to my supervisor. I think that's always been the case. I'm pretty sure that it's the case for most people actually, because it brings us into contact with our superego. We are there to be judged; whether or not your supervisor says, 'There's no judgement here, there's no wrong or right answers,' you're sitting there thinking, 'Well, that's easy for you to say, but I've got to present this meagre account of all these horrible things that I did that are completely wrong and against the grain.' It's very exposing isn't it, to be the supervisee?

Luke: What about your first supervisor? What was your experience?

Andy: I'm remembering my first music therapy supervisor in adult mental health. We sat in this room, which bizarrely had all the pianos from the hospital. So, we sat in a room full of broken pianos and had our supervision. I think I was hopelessly naive about the process. And she really pushed me back to a professional distance. I suppose I did my best with it. I remember saying, at one point, 'I wasn't sure whether that was my stuff or the patient's stuff,' and she said, 'What do you mean by that?' I thought, 'Well, I'm not sure that I know, because actually it's a very complicated thing to talk about, isn't it?' It's exposing, on the one hand, your magical thinking, the 'mad' parts of yourself, or, on the other, the possibility of trotting out a lazy trope, that this was 'countertransference', when in fact it was my transference on to the patient to avoid feeling like it was my fault. There are moments in supervision where it feels as if one's whole worldview is under threat. It's almost unbearable!

Luke: I'm reminded of another moment in my supervision process with you. The patient I was working with was very interested in me and why I was there. He said, 'Why are you here instead of going and making money playing music? Are you like George Michael? Are you doing community service?' And I brought this to supervision. I presented it as humorous, perhaps expecting you to laugh with me. But your response was slightly stony-faced. You said, 'Well, what are you doing here? What is *your* "drugs bust" [that's led you here]?' I think that was your question, taking the client's metaphor and going with it, with a sort of deadpan humour. This idea that the client is on to you was powerful for me. You had another image you'd evoke, which I sometimes use today with supervisees: 'Nobody's wearing the white coat.'

Andy: What do you mean by 'Nobody's wearing the white coat'? Wearing it internally?

Luke: Yes, exactly. It's about the fantasy that you're like a consultant psychiatrist or something, swanning in, doing the session, that you understand all. Of course, the power dynamic between you and the client is real, but it's also pretend. The client sometimes works hard to break it down. You might work hard to maintain it, but the idea that you're above it all is pure fantasy, isn't it? Pure escapism?

Andy: That's right. I think, if you're going to do any useful work, it's not from that position. It's in the fear, isn't it? There's that Bion quote: 'In every consulting room there ought to be two rather frightened people: the patient and the psychoanalyst' (1973, p.10). The patient is picking up a lot, in the case of psychosis, particularly. There's a telepathic aspect to psychotic patients, where everything that you do is of such importance, until people are heavily medicated out of that. While they're in that acute phase, and they've got dopamine and serotonin shooting all over the place, they can be more aware of your internal state than you are, which is really quite anxiety provoking, and the only way to manage that is to evolve yourself, to be able to empathise with where the patient is genuinely at, you know, and I think all patients provide a challenge in that way. How do you develop an appropriate intimacy, in which epistemic trust and real containment, and therefore honesty, reflexivity and working through, are present? The only way to do the work is to be in a place where the patient understands that you understand them, that you can bear to be with them. That takes quite a lot of doing. This suspicion that the patient came in with, that you're just doing some kind of community service, and that you should be out there playing, is such a powerful argument for us, isn't it? Yes, we'd love to be rock stars playing all over the world and so on. But life is busy making other plans for us. And, yes, we have ended up in this hospital. But actually, despite how sort of dodgy that looks, we are actually really interested to be here.

Luke: That's interesting, that that looks 'dodgy'. I like that! Because I think that the fantasy for a lot of people training as music therapists is that they've discovered something more meaningful than being a 'rock star'. They might feel that this is more important work, but it's not that simple, is it? It might be more important; it might not be. Why wasn't Keith Jarrett a music therapist?

Andy: He'd have made a good one, wouldn't he!?

Luke: Well, I don't know, but certainly he had all the musical tools. And I can think of lots of musicians that could be potentially really good music therapists. So why aren't they, if it's so great? What is our 'drugs bust', coming back to that? Maybe it is a bit 'dodgy', as you put it.

Andy: But the sort of gratification and adulation that you might desire to find out there in, say, the fields of Glastonbury is also questionable, in terms of one's desperate need for validation. And then, the question for the music therapist is, how are you different? If you carry a narcissistic, rock-star attitude into the work, you might do quite a nice bit of arts in health. You might get people motivated, but, in terms of insight and that person understanding themselves better, it's not going to reach that level of functionality and new growth for them. It's just going to be a diversion between the pills.

Luke: I suppose most music therapists come to training as musicians first. And they're thinking, 'What do I do with my music? How can I use my music in new and interesting ways?' I think that was the motivation for me. I don't think it was altruism. Much as I'd like to have been touring with my own band, playing my own music to appreciative audiences, that didn't seem to be happening as much as I'd like. I was doing a lot of stuff that I wasn't all that interested in. Rather prosaically, it was time to find something else to do as well, which I might find more interesting and engaging than, for example, teaching saxophone to children.

Andy: Kids not doing any practice and so on.

Luke: At least in music therapy, when it isn't going well, you can take it to supervision!

Andy: Exactly. You can consider the emptiness. I think that it does provide a kind of evolution for your own character, and hopefully for the patient. There's this real sense, as I said before, that we have to evolve in order to be able to be recognised by the patient as useful. There are things that we have to change in ourselves in order to be able to help the patient. How can you identify with somebody who's ostensibly very different from you, or appears to be, through gender, race, or any number of different ways? It's by evolving with that person to understand where the barriers are to that flow of trust. That takes a certain attitude, doesn't it, which is the reverse of narcissism? It's almost as if it's coming from your own shame, enabling you to bear that exposure.

Luke: Yes. We learn from our clients, don't we? The patient's 'community service' comment raised quite a profound question which I didn't see at first. Then I went to supervision with an attitude of 'Isn't it funny that they said this?' Well, it is funny, because it's true. That seemed to me an important part of our supervision process, a tipping point.

Andy: Thank you for saying that. And I'm glad you survived it. God, I sound terrible. I suppose whether you felt destroyed by me or whether you felt held, I wasn't intending to be cruel. I was intending to be honest, in the way that Bion would understand. Make the interpretation you most fear, otherwise 'one wonders why [you're] bothering to find out what everyone knows' (Bion 1973, p.10). It's getting under the surface, isn't it?

Luke: Well, I think an important reason why I wasn't squashed or destroyed and didn't feel it to be negative, was that I think you always approached it with a sense of humour. I think I got the joke, and that seems crucial to supervision, actually. I don't think jokes are an escape. I think they are a way of getting closer to something real. I think that

'Well what is your drugs bust?', despite the seemingly serious tone, is a good joke. It's about making meaning as well. I think it was you who first said to me that everything that happens in the session is to do with your relationship with the client. Some of the difficulties that the profession of music therapy is encountering at the moment, particularly where questions of ableism are being considered, are to do with a failure to identify with the client. If you think you're able, and the client is disabled, and that you're helping them, then that's a narcissistic fantasy, isn't it? Psychodynamic thinking can help us get out of that and 'take off the white coat'.

Andy: Just before we end there is one important addendum to one of the things we were talking about, when considering what it was like for me in supervision. The other thing, apart from it being terrifying, was the endless repetition. I found that I was having the same conversation with my clinical supervisor as I was having with my local manager, as I was having with the head of the arts therapies, as I was having with the psychology lead. It's as if I was having the same conversations, asking what they thought. 'What do you think?' 'What do you think?' 'What do you think?' It was quite a weight having all these different opinions, quite a barrage of different influences.

Luke: But remember that they're all wrong, so it's okay! You needed to get all those voices out of your head.

Andy: Well, as many as possible, because you do have to be able to hear and trust your own voice. In sessions, you have to be confident in what you're feeling. Coming back to that academic principle, the basic dictum of academia is that, on the one hand, somebody says this, on the other hand, somebody says that, and then, what do you think? It can take people a bit of time to be confident in what you think.

Luke: That's where reflexivity is crucial. The hardest part for trainees, in my experience, is understanding what reflexive processes are, which are so important to being a therapist. What does this person say, what does that person say? What do you think? But also, why do you think it? What has it got to do with you? What's in it for you? That's not just 'thesis, antithesis, synthesis'. You've got a whole load assumptions, desires and fears, as a therapist. You've got to acknowledge your position.

Andy: Yes, your part in the transference. There are some important ideas, and then there are things which are just psychically true, and it's about getting to grips with those things. It's not simply a matter of an academic discourse, it's growing a set of tools that you can use practically. That's when you start to become productive.

CONCLUSION BY ANDY LALE

In conclusion, I would like to say, having had such a warm and honest conversation with Luke, that finding a clinical supervision situation where you can feel free to fail is not easy.

As a clinician providing clinical supervision, I do of course have my preferences. They tend to be around engagement in subconscious processes and how to work in the transference.

Those of us working in large institutions, like the NHS for example, may experience little or no separation between the clinical discussion and line management accountability. What Luke has shown here is the courage to examine his half of a psychodynamic and empathic transference field. As a result, the potential to find the patient, pathology and all, in the therapist's mind, and body, through trial identification becomes possible. Once the patient feels accepted and understood, the work usually goes very well. Try again. Fail again. 'Fail better', as Samuel Beckett put it (1983).

REFERENCES

Annesley, L. (2016) 'Your Supervisor is Always Wrong' (blogpost). Available at: https://jazztoad.blogspot.com/2016/05/your-supervisor-is-always-wrong.html. (Accessed 13 September 2023).

Annesley, L. (2019) Two kinds of music therapy: Exploring 'genre' in the context of clinical practice. *British Journal of Music Therapy*, 33(2), pp.74–79.

Beckett, S. (1983) *Worstward Ho*. London: John Calder.

Biacsi, F. (2020) Exploring Supervision: Experienced Music Therapists' Recollections of their First Clinical Supervisory Relationship in Training [unpublished master's dissertation].

Bion, W. (1973) *Brazilian Lectures*. London: Karnac Books.

CHAPTER 2

Spiegel im Spiegel

The Experience of a First-Time Placement Supervisor

ANNA MACKEN AND TRAINEES

FOREWORD

When planning this chapter, I spent a lot of time procrastinating. I realise now that the procrastination enabled other deeper processes to take place, and created space for me to think, reflect and think again about my first experience of supervision in music therapy. *Spiegel im Spiegel* means 'mirror in the mirror(s)'. It is a reference to Arvo Pärt's composition for violin and piano and I hope the reader will see how it applies to this story.

INTRODUCTION

This chapter explores how it felt to supervise two trainee music therapists in their first year of training. It focuses on three themes, drawing strong parallels between the experiences the trainees described, and the experiences I was having at the same time, while engaging in a supervision training myself. Through discussions with my peers on the training course, and also the course trainers, it became apparent that there was more shared experience of the emergent themes from all these people than expected.

Three key elements shaped our experiences and professional development together as supervisor and supervisees: fear, universality and compassion. As a trio we experienced and shared a healthy dose of fear; with our colleagues and peers we shared the universal experience of professional and personal development during a global pandemic; and alongside their clients, our colleagues, and my peers we learned how to be more compassionate, particularly towards ourselves, at a time of deep uncertainty.

To ensure that the voices and the experiences of the then trainee therapists are heard and are part of the conversation I have based this chapter on a discussion we had, reflecting on our shared experiences as they were heading into their second year of training. The discussion is summarised in our words at the end of the chapter. Each of us agreed that our experiences lent themselves to much inner reflection, learning and growth. This is something that has continued well beyond the placement and supervision training, into our current work and thinking. I would like to express my gratitude to the now qualified music therapists Eleanor and Marie (not their real names) for their tenacity, courage and skill in what came to be a deeply rewarding experience.

Throughout this account I will also refer to the poetry and creative prose that has helped me to reflect and understand my process, and how I was able to share this with supervisees as well. To start with, I have found this poem inspiring. It is cited in Shohet's book *Passionate Supervision* (2008, p.195)

Come to the edge Life said.
They said: We are afraid.
Come to the edge Life said.
They came.
It pushed them…And they flew.

(APOLLINAIRE 1971)

CONTEXT

Just before the Covid-19 pandemic took hold of our daily lives I had applied to take a continuing professional development (CPD) course on supervision training for music therapists. I planned to use the training to gain the competence to supervise a group of community musicians with whom I had been delivering projects for our local Music Education Hub, and a music therapist in training, whom I could support at a local special school where I was already working as a therapist. My feeling then was that it would all be lovely and easy, and not too challenging. Then the lockdowns began, and life turned upside down.

When the CPD course began in autumn 2020, I was no longer delivering projects with the Music Education Hub, nor had I returned to the school as a therapist because of Covid restrictions. In fact, I was not working at all.

I did think about deferring the training. However, because restrictions were beginning to lift, I decided to approach the two local special schools again. Neither school team felt able to accommodate a trainee therapist. Instead, I turned to a school where I was known, but where I had not yet established a working relationship. This school specialised in supporting boys aged eight to sixteen years old living with social, emotional and mental health needs. Many of the children had a range of additional needs, including autism, attention deficit hyperactivity disorder (ADHD), attachment issues, anxiety, and speech and language delay. The ethos of the school was and is to deliver a holistic, well-rounded vocational education for the boys attending.

The school management team were delighted at the prospect of therapeutic support at such a difficult time and were eager to explore how music therapy might support the students in their care. I too was eager; I was keen to embark on the supervision training course, to maintain a feeling of connectedness to the music therapy community and to develop new work for the future.

The placement began with online delivery from the trainees but as restrictions lifted further in May 2021, the three of us; Eleanor, Marie and me were able to attend the school in person. We would visit together on delivery days, and held our one-to-one supervision meetings online, later in the week. This gave time for the experiences of the session to settle.

The placement was very brief: it only ran for eight weeks, with two initial sessions online with two individual boys, followed by six sessions with them on the school premises. We approached this brief therapy as a form of assessment or project to explore the appropriateness of a music therapy intervention for the referred clients. As a freelance music therapist, I felt strongly that it would be helpful for Eleanor and Marie to be as involved as possible in the process of setting up the placement, to take part in meetings and develop an understanding of some of the paperwork and issues that can arise in setting up a placement or a piece of work. I have found that sometimes aspects of these processes can be difficult to understand when one first starts working professionally.

I was feeling pleased about my inclusive approach to training, and all seemed to be going well. However, when discussing potential clients, the liaison teacher began to describe the children that he felt would be suitable and benefit from working with Eleanor and Marie as the 'least difficult or complex'. He emphasised how the school was often the last port of call for the children attending: what was clear was that their attendance was felt to be a last opportunity in the local education system, potentially their 'last chance'.

FEAR

It was here that I felt my first personal flutter of fear. If I 'messed up' as placement supervisor, what might that mean for the potential clients, for the trainee music therapists…and what might it mean for me?

Fear was a feeling that we collectively acknowledged experiencing in the setting, because of the sometimes chaotic atmosphere in school, with children and staff trying to manage the experience of returning to school after the extensive lockdowns. In addition, we shared feelings of fear around our individual abilities and capacity for the work we were undertaking. We were able to acknowledge that we shared a variety of concerns: around supporting and facilitating change for the clients; about our capacity to support the setting while demonstrating how music therapy interventions could support their students; about our personal desire to do well in our training; about receiving positive feedback from peers and tutors; and about achieving good marks in our assessments, to be good enough to pursue our different roles.

My main assignment in order to pass the supervision training was a themed viva presentation, and I found it helpful to base the presentation on the topic of fear, addressing how acknowledging its presence in the work had facilitated a release, and an ability to let go and develop a deeper trust of my own judgement, experience and intuition.

When reflecting on the work more recently I've also been able to think about feelings of fear present for school staff – for example, judgement by visiting professionals during the time following a second lockdown, and, as I later found out, following a difficult school inspection a couple of years before. As far as the school and the staff were concerned, we were experts entering their school; maybe we were to be feared, maybe we would be making judgements about them and their school community.

I reflected at the time that visiting the school felt a little like entering the world of the Lost Boys from the novel *Peter Pan* (Barrie 1911), although it was clear to me that the staff were doing their best for those in their care while the world remained in the throes of an unprecedented existential threat. Still, it felt as if the school was somewhat out of sight and out of mind, and there was a sense that the teachers had been left to it – bringing Stevie Smith's poem 'Not Waving but Drowning' (1957) to mind. I realise now that everyone was frightened, everyone was feeling overwhelmed, and the burden of responsibility weighed heavily everywhere.

One example of a situation evoking fear for both the trainees and me was the moment the school team shared the clients' Education, Health and Care Plans (EHCPs), which they did immediately. I found myself wishing that the reports had only been shared with me initially, allowing us to digest the information about their clients together later. I had thought that the fears we experienced here were different. My fear was that I had got it totally wrong, that I had made a mistake in setting up this as a placement and wasn't experienced or knowledgeable enough to support trainee therapists to work with children in this setting. Marie and Eleanor's fears stemmed from the information on the page, which tended to present the children and their experiences as 'frightening'. I now recognise that these were my fears too. Marie and Eleanor had not yet had any experience of supporting children therapeutically in sound and music and they were presented with the most difficult parts of their clients' lives so far, and I was responsible. What I see retrospectively is that Marie, Eleanor and I weren't so different in terms of our fears, and in fact we had more in common than not.

Both clients presented with complex needs, and complex and traumatic histories. Supervisees and supervisor were naturally immediately drawn to the difficult information presented. I felt deep concern around the supervisees' initial perspective of each client, gleaned solely from the information in the EHCP. The trainees had not yet met their clients but were privy to so much information about them, and the initial feelings of fear brought up by the paperwork stopped us all seeing what was right in front of us on the page. For example, one client's goal was simply to be able to go for a sleepover with his friends. It was as if the child disappeared under the weight of the information presented within the EHCP. In retrospect, it felt totally overwhelming.

UNIVERSALITY

When my first feeling of being overwhelmed started I phoned my supervisor from the supervision training course. I was not sure what I wanted them to tell me or to do, or even why I was ringing. I just wanted someone else to take the weight of the responsibility away from me. I do remember saying, 'Actually it's okay, I think I was just overthinking', or something along those lines. This was perhaps a shame or defence response, and I had a sense of being an imposter presenting themselves as expert. In parallel, this was reflected in experiences brought to supervision by the trainee therapists. They had questions about their work with their clients such as 'Am I making enough music?', 'What do I do; they don't want to make music?' and 'They didn't come to their session.' Additionally, there were external experiences, such as the group supervision sessions ('clinical seminars') where trainees presented their work back at their training institution, experiences which Marie and Eleanor also brought to their supervision sessions with me.

Both supervisor (me) and supervisees (trainees) were able to acknowledge, in our subsequent conversations, a collective fear of being judged, assessed or deemed not good enough to move into year two of training or to succeed at the CPD qualification. For Eleanor and Marie, there were suggestions and assurances from peers in the clinical seminar group such as 'You should take the lead more; you should take control' or 'The music *doesn't* seem chaotic!' For me, I fantasised about judgement from clinical seminar leads, such as 'I wouldn't do it like that.' Of course, with hindsight, I might say the same!

Attending a supervision training day later that month, I was surprised that the course leader spontaneously talked about how even very experienced music therapists could feel 'imposter syndrome'. It almost felt as if this discussion had been scheduled as part of our learning. I was reminded of Yalom's writing about universality (1995), as the experience provided me with the understanding that my own feelings, experiences and frustrations were not in fact unique, and this gave me a powerful source of relief. I was not alone; we were not alone. If imposter syndrome was being experienced more widely, then maybe fear was too. And of course, why wouldn't it be? We were all learning to live through a pandemic.

The relief of this conversation lifted the gauze of fear from my eyes. The reassurance of knowing that it was not just me feeling like a fraud was tremendously helpful.

There were other conversations in our supervision training group which felt reassuring during this time of pandemic and professional uncertainty. I was conscious of the humility of our tutors and my peers, especially their ability and willingness to share when things had gone wrong or felt overwhelming. I remember the power of a simple story when we were discussing core beliefs in supervision. This described someone hanging out their washing in a hot climate, believing the locals were getting it wrong because they turned their clothes inside out, only to discover that it was the storyteller who found her clothes bleached by the blistering sun.

Over time, I realised that this opportunity to listen, observe and relate my own experiences to the experiences of my peers, tutors and supervisees acted as a form of permission, giving me a quiet confidence to share my own feelings about the placement with the trainee therapists. This then allowed me to explore more deeply on a personal level where my personal fear was emanating from: the setting, or the pandemic, and the potential to do damage or get it wrong.

It enabled me to think about any initial assumptions I had made as a trainee supervisor about the student supervisees. These included my internal response to perceptions of their apparent calmness, while understanding that like a swan on a lake, feet would be working hard under the lake's surface to control feelings brought up by the clients and the setting. There was also my perception of their apparent confidence, and I realised that this might be disguising an initial fear of theirs about the risk of being therapeutically and emotionally engaged.

Both aspects I could relate back to myself as a trainee therapist a few years before, and as a trainee supervisor.

COMPASSION

John O'Donohue described his sense of compassion as an 'ability to vitally imagine what it is like to be an other, the force that makes a bridge from the island of one individuality to the island of the other'. He encouraged listeners to 'step outside your own perspective, limitations and ego, and become attentive in a vulnerable, encouraging, critical, and creative way with the hidden world of another person' (Nurrie Stearns 1991).

I was conscious of wanting to show compassion to the clients and supervisees on the placement. However, I had perhaps neglected compassion for my own experience. I became aware of this during an experiential peer supervision session exploring my own clinical work through the Ahonen method of supervision in groups, and this experience felt pivotal to enabling me to 'let go' or 'come to the edge'.

The Ahonen method invites a practitioner to bring a dilemma to their peer group, who then express their response to the dilemma through musical improvisation (Ahonen-Eerikainen 2003). The practitioner bringing the dilemma presents it as a sentence. I asked, 'Why aren't you listening to me?'

My peers began to play, and I joined in, finding myself sat on the floor using instruments in a way that brought to mind the phrase 'a square peg in a round hole' because the instruments in my hands felt deeply unsatisfying and frustrating, and I felt a strong sense of incongruence. I couldn't create the sounds I felt I needed to connect, and there was a tension in the way I was trying to make those sounds. I didn't understand why I had felt drawn to crouching on the floor. I felt small.

When the improvisation came to a natural end, and we began to talk about the experience, I explained the scenario that had inspired my dilemma question. My peer responded with what felt to be some energy, expressing that she felt angry and frustrated on my behalf, that I was not being listened to. Whether knowingly or not she reframed my initial question, saying back to me, 'Why aren't you listening to Anna?'

Hearing the question spoken in this way facilitated a shift in perspective for me, because what I realised was that it was 'Anna' who was not listening to Anna. Instead, my thinking and judgement had become eclipsed by the noise of the fear of failing everybody and of not being good enough. This peer supervisory experience enabled me to refocus and come back to the understanding (obvious as it may seem) that to experience successful and meaningful therapeutic and supervisory relationships I must also be compassionate towards myself. Unless I acknowledged this, I would continue to feel like that square peg in a round hole, and inauthentic in my practice.

I had recently watched a documentary film about the life and work of Dr Oliver Sacks (*Oliver Sacks: His Own Life*, 2020), whom I greatly admire. I was moved by observing his life experiences; the stories of his patients and associates, the very deep love, compassion and vulnerability that existed within those relationships. I was most struck by his honesty and courage in how he talked about his own difficulties, sorrows and neuroses *with compassion*.

This made me reflect again on the experience of the placement, and the necessity for compassion for every person engaged at every level of the therapeutic process. For us to really 'hear' and support the clients, the trainee therapists and I had also to observe and acknowledge ourselves within that process, with compassion. I was coming to understand Shohet's words:

> Fear covers love, a love that is not ephemeral, but the naturally compassionate essence of who we truly are. Passionate supervision offers a space to bring fear into consciousness and dissolve it so we can enter into a space where loving presence can bring healing for supervisor, supervisee and client. (Shohet 2008, p.79)

I recommended a book to the supervisees: *The Invisible Child* by Tove Jansson (1962), a Moomin story where a small child has been frightened 'the wrong way' by a lady who has taken care of her without really liking her, and who because of being frightened so very often becomes invisible.

As a result of her treatment, the child has all but disappeared, with all that remains a small silver bell, hung around her neck on a string. The Moomin family only know of her presence by the tinkle of that bell – and it falls to the Moomin family to help the child to reappear, to feel and to play again.

I shared this in the belief that the story is a great allegory for the clients we meet in our work, and particularly young people who have been affected by trauma, and that what we music therapists look for in our work are those moments of connection in sound and music. However, I was not attending to the helpful message I might have received from myself, had I been listening at the time, about the capacity for my own fear to render me, the expert, invisible. I was too busy trying to ensure that everyone else had a 'good' and risk-free placement. This reminded me of Shohet's words: '[by] attempting to make the world a place of safe certainty, trying to avoid risk we reinforce fear...conditioned fear, imagining fearful futures... not trusting our own experiences, our intuition because others know better' (Shohet 2008, p.84).

The realisation I was afraid prompted many questions. What was I afraid of in my role as supervisor? What was I trying to keep safe and certain? How much fear was I responsible for creating? Was I picking up fear from the clients or Marie and Eleanor? As a result of the support I felt from tutors and my peers on the supervision training, I became freer to support Marie and Eleanor to think about their feelings, and to begin to recognise transference.

I also found myself doing some deeply reflective personal work in the process, not through personal therapy but because of the reading, the experiences and the greater self-awareness I felt myself to be developing as part of the supervision training, calling on my internal therapist to explore, with compassion, why I felt the way I did. I came to understand that I hold a core belief relating to responsibility for others which instils a sense of fear because it is painful. This relates to experiences in my childhood, causing me to assume that it was my responsibility to look after everybody. However, I felt I was not very good at it because things did not work out whichever way I tried to fix them, leaving me and my needs invisible in among the noise of the emotional needs of others. Through my personal musings I deduced that my core belief was this: responsibility for others is overwhelming and I am an imposter. I realised that I felt like a supervisor/therapist occupying a role of knowing and being 'expert' while convincing myself that I do not know anything and that I am not right for the role.

The thing is, on this placement I didn't know. Everything was different, uncertain and hard – but I felt utterly committed to making this work.

Listening to 'Anna' and experiencing my sense of being overwhelmed without allowing it to be the dominant voice enabled me to place the client at the heart of my thinking and feeling more easily. This decision acted as both a form of permission and of release. I like to think that I enabled the facilitation of space within our supervision sessions for supervisor and supervisees alike to embrace the uncertain and fearful feelings that came up during the placement. I tried my best to model a way of being to Eleanor and Marie, demonstrating that it was fine not always to know the answer and to share vulnerabilities. I could show that I trusted the relational musical processes of music therapy and had faith in their ability to engage their clients musically and emotionally with a complexity appropriate to their experience and year of study. In supervision sessions, it was more possible to support the trainees to feel held by making music with them following therapeutic delivery, when sometimes words were not enough. I took time to gently remind both supervisees (and myself as a result) that this initial experience was about looking to develop a relationship in music, meeting the person in the room as they are, trying to glean an insight into their interior worlds, not to slip into making a judgement or decision based on the narratives of others. The client must be the heart of the work. From here I believe we developed a stronger and rewarding working alliance.

MARIE

Supervision was really important for me because it gave me a lot of confidence in my ability, because there were times where I was like, what am I doing? And a little bit like, not panicking but worrying about what to do next, or whether I was doing enough music? Or whether I was doing it as I thought I should be? And I don't know how to explain it but it was like a wheel of continuous self-doubt. Having someone come in and break that was really refreshing, and it gave me a lot more confidence in my own work, how I work as a musician, and how I work as a therapist. I thought it [supervision] was really, really helpful. And because [the placement setting] was such a complex place it has given me a lot more confidence in my next placement.

ELEANOR

It's strange because it doesn't feel like long ago, but it also feels like a long time ago now. Just to sum it up really, it was a difficult placement. I think it was definitely the most difficult placement considering our whole year group, and comparing other students' experiences. And it was difficult for me as well personally; I felt as if there were lots of similarities with being in a psychiatric hospital, which I wasn't really expecting. A lot of those sort of feelings got brought up for me. I explored that in personal therapy as well as supervision, which was useful; it was just so challenging.

But I enjoyed it, and I've been thinking about it recently – I feel that I've learned so much from it. And it's taken a while to process it as well.

I think it was special how we were all new to the school, and it felt like we all had this bond together where we were experiencing something like this for the first time, something so new and, yeah, it just felt on a different level really [laughing]!

ANNA

There is little mention of the clients in this chapter, or the outcomes of their initial experiences of music therapy with Eleanor and Marie, other than to say it felt like a helpful experience for them as it created a space for both individuals to express themselves their way, and to be listened to attentively. In terms of the school community, I feel real gratitude; they welcomed us in and were willing to take a risk, to trust our presence and our profession as a means to support their students. I hope readers will be assured that those clients and their needs were kept firmly at the heart of the intervention.

I'm glad to share that because of Eleanor and Marie's work, the school have embraced music therapy as a support modality for their students and now have a resident music therapist in post one day a week. They also have a rock band, a choir and a visiting spoken word artist – and are in no doubt about the power of musical interaction to support and nurture the students in their care.

FINAL REFLECTION

This, my first official supervisory experience, facilitated new beginnings as we emerged from the pandemic, and a different and perhaps greater understanding of myself. It was an opportunity to learn more while supporting, observing and working alongside Eleanor, Marie and their clients. As a professional development experience, it was an opportunity to observe elements of myself being mirrored back both in supervision sessions with the trainee therapists, and in my peer supervision group.

Together we found our way through and were able to experience a beginning, a middle and an end, and see an important short piece of work to its fruition. In retrospect, this felt like a helpful intervention for the clients, and successful for each of us, despite the difficulties of the pandemic, the feelings and worries brought up by the placement, and the critical internal and external voices that created doubt along the way. I can conclude (and aim to remember) that just as in our therapeutic relationships, every supervisory relationship may offer intimate and potentially transformational new beginnings as we support those we work alongside, whether client, supervisee or peer, observing the inner worlds of others together, while also contemplating our own.

What did I learn? To attend carefully to the words, advice, expertise and experience I choose to share in future supervisory relationships. Those words may also be meant for me.

REFERENCES

Ahonen-Eerikainen, H. (2003) Using group-analytic supervision approach when supervising music therapists. *Nordic Journal of Music Therapy* [online], 12(2), pp.173–182.

Appollinaire, G. (1971) 'Come to the Edge.' In R. Shohet (ed.) (2008) *Passionate Supervision*. London: Jessica Kingsley Publishers.

Barrie, J. M. (1911) *Peter Pan*. London: Hodder and Stoughton.

Jansson, T. (1962) 'The Invisible Child.' Excerpt from *Tales from Moomin Valley*. Special edition of two Moomin stories published in October 2017 in support of Oxfam. London: Sort of Books.

Nurrie Stearns, M. (1991) The Presence of Compassion. An Interview with John O'Donahue by Mary Nurrie Stearns. Available at: www.personaltransformation.com/john_odonohue.html (Accessed 12 December 2023).

Oliver Sacks: His Own Life (2020) Directed by R. Burns. Available at: Amazon Prime. (Accessed 12 December 2023).

Shohet, R. (ed.) (2008) *Passionate Supervision*. London: Jessica Kingsley Publishers.

Smith, S. (1957) *Not Waving but Drowning*. London: Andre Deutsch.

Yalom, I. D. (ed.) (1975) *The Theory and Practice of Group Psychotherapy* (second edition). New York, NY: Basic Books.

CHAPTER 3

In Correspondence

Co-creating Reflexive Spaces Through Improvisation
in Music Therapy Supervision Seminars

NICKY HAIRE
with contributions from Ade, Alis, Geoff and Susan

IMPROVISATION: BEGINNING

When the playing begins, there seems to me an equality of voices between the five of us. No one voice appears to be leading and the sounds are sporadic. It's difficult to get a sense of the feeling in the room and, as I listen back to the recording, I'm unsure about who is playing what, including myself. A piano line emerges with a small swell, then a guitar carries this on. As the sounds become more cohesive, there also appears a secure sitting with silence and space. Sparky interjections follow this, and percussion leads into a more playful turn-taking in the group. It starts to sound like we are having a lively conversation. The improvisation ends soon after this with lots of coughing.

INTRODUCTION

This chapter offers a dialogic reflective account of a shared exploration of the experiences of introducing improvisation into small group supervision seminars with music therapy students at Queen Margaret University (QMU), Edinburgh. The exploration incorporates my own reflections alongside and in dialogue with music therapy students in the group: Alis, Ade, Geoff and Susan. Geoff was happy to use his given name in this chapter. Alis, Ade and Susan chose to be referred to using a pseudonym.

When the students I was working with in this group shared their interest around improvising in the space, I was curious to see what it would be like to play together as well as talk in supervision. I suggested that we record our improvisations and subsequent reflections at the beginning and end of our supervision seminars to see what they might tell us about processes in supervision. Within this intention we remained open to what might emerge, and I am grateful to be able to reflect on the purpose of our exploration in this chapter.

I use an auto-ethnographically informed approach in dialogue with students in which I draw from Linda Finlay's (2002) notion of collaborative reflexivity and build on previous co-creative work (Annesley & Haire 2021). In this, I write from my own position as a Scottish/Irish, white, gay, non-disabled person, and acknowledge the privileges inherent in some of these identity markers. Uncovering how these aspects of my being in the world influence my thinking, teaching and music therapy practice, especially in relation to normative practices in improvising and sound-making with others, is ongoing. One aspect of this process, key to the project detailed in this chapter, involves how to balance a fluid movement of being-with-in-sound within the role of supervisor in an educational context. Tim Ingold's (2021) articulation of correspondences provides a useful frame for the overall process of learning and knowing through doing with.

It is important to say that the explorative project outlined in this chapter was not considered research; therefore, ethical approval was not required. Nevertheless, consent to be involved in the exploration and write-up of the process was sought on an ongoing basis. Although the idea of using musical, or sonic, improvisation as part of our supervision process was initiated by the students, I felt it was important that I took responsibility to ensure that any work we did together thinking about improvisation and supervision did not adversely affect the supervision they were engaged in.

I am hugely thankful to Geoff, Susan, Ade and Alis for their openness in jumping into this exploration so enthusiastically with me. I would also like to acknowledge Geoff in particular and thank him for his time and ongoing willingness to continue dialoguing with me about his experiences, thoughts and words.

RELATED LITERATURE

When I took up my role as a lecturer, I was interested in how to develop a supervision space within an educational context. The complexity of this for music therapy students is articulated usefully by Eleanor Richards (2009), and as Peter Hawkins and Robin Shohet (2007) explain, there are also many layers involved in supervision practice for talking therapists, and these can include educational support, professional development, contextual dynamics and relational learning, along with the ongoing development of emotional resources. However, supervision in an educational context seemed to me to offer possibilities for a particular kind of experiential learning.

For music therapists, using musicking reflexively as part of a supervision process is not a new idea and has been documented (Lee & Khare, 2019; Priestley 1994; Turry 2019). There are various accounts in the English language concerned with music therapists using music and improvisation in their supervision, both in training and once qualified (Bunt & Hoskyns 2002; Forinash 2019; Lindvang 2013, 2015; Odell-Miller & Richards 2009; Pederson 2009; Priestley 1994; Sutton & De Backer 2014; Young & Aigen 2010). This literature, while not extensive, spans music therapy approaches, addresses individual and group supervision and offers different models within which music can be used to illuminate and work through experiences and occurrences in therapeutic work.

Laurel Young and Ken Aigen's (2010) exploratory project investigating parallel processes in supervision training is useful, though I came across their study after engaging in the project detailed in this chapter. Young and Aigen (2010) approach their investigation from a shared reflexive stance (as supervisee and supervisor respectively) and embody a co-creative focus which celebrates the development of thinking and practice through open dialogue. Their study encompasses music-centred philosophy, psychodynamic thinking and a pragmatic approach.

As supervisor and supervisee, Young and Aigen (2010) focus on specific examples of shared improvisations during their supervision process and consider possible transferential dynamics that are being played out in both their supervision process and the supervision process Young is engaged in with her students.

Young and Aigen's (2010) context is higher education, with students who are studying music therapy, and their spontaneous and exploratory orientation is especially relevant to this chapter. That said, their focus on parallel psychodynamic elements involved in these particular relationships diverges from the project detailed here, which, on reflection, could be thought of as involving an earlier stage; namely, the development of an internal supervisor-self for music therapy students.

THEORETICAL FRAMEWORK

When I engaged in the project detailed in this chapter, I was midway through my doctoral study (Haire 2022) and so questions around improvisation as an arts-based method of sense-making were very alive for me. *Thinking through improvisation* as it emerged through my doctoral research invited 'a balance between "dreaming and doing" (Milner 2011) through playing (mostly my violin) where new knowing and surprise could occur' (Haire & MacDonald 2021, p.13).

Further: 'With audible resonance to free association, thinking through improvisation as method, methodology and personal philosophy, has enabled deep exploration of self and selves within sound, in turn deepening awareness of relational processes in music therapy practice' (Haire 2021, p.69).

During my PhD, I was using thinking through improvisation to make sense of communications beyond words, and so I considered 'thinking' as a whole mind-body act. This has led me on an ongoing quest beyond music therapy into queer theory (Czyzselska 2022), critical disability studies (Clare 2015; Gallop 2019) and neuroqueering (Walker 2021) to find more expansive, inclusive and fluid frames of reference beyond purely arts-based methodological positions.

When the MSc Music Therapy programme at Queen Margaret University was revalidated, we joined the Person-Centred Practice Framework (McCormack & McCance 2017) as a learning pathway. Within the Person-Centred Practice Framework (PCPF), attentiveness to ways of knowing, being and doing enables practitioners to reflect on their continual becoming as persons (Robinson *et al.* 2021). Consequently, *becoming* is felt and seen as an infinite process of unfurling, as new situations, interactions and experiences transform individuals, their colleagues and those they work with.

THE PROCESS

When we initiated this project, I was a new member of staff, the students were relatively new to the course, and we were working within a new theoretical framework.

During the music therapy training, students attend a small supervision seminar group that meets weekly throughout both years of study to reflect on ongoing music therapy work they are engaged in with persons on placement. I use the term 'persons' for those engaging in therapy with students on placement. This aligns with the Person-Centred Practice Framework (McCormack & McCance 2017) followed at Queen Margaret University. The groups are facilitated in the group; therefore, this is a pastoral role as well as a teaching and supervisory role. Usually, there are four or five students in each group. In their first year, Geoff, Alis, Susan and Ade were assigned to my group.

After discussion with the students around incorporating improvisation into our group sessions, I suggested audio-recording improvisations and subsequent verbal reflections from the beginning and end of three of our supervision meetings over the course of one month towards the end of the academic year.

Due to the Covid-19 pandemic, these recordings were put aside for a couple of years, and we revisited them again during late 2022. I contacted the students who had taken part – now music therapists practising in different countries – to check whether they were still happy for me to engage with our recordings and to see whether they were interested in contributing to the chapter.

Three of the students, while still happy for me to incorporate their improvisations and reflections, did not have enough time to devote to revisiting the project in any depth. However, one student – Geoff – was keen to revisit the project and we both re-engaged with the recordings. Following this, Geoff and I corresponded over email and Geoff shared some written reflections. We eventually met over Zoom to discuss the overall process, using our reflections as a starting point.

OVERALL REFLECTIONS

Listening back to the audio recordings was uncomfortable and enlightening. I was very struck at not being able to identify myself at times during some improvisations when I listened back. There was a rich mixture of different instruments (including tuned and untuned percussion, harmonic and single-line instruments) and so I sometimes found it difficult to identify my own sounds. This added a hazy feeling to the recollection of a meaningful experience.

It has nevertheless been constructive to look back and listen to where I was and where we were then; I have been able to recognise how my ways of working as a personal academic tutor have developed. This feels important, as during the project I remember feeling 'very young at this'.

At the time, following the students' curiosity to engage in

improvisation and document this, I can see that I worked hard to keep a focus to the exploration. This may have felt stultifying. The questions I put to the students about what improvising as a group brings to the supervision process, and what we might learn about supervision through improvisation, seemed to serve to hold the exploration. Yet, I wonder now whether my questions were congruent with the students' curiosity. I certainly remember feeling concerned that I was in a position of responsibility for their learning and working to articulate this.

Our final supervision session happened online due to the first Covid-19 lockdown in the United Kingdom (UK), and I was left with many questions about what listening means in an online context. I remember feeling hopeful about what we could learn from what I felt was missing, and at the time I didn't find it a completely dissatisfying experience, but the agency of Zoom must be allowed for, which throws up interesting questions when improvising in a group (MacDonald *et al.*, 2021; Williams *et al.*, 2021). For example, aside from the latency which is experienced when playing online, the Zoom platform also 'decides' which voice will be privileged. Added to this, it is very difficult to know in the moment how what one is playing is being received through the platform by others in the group.

Geoff commented:

Listening back to the recordings from QMU, I was reminded of how reverential the atmosphere around the whole supervision (including the improvisation parts) was. Hushed voices, long silences. I think, for me, this had to do with the level of respect for, and honouring of, the persons that we were working with on placement, and then bringing into the room to be discussed. At times I felt that perhaps that discouraged others in the group from being more forthcoming – possibly nervous about saying the wrong thing. Although the feeling around the musical improvisations was special, reverential, thoughtful – and I appreciated the seriousness with which I felt we approached the whole process – I wondered if, in some way, echoing the structure of the formal supervision, or bringing into the improvisation a sense that we were all going to try on different roles within the music, might have helped stimulate the conversations within supervision.

THREADS OF EXPERIENCE

In what follows I offer reflections around five threads that emerged from listening back to the recordings and corresponding with Geoff. I hope this format invites the reader to continue to think about the ongoing unfolding of ideas from our experiences *then* and reflections *now*.

LISTENING AND TUNING IN TO EACH OTHER

Several times, students mentioned that the process of playing before and after supervision offered us a way of attuning to each other. This had seemed to have an impact on how the group felt when moving into more detailed verbal supervision processes.

Geoff wrote about this in relation to the purpose of our improvisations, and after the initial improvisation in our first meeting, he observed that the improvisation had grown from Susan tuning up her instrument. Susan responded that she felt we were 'tuning in to each other and getting ready' for sharing reflections about work.

Listening back, Geoff had observed a sense of coherence in the improvisations that he had been less aware of at the time. We spoke about this together and I wondered whether improvising in groups allows for a kind of mutual 'tuning in' to each other in whatever way might be necessary for that individual. In this, perhaps there is also something about how we learn to respond as music therapists.

Thinking further about how improvisation works in (or as) a supervision process, during our first session, Ade pointed out that improvising could model a way of reflecting and responding in dialogue without necessarily arriving at 'right or wrong [...] Maybe it's a more accepting mindset [that] enables you to do that without then also having to process other things that are usually in the musical... "Am I playing in a particular key/genre?" You can be freer so you can focus more clearly on those internal aspects.'

This provoked an interesting discussion between the students which took us back to the purpose of improvisation in this context. Geoff returned to this in his written reflections: 'Maybe it would have been useful to articulate what that [tuning in...getting ready] actually meant (as I don't remember that we did that). For me it would have meant both an authentic "showing up" for supervision, but also a willingness to share and add thoughts to the discussion.'

READINESS

Over the course of our improvisations, the importance of getting ready and being ready to improvise and engage with others in this way was voiced repeatedly. This seemed closely linked to listening and tuning in to each other, and yet something further about how to prepare for supervision (and improvising?) is interesting to reflect on, especially with relevance to developing this capacity. Susan first articulated this during our second meeting: 'For me, as well as arriving, there was a sense of acknowledging one another that enables me to be more ready to be able to talk together.'

In this session, Geoff also mentioned this in reference to feeling ready in terms of the physicality of playing his instrument (trumpet) in the group: 'I felt mentally ready but not physically ready to play and I found it frustrating. Thinking about people [persons] I work with and their own states of readiness or not. Wanting to be in a state of readiness but not being there. Something about that...'

When Geoff listened back to the recordings initially, he wrote:

> I had a cringe when I heard myself say, in the discussion, that people [persons] I work with might 'not be ready' for music therapy. I think I was trying to articulate something about the feeling that if you have something that you want to 'say' musically, you might not have the skills to be equipped to do so, or you might not – because of a perceived lack of skills or experience – particularly have anything to say, and trying to get a sense of what it might be like for someone coming in to music therapy. A sense of not ready-ness, or incompleteness, that might get in the way: this is definitely a projection of my own stuff but might also have something useful to say about the experience of the person 'receiving' therapy.

In our conversation, he expanded on this further to describe improvisation in supervision as something that moved him away from a more critical stance:

> Someone was saying something about the getting ready...music as a getting ready for supervision... if I was a bit more conscious of those sorts of prejudices at the time, maybe I could have used that musical improvisation as a way of like getting myself ready in terms of being more aware of 'okay this is how judgemental you're being...'

DEVELOPING AND DIALOGUING WITH
AN INTERNAL SUPERVISOR

The process of improvising and reflecting together highlighted complex experiences of decision-making in the moment, involving intrapersonal, social, relational and aesthetic frames. In this setting, learning how to navigate participation, silence, group dynamics and inner dialogues was often at the forefront of discussions.

In conversation, Geoff drew attention to this:

> The thing for me with this whole process, the thing that's been the most illuminating from this is it's flagging up just how judgemental I am. Judgemental about music, and judgemental about people [persons] is something I really have to keep an eye on and work with. And that relates to that sense of space and silence... Because, all the time, whether it was in the music or in the sort of formal supervision, I'm always thinking like, who's contributing, what are they saying, how much are they getting involved, how much am I getting involved? Should I be talking now? I have something to say but I don't want to take up space for someone else...particularly from someone who maybe doesn't have as much privilege as I do for whatever reason...

Observing this ongoing decision-making process was echoed in my experiences as a new supervisor, and making sounds with students highlighted the intricacies of this. In response to Geoff, I wondered aloud about his use of the term *judgemental*: '"Judgemental" sounds like quite a definitive term and what I'm hearing from you is a bit more expansive and reflexive...'

Perhaps what we're identifying here is something around a learning process in these supervision seminars that goes on in relation to how to make conscious, listen to, dialogue with, and use the voice of an internal supervisor (Casement 1985). The intrapersonal dialogue (or 'inner debate' as Prévost (2004) terms it) that happens when improvising with others seemed to occur in a similar way for the students and myself and yet was also framed by the roles we were occupying.

For example, during the closing improvisation in our second meeting, there were moments when I felt I was dominating the group and I do remember worrying at the time that I had stopped listening in order to communicate something in my music. My pianistic flurrying did not last long but felt uncharacteristically dominant at the time.

When this improvisation finished, there was a pause of around four minutes. The silence felt rich to listen to on the recording and I remembered the palpable sense of tiredness in the group. At the time, I felt we were all processing our own experiences. On repeated listening, I found myself wondering if my piano playing *had* been dominant or somehow self-centring and what that meant in my supervisory role. Perhaps my 'Keith Jarrett' moment deserved more discussion?

Along these lines, the experience of an internal discussion becoming explicit was also expressed by Geoff:

> I struggled often on the course with feelings around leadership...wanting to take on and demonstrate qualities of leadership, but also giving support and space to others to be able to take that on, too. In the discussion around the first improvisation Alis picks up my description of my playing as 'leading'. I certainly felt that in that moment in the music I did consciously take on a leadership role, but I would be interested to know whether Alis, and everyone else in the group, had the feeling that I was leading at this point. It's taken and not questioned in our discussion. I want to know! Perhaps narcissistically. But also, how was it for the rest of the group, if it was the consensus that I was leading, and everybody else was following, to be in this musical relation to me? Was it welcomed? Some level of second-order positioning in the group would have been really useful for me. I would have loved to know if other people were also having these sorts of internal struggles – both in the music-making and the supervision.

IDENTITY, ROLES AND RELATIONAL KNOWING

Geoff's written reflections above along with my questions around dominance speak to how we come to know ourselves through relationships with others in a group; what this means in terms of roles and how our interactions through sound can identify aspects of knowing that were implicit.

In our conversation, Geoff described making music together in this project as adding 'relational layers' to the experience, yet he and I also discussed finding it difficult to identify when we were playing when we listened back to recordings: 'My identity has dissolved somewhat into the group,' he observed in our discussion.

I was interested that the overall focus during the project remained largely on the dynamics and experiences within the group (rather than moving more fully into students' experiences on placement), and I wonder if this was down to my facilitation and interest in thinking through improvisation. As a group we came to know each other differently through this exploration, but we did not meet fully with the persons students were working with at the time. Our reflections circled around individual experiences in the improvisations, and we tended not to make explicit links to music therapy work on placement.

There was, however, general discussion about dynamic musical processes students were engaged in on placement. For example, after the closing improvisation during our first meeting, the students were curious about what it might be like to try and play like the persons they were working with. Ade voiced an idea around using the improvisation to embody 'musical proximity to someone in your sessions... How does it feel to do what they're doing? [...] What does it give me in relation to that work, that person?' He went on to observe that in that particular improvisation, he had been trying to put into practice some of what we had been talking about in supervision 'like leaving space, and not musically shadowing so much'.

Overall, my ideas about my developing role as a supervisor are mixed in with students' ideas about levels of engagement and perceived authenticity in interactions. I wonder if this is common in this kind of experiential learning. I do remember at the time feeling very responsible for the students' wellbeing, and as mentioned I reflected openly on the potential riskiness of the project and my own responsibility in it several times.

The group responded to my concern around my involvement in playing with curiosity. During the second improvisation in our second meeting, Geoff stated:

> You were talking before about whether you should really be a part of music-making. Think there's an element of like, professional distance of yourself to us as a group, which I think makes it, I don't want to like ask you in detail like 'how was your weekend?'[...] but in a way, doing the musicking together offers an honest communication without necessarily having to disclose too much possibly... So maybe that music facilitates the supervisory relationship in a positive way.

Ade echoed this:

> Music improvisation allows for other things to come other than the perfunctory-ness... [like] a perfunctory 'how are you doing?' [You're] considering the past/future as well as the moment and what somebody just played, what you're playing right now, how you might respond/what you might introduce... Improvisation invites a more 'open time' to be in.

Geoff and I returned to this when we met later in the project. In response to my sense of responsibility, he observed:

> You are not only considering our wellbeing as trainees, but you're also indirectly responsible for the people [persons] that we're working with as well, and so there's maybe something I've lost sight of in the thinking about this project. Knowing that you have that responsibility to make sure that we are being supervised adequately in order to support the people [person] we're working with... That's primary directive number one, basically.

SUPERVISION STRUCTURES

During the course, students are involved in many different group formations involving shared music-making and verbal reflections. Our final session took place online over Zoom and, among other things, something about this experience heightened my awareness of the kinds of structures which are required in supporting reflexive supervision spaces. We did not have the same physical structures around us, and I felt somehow that we had to work harder to listen to the in-between dynamic processes that might be involved. Certainly, I felt that experiences of improvising online drew attention to our sonic 'norms'.

When we first engaged together, it was clear that we were all trying to find how to engage with each other online. Geoff observed in the moment how it was 'bringing this experience into my own home...rather than the dedicated supervision space. In a cramped home office, I don't have any room to move. It is separate but I'm feeling boxed in.'

Ade responded to this:

> ...boxed in by the other screens as well and what we can see... Not being able to take in other people's movement. It all becomes quite

'brain-based' rather than 'body-based'. [It's like] Potential space – how big the distance is. But still there's a sense of movement and exchange…

Having to improvise online was completely unexpected at the time, and I would not necessarily have chosen this way to engage had we not been at the beginning of a national lockdown. However, I was moved and interested that all the students came prepared to play with their instruments, each ready to explore further, and I continue to wonder about what this way of engaging can reveal about how we listen to each other in person.

IMPROVISATION: CLOSING

In our closing improvisation online, we give ourselves time. Although it still sounds as fragmentary as our first improvisation two hours ago, as we all try to find a place in our 'gallery view', there is a more reflective quality to our sounds. It reminds me of that group activity where everyone is invited to try to play in the silent spaces. There seems to be room for responding on Zoom but only one response can be heard fully at a time. I feel I am listening underwater and it's difficult to tell what sounds are intentional or to do with strength of individual WIFI signals.

Overall, I have a sense of threads imagined and almost meeting. Geoff and I try a short flurry of dialogue which works. I hang on to the consistency of inconsistency. Our ending feels pragmatic and almost happens without happening.

CONCLUDING REFLECTIONS

The exploratory nature of this project offered an open-ended invitation to see what improvisation could tell us about supervision in a music therapy training context. Through the experiment, we experienced a creative approach to supervision, along with a collaborative approach to learning and an arts-based movement towards inquiry. Each of these ways of being seems relevant to meaning-making processes in music therapy and music therapy supervision.

For me, a small group supervision seminar provides a creative and relational space where students develop reflexive skills and are empowered to grow their own music therapy selves. In the project described in this chapter, the iterative process of playing and reflecting together in these supervision seminars was mirrored in the reflexive mode of dia-logic inquiry; we used improvising together to think about improvising together in this context.

As the project was finishing, I found myself both apologising for the openness of the exploration and underlining the importance that we keep it open. It was difficult to know what we had found, and what we had explored, but learners responded with energy to this. Geoff observed, 'I found the whole process very interesting… I don't know how it changes the supervision dynamic or the whole process of it but I'm very pleased to have done it.' Ade echoed this: 'Likewise – I had the feeling that it's been very valuable to do but I don't think I have the sense of what the value is yet…'

Working openly in conversation with students and using an auto-ethnographically informed position has offered an opportunity to bring to the surface knowing about intricate learning processes that occur in an educational supervision space, both for myself as supervisor and the students involved. What has emerged is less a model of how to do music therapy supervision or be a music therapy supervisor but more an indication of the breadth of experiential potential in this way of working, along with the similarities between supervision and collab-orative reflexivity informed by auto-ethnography.

Through further correspondence with one of the students involved, Geoff, I was able to draw attention to the different aspects of educational-supervisory processes that were surfaced through improvising together as part of supervision seminars. These included:

- listening and tuning in to each other
- readiness
- developing and dialoguing with an internal supervisor
- identity, roles and relational knowing
- supervision structures.

During this brief exploration, we seemed to use the group to discover our own identity-edges within music therapy practice and training, while at the same time developing a shared sense of purpose as persons in the world. It would be interesting to delve more into the usefulness of thinking through improvisation in correspondence with the idea of auto-ethnography as supervision as a way of articulating the dimensional aspects of processes that are fluid, relational, nuanced and profound.

REFERENCES

Annesley, L. & Haire, N. (2021) Experiences of music therapists sharing improvisation remotely during lockdown. *Journal of Music, Health and Wellbeing*, autumn. Available at: https://eresearch.qmu.ac.uk/bitstream/handle/20.500.12289/11672/11672.pdf (Accessed 6 January 2024).

Bunt, L. & Hoskyns, S. (2002) *The Handbook of Music Therapy*. Hove: Brunner/Routledge.

Casement, P. (1985) *On Learning from the Patient*. London: Tavistock Publications.

Clare, E. (2015) *Exile and Pride: Disability, Queerness, and Liberation*. Durham, NC: Duke University Press.

Czyzselska, J. C. (ed.) (2022) *Queering Psychotherapy*. London: Karnac Books.

Finlay, L. (2002) Negotiating the swamp: The opportunity and challenge of reflexivity in research practice. *Qualitative Research*, 2(2), pp.209–230. Available at: https://doi.org/10.1177/146879410200200205 (Accessed 6 January 2024).

Forinash, M. (ed.) (2019) *Music Therapy Supervision*. Gilsum, NH: Barcelona Publishers.

Gallop, J. (2019) *Sexuality, Disability, and Aging: Queer Temporalities of the Phallus*. Durham, NC: Duke University Press.

Haire, N. (2021) Improvising the self. *Journal of Critical Psychology, Counselling and Psychotherapy*, 21(2), pp.61–70.

Haire, N. (2022) *'How Can you have Music Therapy Without Humour?!': A Phenomenologically Informed Arts-based Reflexive Study Exploring Humour in Music Therapy with Persons Living with Dementia* [doctoral thesis, University of Edinburgh]. Available at: https://hdl.handle.net/1842/38803 (Accessed 6 January 2024).

Haire, N. & MacDonald, R. (2021) Thinking through improvisation: How arts-based reflexivity can offer new knowing about music therapists' experiences of humour in music therapy. *Voices: A World Forum for Music Therapy*, 21(2). Available at: https://doi.org/10.15845/voices.v21i2.3104 (Accessed 6 January 2024).

Hawkins, P. J. & Shohet, R. (2007) *Supervision in the Helping Professions* (third edition, reprinted). London: Open University Press.

Ingold, T. (2021) *Correspondences*. London: Polity.

Lee, C. & Khare, K. (2019) 'Music-Centred Supervision of Clinical Improvisation.' In M. Forinash (ed.) *Music Therapy Supervision* (second edition, pp.261–276). Gilsum, NH: Barcelona Publishers.

Lindvang, C. (2013) Resonant learning: A qualitative inquiry into music therapy students' self-experiential learning processes. *Qualitative Inquiries in Music Therapy*, 8, pp.1–31. Available at: https://barcelonapublishers.com/resources/QIMTV8/QIMT8-1_Lindvang.pdf (Accessed 6 January 2024).

Lindvang, C. (2015) Group music therapy – A part of the music therapy students' training at Aalborg University. *Group Analysis*, 48(2_suppl), pp.36–41. Available at: https://doi.org/10.1177/0533316415583262g (Accessed 6 January 2024.)

MacDonald, R., Burke, R, De Nora, T., Sappho Donohue, M. & Birrell, R. (2021) Our virtual tribe: Sustaining and enhancing community via online music improvisation. *Frontiers in Psychology*, 11, 623640. Available at: https://doi.org/10.3389/fpsyg.2020.623640 (Accessed 6 January 2024).

McCormack, B. & McCance, T. (eds) (2017) *Person-Centred Practice in Nursing and Health Care: Theory and Practice* (second edition). London: John Wiley & Sons.

Milner, M. (2011) *A Life of One's Own*. New York, NY: Routledge.

Odell-Miller, H. & Richards, E. (eds) (2009) *Supervision of Music Therapy: A Theoretical and Practical Handbook*. London: Routledge.

Pederson, I. N. (2009) Music Therapy Supervision with Students and Professionals: The Use of Music and Analysis of Countertransference Experiences in the Triadic Field. In H. Odell-Miller & E. Richards (eds) *Supervision of Music Therapy: A Theoretical and Practical Handbook* (pp.45–66). London: Routledge.

Prévost, E. (2004) *Minute Particulars: Meanings in Music-Making in the Wake of Hierarchical Realignments and Other Essays*. Harlow: Copula.

Priestley, M. (1994) *Essays on Analytical Music Therapy*. Gilsum, NH: Barcelona Publishers.

Richards, E. (2009) 'Whose Handicap? Issues Arising in the Supervision of Trainee Music Therapists in their First Experiences of Working with Adults with Learning Disabilities.' In H. Odell-Miller & E. Richards (eds) *Supervision of Music Therapy: A Theoretical and Practical Handbook* (pp.23–44). London: Routledge.

Robinson, B. A., Lynch, B. & Murphy, J. (2021) 'Knowing, Being and Becoming in Person-Centred Research.' In J. Dewing, B. McCormack & T. McCance (eds) *Person-Centred Nursing Research: Methodology, Methods and Outcomes* (pp.93–102). Cham, Switzerland: Springer.

Sutton, J. & De Backer, J. (2014) 'Supervision in Music Therapy: The Jumping Off Point.' In J De Backer & J. Sutton (eds) *The Music in Music Therapy. Psychodynamic Music Therapy in Europe: Clinical, Theoretical and Research Approaches* (pp.300–319). London: Jessica Kingsley Publishers.

Turry, A. (2019) 'Supervision in the Nordoff-Robbins Training Programme.' In M. Forinash (ed.) *Music Therapy Supervision* (second edition, pp.335–361). Gilsum, NH: Barcelona Publishers.

Walker, N. (2021) *Neuroqueer heresies: notes on the neurodiversity paradigm, autistic empowerment, and postnormal possibilities*. Fort Worth: Autonomous Press.

Williams, J., Ruddock, E., Mohseni, A., Gibson, S. J. *et al.* (eds) (2021) Musicking through COVID-19: Challenges, adaptations, and new practices [special edition]. *Journal of Music, Health and Wellbeing*. Available at: www.musichealthandwellbeing.co.uk/musickingthroughcovid19 (Accessed 6 January 2024).

Young, L. & Aigen, K. (2010) Supervising the supervisor: The use of live music and identification of parallel processes. *The Arts in Psychotherapy*, 37(2), pp.125–134. Available at: https://doi.org/10.1016/j.aip.2009.12.005 (Accessed 6 January 2024).

PART 2

DIVERSE CULTURAL PRACTICES IN SUPERVISION

CHAPTER 4

Affinity Groups for People of Colour: Longing for Belonging

The Antidote to White Supremacy in Music Therapy Supervision

DAVINA VENCATASAMY AND MICHAELA DE CRUZ

INTRODUCTION

Race, or ethnic identity, is a key element to supervision; it is a fundamental and inseparable part of identity (Swamy and Kim 2019). For the last decade or so there has been a sustained conversation around race and music therapy, including its relationship to culture and other intersectional forms of oppression in North America and Australia (Belgrave and Kim 2020; Hadley 2013; Leonard 2020; Norris and Hadley 2019; Whitehead-Pleaux and Tan 2017). Despite this, at the time of writing it remains largely unaddressed in music therapy publications in the UK, perhaps due to the predominantly white, female, able-bodied demographic of the music therapy profession (Langford, Rizkallah & Maddocks 2020). As a result, both our supervision experiences in the UK have occurred within a Eurocentric frame of therapy, and solely with white supervisors. The dearth of supervisors of colour reflects the lack of diversity in the profession, even though there is currently no research data to support this (Ruck 2023, personal correspondence). In our lived experiences, we have both experienced racism and racist microaggressions, and been racialised within white music therapy spaces. Racism can be expressed in subversive ways and is rarely explicit (Taylor 2023). In the supervisory space, it can be experienced in psychodynamic processes such as transference and countertransference, interpretations of which are subjective, leaving the supervisee of colour vulnerable to gaslighting and internalising wider systemic forms of oppression (Báez-Powell 2023; Turner 2021).

While overt racism does occur in supervisory relationships (Langford *et al.*, 2020), often it is the more insidious act of dismissing racist encounters that can cause wide-ranging harm. The indeterminate (and yet inflammatory) nature of these encounters further excludes them from being spoken or written about, which adds to the difficulty of conveying its seriousness and emotional impact in a text such as this which demands a level of academic rigour. When supervisors inadvertently cause or turn a blind eye to painful racial attacks in the therapy space, this can leave the supervisee feeling unseen and unsupported (McKenzie-Mavinga 2016). Unbalanced power dynamics in individual supervisory relationships can amplify this harm.

We endeavour to contextualise these experiences to offer insight into how supervision in the form of affinity peer groups can counter white centralisation, white dominance and white supremacy, and flatten the power dynamic by offering a rich supervisory opportunity to people of colour (POC). We also bring attention to our responsibility as music therapists to consider our training and practice within an anti-racist and anti-oppressive frame (Norris 2020; Pickard 2022).

Writing this chapter has been an illuminating journey. We started with an intention to share experiences of racism in supervision, to shine a light on failings in praxis and to precipitate change and discourse with the rest of the music therapy community. We found that the direct naming of racism in supervision practice activated a range of difficult emotions from those who believe their practice is not impacted by the colour of someone's skin. This seems to be echoed in the wider political context within which we practise our profession in the UK (Sewell 2021). However, fruitful conversations are occurring between POC who have experienced damaging and harmful supervision, alongside engagement with allies who recognise and understand that both systemic and individual racism does happen.

We are inspired to propose a supervisory model in the form of affinity groups, which supports therapists of colour in exploring the pervasiveness of racialised experiences and their potential to become vessels for growth. Through community building and seeking each other out, we lovingly water the cracks in the scorched earth left by the coloniser and watch as our nurturing efforts begin to flower.

These rare healing spaces provide enrichment in ways that traditional supervision models have failed to do for us. For my professional and personal growth, I (Davina) engage in a diverse array of supervisory models including affinity groups, peer supervision and 1:1 supervision with supervisors of colour. These spaces come with a level of mutual understanding of the experiences I share without having to engage in a process of educating the supervisor, cultivated from their own lived experiences of being a person of colour. I hold a supervisory practice that proactively encourages discussion about race and racial identities, both from the client experience and from the therapist's perspective.

I (Michaela) have witnessed the life-changing impact of discussing clinical material with peers of colour, and with my current supervisor who is Black and Queer. When racist acts and intentions are recognised for what they are, the resultant emotional collateral damage can be addressed openly, without fear of gaslighting. There is an ineffable relief that comes with that, which in turn feeds into a more authentic and robust consideration of clinical work.

Good supervision, affinity groups and peer support can be supportive and counteract experiences of harm. Safe spaces are necessary to recount experiences and express opinion freely, without risk of being othered or silenced. In writing this chapter, we gave ourselves room to breathe and offered each other the safety to explore both our and our peers' experiences of supervision with white supervisors and the contrasting practice of supervision in affinity groups with POC.

POSITIONALITY STATEMENTS

Michaela: I identify as a Brown, mixed-race, nondisabled, neurotypical, cishet woman. I was born and raised in a previous British colony in Southeast Asia and communicate only in English. The transgenerational trauma I carry includes the loss of my ancestors' traditions, customs and language. Supervision has felt both supportive and intimidating to me. I am now aware of the ways in which racial elements amplify the already inequitable power imbalance in 1:1 supervision and emphasise that this must be explicitly acknowledged (Imeri and Jones 2022; Jordan 2004). As an immigrant to Britain, the complexity of my story requires a supervisory space that is both open to understanding the repercussions of colonisation and racism on myself and my work, and also a commitment towards decolonising music therapy practice. I believe that supervision within peer affinity groups of colour fits into that pathway forward.

Davina: I locate myself at the intersectionality of being a British African of indentured Indian descent; a Brown, able-bodied, queer, cis-gender female. I am a second-generation immigrant who has uncovered several facets of my transgenerational trauma, including displacement, poverty and slavery, which continues to inform how I experience the world. My experiences of supervision have been both helpful and damaging, perplexingly not always exclusive of each other. Acknowledging how supervision has felt punitive and damaging feels uncomfortable but important. It allows us the capacity to understand the wider processes at play within the supervisory relationship, particularly in its potential to become spaces of further oppression.

MAKING THE CASE FOR PEER SUPERVISION AMONGST PEOPLE OF COLOUR

I found a place to build my house since I couldn't go back home[1]
RHIANNON GIDDENS

In a paper exploring race and racism in supervision spaces for Black music therapists, Imeri and Jones (2022) uncovered that over and above the immense vulnerability, exasperation and feeling of being an outsider in an unchanging oppressive system, discussing race in and out of supervision also routinely evoked the defensiveness of white supervisors and other professionals. Additionally, they found a lack of commitment to action even when racism and white privilege were discovered.

Many music therapy supervisees use only one source of supervisory support. The peer supervision model provides much-needed support of other therapists without regular financial output. However, financial motivation is not always the sole reason for pursuing peer support. Gaining insight from several people actively working in the field, compared to just one individual supervisor, may be a more extensive method of garnering expertise.

In training to become a music therapist, group supervision or

---

[1]   From the song 'Build A House' composed for the 155th anniversary of Juneteenth and performed with renowned cellist Yo-Yo Ma.

reflective practice groups can be used as pedagogical approaches to enable groups of trainees to obtain exposure to as much clinical case material as possible. This allows a concentrated volume of supervision to happen within the short time frame of a music therapy master's training. Wilkins suggests that group supervision can offer opportunities to have more in-depth, practice-focused conversations which can contribute to wider cultural change within organisations (2017). Pre-Covid-19, the expectation of face-to-face supervision meant having to prioritise geographically accessible supervisors. This sometimes came at the expense of relevant expertise or personal compatibility. Post-Covid-19, online supervision is more common. This has some obvious disadvantages for music therapists, for instance complicating the ability to make spontaneous, responsive music together, and/or obscuring certain psychodynamic, non-verbal elements which may be more palpable in a physical space with another. However, the advantage is that it presents more choice, such as a supervisor who has the related competencies, aligns with personal communication styles, and/or is a supervisor of colour, no matter where they may reside in the world.

In our ongoing commitment to decolonise our lives and work, we recognise the parallels that could be drawn between the championing of 'individualism' in Western culture and the degrading of 'community'. Colonialism requires the disintegration of community so that power can be delivered into the hands of a few individuals (Lorenz & Watkins, 2003). The birth of psychology coincided with early colonial intent, and theories of individualism have arguably served its development (Kirmayer, Adeponle & Dzokoto 2018). Our desire to connect with community and affinity groups has therefore been an organic part of this decolonising process. We view peer supervision as a decolonised approach to supervisory practice.

WHAT IS AN AFFINITY GROUP?

Affinity groups are groups of people who share a certain set of life experiences and histories of trauma and resilience. They understand how existence and identity are directly forged by these experiences and histories. For us, affinity groups are spaces where the entirety of ourselves (our identities, histories, joy, trauma, losses and reclamations) has been accepted unquestioningly and require little translation.

Context

Movements such as the Black Creative Healing Project founded by Dr Natasha Thomas and Dr Adenike Webb in the USA and We Are Monster (www.wamonster.org), a global music therapy network for POC, have blossomed out of a need for spaces protected from the white gaze. We explore the freedom inherent in these spaces as we discuss peer supervision affinity groups and what they bring to us as therapists of colour. We recorded our Zoom conversation, and the following transcript has been edited to ease the reading flow.

We began by defining peer supervision as we understand it: a model where there is no one person in a position of authority. This contrasts with traditional individual supervision, or supervision with a group facilitator. It usually occurs without payment exchange, which flattens hierarchy, equalises power dynamics, and embraces the idea of needing a village to raise a child. We explore how this non-hierarchical dynamic, particularly amongst an affinity group of POC, can grant the safety needed in discussions of race and racism. Because we speak about supervision and affinity groups within both UK and US contexts, we may represent a more global outlook.

Dialogue

M: What does your clinical supervision affinity group with POC bring for you that you may not get from traditional 1:1 supervision?

D: You already know that all my previous 1:1 supervisors have been white and my affinity supervision group is with POC [from the USA]. So, the difference is going to be stark, no matter what. Affinity groups for me are about being able to *BREATHE* in a space and have the freedom to bring anything, without being afraid of framing it within a racial lens from the outset. And within the group that I'm part of, it's very easy to start off from a place of race, come back out into other spaces, and then recontextualise as we go along. But I know that in white spaces that whole process gets cut out completely. I simply don't bring it in and that's not because I don't want to talk about it, because I clearly do, *all the time* in my affinity group – just that in a white space, it feels too much of a burden on me to open up that conversation; to not know how that other person is going to receive what I'm saying, and then place the burden on me to teach them.

I didn't know I was entering into an affinity space. It wasn't like I subscribed to a group that called itself that. I started within a supervisory relationship with someone of colour, Dr Natasha Thomas, which was already a new experience for me, and she brought people together who were talking about the same things. So, we ended up in a group and we now have a space which we all value highly and use for clinical work as well as personal reflections on race.

M: You've mentioned the difference between being in white spaces and spaces with POC. But what is the difference between that 1:1 relationship and the group community experience; whether hierarchical or not hierarchical? What does community bring?

D: I'm not quite sure how I would compare because everyone else in my peer supervision group is Black and I'm the only Brown person, and they're all American as well. In 1:1 sessions, there is the ability to dig down and the time is all mine, which seemingly should be an advantage. But I get so much more from the group because what is mine is theirs, and what is theirs is mine too. So we have four or five people sharing and we're all connecting with everything. It's fivefold rather than just this 1:1 environment. My experience of the 1:1 supervision environment has been drier because I haven't been able to talk about the stuff that really connects with me. All I've been able to talk about is the client. Maybe it's hard to see why that would be a problem, because perhaps it should always be about the client, but there's an argument that if we're not bringing our whole selves into the space, or at least the part that we are getting impacted by on a daily basis, we are not fully in the process. I don't want to say that we can't have supervision without having this profound connection, but in a Brown and Black group, the profound connection is there, *and* you get the supervision. Whereas in the white space, that part of me that I cut out, takes some of the depth away from talking about the clinical work. Because when I'm in the therapy or supervisory space, I am there – *all* of me. So whatever is happening or whoever is in the room, whether I like it or not, they are reacting to me as a Brown woman, because I can't hide that part of me. However, do we get to process it? No. In the affinity group we prioritise that processing through creative means – music, art, poetry, writing, dancing; indigenous and ancient ways of knowing connected to pathways that existed before colonisation destroyed them. We see those modes of creation as extensions of who we are as POC, and we draw from them as ancient, natural, wisdoms. This is very different from the intellectual methods of processing and theorising we're trained in. Being able to do that in a group means that we can relate to each other in community, and you don't get that in the same way in the 1:1 relationship.

M: It really struck me when you said, 'what is mine is theirs, and what is theirs is mine'. It made me think about an earlier version of this chapter: we talked a lot about the significance of *being seen* versus *not being seen*. When I say 'being seen' here, I mean being humanised and validated as rich, complex human beings – not being reduced to the stereotypes that POC endure or being made invisible because of our difference. And I can imagine if your experiences are being owned and mirrored by a group of people, then that really makes you and all your many layers feel *seen!* Especially if you're also being given the space to express yourselves in artistic, creative and embodied ways as well. I wonder if that allows your therapeutic decisions and everything that goes on in the room with your clients to be seen through that lens?

D: I think it's a really important point to say out loud. Being seen is highly underrated because the people who feel seen are already part of the dominant narrative. It's the marginalised and oppressed who don't have a voice and are not able to articulate what it feels like to be seen. I think being seen within that group has boosted everything else: confidence and a stability to feel belonging, to have a place. We under-estimate how important these things are to have when walking through the world. So, it's much, much more than just a supervision group. It is very much more about growing and healing as a Brown person, and through that the clinical work changes shape and changes meaning. We're all music therapists who have gone through a process of profound change and growth by becoming therapists. But that change takes on something new in these affinity spaces.

Now I have some questions for you! So, at the 2024 BAMT conference, I spoke about this affinity group and my experiences within it. Luckily enough, two members of the group were able to come over from the US and one member was online, and we spoke about the experience of being part of something that has Black healing and creativity at its core and how we deal with conflict and change as a group. I noticed that you reacted to that because you were in the audience...

M: I was weeping...

D: Yes! Can you say more about this?

M: Your session sat in the middle of a conference which we were moving through as an affinity group already, because we were there with so many members of our We Are Monster network. That experience in itself was a shock to the system, in the best way, because being with my community in a space where I'd otherwise have felt like an outsider was brand new and unexpected. Your session then sparked further feelings around what clinical work can look like when it is viewed through the lens of race, creativity, affinity and community. For me, it felt like a longing for belonging within a clinical space because, like you said, within that group you don't just talk about the clinical, you also have the freedom to talk about the personal. We try so hard to separate that in the therapy world. I'm not suggesting that we shouldn't be implementing certain therapeutic boundaries, but our identity seeps into everything. So, I think the weeping was about a longing for a space where I could bring myself in without the worry that I am bringing *too much* of myself in, or that I must maintain some sort of overly professional demeanour to participate in supervision. The relationship that you all so generously shared with us really showed me that it's possible to analyse your clinical work with so much *LOVE*. That felt extraordinarily powerful. The love amongst the group entered the room, and I can imagine that it also revolutionises the way that you in the group look at your work.

D: Absolutely. I like what you said there about being professional. I think there's a risk that people on the outside look in and say well, this is just a chat between people who share a commonality, which I guess is what affinity groups are, but also, we can be professional and hold those clinical boundaries in the same way as any supervision group does. I think for us, Natasha [Dr Natasha Thomas] brings a level of kudos people won't question because she has the respect of the profession. And yet the idea of talking in this way with 'love' as you say might be really challenging for the profession.

M: In a space like this it feels like you have the respect and autonomy to bring your whole self in, together with your pain and your joy, in the ways that it relates to what you do clinically, which might be risky in traditional supervision. I'm also thinking about how clinical seminar groups during training may set up what you believe you are allowed to bring into supervision once qualified. Can we be audacious enough to imagine a space where we give ourselves the permission to be fully there?

D: You have been qualified for a shorter time than me and have less experience in supervisory spaces. I also know that all your previous supervisors were white. Where do you think the gaps have been in your white supervisory spaces that you might find in an affinity group? What is the belonging that you are longing for?

M: I think this goes back again to 'being seen'. If as a person of colour I am expected to leave so much of myself at the door, I can never enter supervision as the full version of myself. I may even make conscious or unconscious decisions *not* to be seen because I never quite feel like I can fit into the idea of what I believe I'm supposed to be. I'm often quite a vocal Brown woman in a country where it's impolite to be vocal in the first place.

In some supervisory experiences, I have been reminded not to be so vocal in subtle and what I felt to be 'British' ways. I don't know if that's a racialised thing. It really did not make me feel safe enough to bring all of myself into the space. So that longing is definitely to be amongst people who won't question the legitimacy, authority and authenticity of who I am. There are always going to be power dynamics in groups, but once you take away that layer of 'I don't understand you, I don't see you, I don't really know what to expect from you', then as you said earlier, you can be and *BREATHE*. I believe that can be nothing but a service to your clinical work.

REFLECTION

The axe forgets...the tree remembers
OLD SANKOFA PROVERB (UNKNOWN AUTHOR)

Ways of knowing, being and healing for POC are continuously evolving, taking shape from ancestral knowledge (Low *et al.*, 2022). Black and Brown wisdoms have been interrupted for centuries and are still constantly under threat within white supremacist systems. Under the white gaze they are often denigrated as born out of wildness, rooted in nature, and ungrounded in Westernised scientific fact. Ancient practices which do get accepted into the mainstream can be conveniently white-washed to serve oppressive, racist and capitalist systems. An example is the way UK yoga praxis has been commodified into an exercise pro-gramme in a gymnasium, largely dishonouring the spiritual discipline it originated from. However, our indigenous, embodied knowledges are persistently emergent and defiant (Smith 2021). Music therapists of colour are reclaiming these ways through community affinity groups, arts-based research (Norris, Williams & Gipson 2021), rap music (Fisher & Leonard, 2022), yoga and meditation healing, and poetry to mention a few ways. Williams (2024) puts it best when she describes how 'incorpo-rating poetic reflexivity into [my] research engages a Black epistemology and challenges the rigid notion(s) of what (and who) constitutes aca-demic/scholarly writing'. Re-communing with our roots and building communities also disturbs the hierarchical power imbalance central to the traditional 1:1 supervisory experience, which becomes more dispro-portionate when one person in the relationship, particularly the super-visee, is a person of colour (Jordan 2004).

> Our understanding of affinity groups and the power they hold to heal and grow Black and Brown bodies feels unquantifiable. How can one measure the importance of being seen, being believed, being able to breathe or being allowed to simply be? Furthermore, how do we grap-ple with what is lost when those elements are cut away, either due to a blindness to how the supervisory space is created or an acceptance of the status quo? When those challenges are levelled and solutions do not look comfortable or recognisable, how do we open our hearts and minds to accept that which is different to what is known?

CONCLUSION

Our intention with this chapter has been to testify to the potency of peer supervision for affinity groups of colour. A person of colour enters any music therapy space without the privilege of being able to hide the colour of their skin, and having access to inclusive and creative supervision that does not need to be convinced of this from the outset allows for a more authentic and in-depth inquiry into the interactions and shifts in clinical work. When experiences of the world are heard and mirrored without the need for justification, confidence and security in the clinical space grow.

Finally, we want to speak to the white music therapists who may be reading this. Our hope is that you come away from this chapter with a deeper understanding of what supervisees of colour may need from supervision. We need allies in the race conversation (Ellis 2021) who can advocate for affinity groups and peer supervision as an evolved way of self-reflection, understanding, learning and development and who will not see it as a threat to their own practices, but rather as a crucial aspect of identity restoration for POC.

REFERENCES

Báez-Powell, N. N. (2023) Decolonizing my therapeutic identity: Going beyond the surface. *Psychoanalysis, Culture and Society*, 28(3), pp.476–486. https://doi.org/10.1057/s41282-023-00376-7

Belgrave, M. & Kim, S. (2020) *Music Therapy in a Multicultural Context: A Handbook for Music Therapy Students and Professionals*. London: Jessica Kingsley Publishers.

Ellis, E. (2021). *The Race Conversation: An Essential Guide to Creating Life-Changing Dialogue*. London: Confer Books.

Fisher, C. & Leonard, H. (2022) 'Unsettling the Classroom and the Session: Anti-colonial Framing Through Hip Hop for Music Therapy Education and Therapeutic Work.' In The Colonialism and Music Therapy Interlocutors (CAMTI) Collective (eds.) *Colonialism and Music Therapy* (pp. 305–334). Dallas, TX: Barcelona Publishers.

Hadley, S. (2013) *Experiencing Race as a Music Therapist: Personal Narratives*. Gilsum, NH: Barcelona Publishers.

Imeri, J. P. & Jones, J. D. (2022) Understanding the experience of discussing race and racism during clinical supervision for Black music therapy students. *Music Therapy Perspectives*, 40(2), pp.174–181. https://doi.org/10.1093/mtp/miab027

Jordan, J. V. (2004) 'Relational Learning in Psychotherapy Consultation and Supervision'. In M. Walker & W. B. Rosen (eds) *How Connections Heal: Stories from Relational-Cultural Therapy* (pp.22–30). New York: Guildford Press.

Kirmayer, L. J., Adeponle, A. & Dzokoto, V. A. A. (2018). 'Varieties of Global Psychology: Cultural Diversity and Constructions of the Self.' In S. Fernando & R. Moodley (eds.) *Global Psychologies: Mental Health and the Global South* (pp.21–38). London: Palgrave Macmillan.

Langford, A., Rizkallah, M. & Maddocks, C. (2020) *BAMT Diversity Report*. www.bamt.org/resources/diversity-report

Leonard, H. (2020). A problematic conflation of justice and equality: The case for equity. *Music Therapy Perspectives*, 38(2), pp.102–111, https://doi.org/10.1093/mtp/miaa012

Lorenz, H. S. & Watkins, M. (2003) 'Depth psychology and colonialism: Individuation, seeing-through, and liberation.' *Quadrant*, 33, 11 -32.

Low, M. Y., Kalsi, G. K., Kuek Ser, S. T., Badri, M. R. M. (2022) 'A Discussion About Colonialism, Music Therapy, and Food in Malaysia.' In The Colonialism and Music Therapy Interlocutors (CAMTI) Collective (eds.) *Colonialism and Music Therapy* (pp.117–135). Dallas, TX: Barcelona Publishers.

McKenzie-Mavinga, I. (2016) *The Challenge of Racism in Therapeutic Practice*. London: Palgrave.

Norris, M. S. (2020) Freedom dreams: What must die in music therapy to preserve human dignity? *Voices: A World Forum for Music Therapy*, 20(3), p.4. https://doi.org/10.15845/voices.v20i3.3172

Norris, M and Hadley, S., (2019). *Engaging Race in Music Therapy Supervision*. In M. Forinash (ed.) *Music Therapy Supervision* (second edition). Gilsum, NH: Barcelona Publishers (pp101-125).

Norris, M., Williams, B. & Gipson, L. (2021) Black aesthetics: Upsetting, undoing, and uncanonizing the arts therapies. *Voices: A World Forum for Music Therapy*, 21(1). https://doi.org/10.15845/voices.v21i1.3287

Pickard, B. (2022) Anti-oppressive pedagogy as an opportunity for consciousness raising in the music therapy profession: A critical disability studies perspective. *British Journal of Music Therapy*, 36(1), pp.5-15. https://doi.org/10.1177/13594575221078582

Ruck, W. (2023) E-mail correspondence, 23 August 2024.

Sewell, T., Aderin-Pocock, M., Chughtai, A., Fraser, K. *et al.* (2021). *Commission on Race and Ethnic Disparities: The Report* https://assets.publishing.service.gov.uk/government/uploads/system/uploads/attachment_data/file/974507/20210331_-_CRED_Report_-_FINAL_-_Web_Accessible.pdf

Smith, L. T. (2021) *Decolonizing Methodologies: Research and Indigenous Peoples* (third edition). London: Zed Books.

Swamy, S. & Kim, S. (2019). 'Culturally Responsive Academic Supervision in Music Therapy'. In M. Forinash (ed.) *Music Therapy Supervision* (second edition), pp.217-238. Gilsum, NH: Barcelona Publishers.

Taylor, F. (2023) *Unruly Therapeutic: Black Feminist Writings and Practices in Living Room*. New York: W. W. Norton & Company.

Turner, D. (2021) *Intersections of Privilege and Otherness in Counselling and Psychotherapy*. Abingdon: Routledge.

Whitehead-Pleaux, A. & Tan, X. (2017) *Cultural Intersections in Music Therapy: Music, Health, and the Person*. Dallas, TX: Barcelona Publishers.

Wilkins, D. (2017) Does reflective supervision have a future in English local authority child and family social work? *Journal of Children's Services*, 12(2/3), pp.164–173. https://doi.org/10.1108/JCS-06-2017-0024

Williams, B. (2024) Poetic awakenings: (Re)imagining epistemic justice and academic writing through a Black aesthetic lens. *Qualitative Studies*, 8(1), pp.58–86. https://doi.org/10.7146/qs.v8i1.136781

CHAPTER 5

The Nordoff Robbins Tradition of Supervision

Cultivating Awareness and Courage to Follow Where Music and People Lead Us

OKSANA ZHARINOVA-SANDERSON AND SIMON PROCTER

INTRODUCTION: NORDOFF ROBBINS SUPERVISION WITHIN THE CONTEXT OF THE APPROACH

Supervision is an integral part of the practice of music therapy in the UK. There are various approaches to the doing of and thinking about music therapy, and it is therefore unsurprising that the specific characteristics of these manifest also in how supervision is done and thought about. In this chapter, we consider how the 'music-centred' nature of the Nordoff Robbins approach (sometimes also termed Creative Music Therapy) is manifested within supervision. In particular, we examine how the supervision process is founded on detailed consideration of the particulars of musical interaction, and how this consideration flows through phases of listening, describing, experimenting and reflecting.

Supervision is an aspect of music therapy practice: what characterises effective supervision also characterises effective practice. Both must be founded on a commitment to enabling the person we work with to fulfil their personal musical potential, and both are based on detailed listening, musical imagination, and the courage and ability to translate intention into musical possibility.

In this chapter, our focus is on what makes Nordoff Robbins supervision distinctive. Like all supervisors, those working in the Nordoff Robbins approach are mindful of assuring the safety of all concerned, safeguarding potentially vulnerable clients, risk amelioration, supporting therapists' wellbeing in relation to their work, and so on: these aspects of practice need to be considered in any form of supervision.

HISTORICAL PERSPECTIVES

In their pioneering work, Paul Nordoff and Clive Robbins emphasised attending to, and learning from, what was actually happening in music therapy sessions. They audio-recorded their work, devoting time each week to listening to recordings of sessions (Aigen 1998, p.24). They developed the practice of indexing: making a detailed written analysis of the musical progression of a session over time, based on detailed listening to recordings (Nordoff & Robbins 2007, pp.182–188). Having to work out the precise components of both client's and therapist's contributions to the music (via repeated stopping and rewinding of the tape) required honest analytic listening. This led to clearer understanding of the client's musical character and potential (as well as ways in which the therapist might be supporting or hindering this) and enabled strategies for further sessions to be identified. Post-session indexing was also a discipline which ultimately served to train in-session acuity of awareness of each moment and helped them to make more informed and appropriate judgements as to the best next steps. A glimpse of this process can be seen in the documentary *Oyvind Can Beat the Drum* (Norwegian Television 1971). Evident here are the collegiate attitude, the shared focus on the client and their potential, and the commitment to hearing clearly in order to imagine what might be possible and how. This attention to musical detail is key to the effective practice of the Nordoff Robbins approach, and so it was natural that when training others, Paul Nordoff and Clive Robbins likewise required them to bring indexed recordings to supervision.

Aigen's formidable qualitative analysis of Nordoff and Robbins' work (Aigen 1998), as well as the writings of contemporary practitioners, informs our contemporary understanding of the approach including supervision. Its key features include the centrality of shared musical work and being playful within it, as well as the need for faith in music: a recognition of music's potential to facilitate change when offered with clarity and precision. The therapist has to draw on their own experience of music 'working' and apply this imaginatively to facilitate connective and enabling musical companionship with their client.

Little specific literature on supervision within the Nordoff Robbins approach exists. Turry (2001) describes supervision within the Nordoff Robbins training programme in New York, while Brown (2009) considers her own supervisory practice, which has clear roots in mainstream psychodynamic and psychoanalytic thought. Nevertheless, supervision has been an integral part of the Nordoff Robbins community of practice internationally and represents a body of knowledge developed and propagated via shared practice rather than being set down in writing. This chapter describes supervision as it has evolved in the UK, and in particular within the UK charity Nordoff and Robbins. A key figure in the evolution of a distinctively Nordoff and Robbins supervision practice in the UK is Rachel Verney. Her commitment to the discipline of the work, her uncompromising focus on the centrality of precise, non-judgemental musical listening, and her conviction that 'musical detail isn't just a "purely musical" matter – it's a concern for exactly what's going on between two or more people in music therapy' (Verney & Ansdell 2010, p.78) has inspired Nordoff Robbins therapists and supervisors around the world. In particular, her insistence on workshopping as an integral part of supervision has been hugely influential.

TELLING A STORY

All music therapists working for Nordoff and Robbins in the UK participate in regular, small supervision groups as part of the charity's quality assurance scheme. The rest of this chapter describes a supervision encounter within such a group, but all identifying details have been changed.

We follow the process through various stages of supervision, told from the perspective of the supervisor (Oksana). The stages are not prescriptive; not all supervision sessions will contain all these stages, and stages may overlap, but we hope this example will give the reader an idea of the process. The case study is interspersed with reflections and explanations.

FRAMING THE SUPERVISION AHEAD OF LISTENING

It's Jean's turn to share her work with the supervision group. She starts by explaining the context of the situation she needs help with.

Based in a primary school for children on the autism spectrum, Jean is experiencing considerable frustration in her music therapy work with seven-year-old Zeb. She experiences Zeb's playing as chaotic: week after week she struggles to find a meaningful connection, let alone a sense of flow in music-making with him. Things came to a head this week when a teaching assistant had observed Zeb's session: Jean feels both ineffectual and judged as such.

Jean explains that she has indexed a section of her recording of the session where she finds Zeb's playing particularly chaotic and she is struggling to make sense of it musically. Her indexing confirms the feeling she had in the session that she is trying to match the qualities of Zeb's playing in order to connect with him, but nothing shifts as a result of this. She sums up her question to the group: 'What can I do differently here?'

I ask Jean a few questions about her understanding of Zeb's life circumstances and how these may be affecting his presentation both within and outside music therapy. She wonders whether his family environment may be contributing to his hyperactivity and lack of focus. Holding this in mind, I ask Jean to share with us the extract that she has chosen as exemplifying the 'chaos' she is describing.

Supervision is a shared endeavour, motivated by mutual concern for the client in question and for the therapist's work in general. The therapist is therefore expected to prepare for supervision, principally by identifying a particular session (or part thereof) that they wish to focus on, indexing it to 'know' it as well as possible. This in turn may help them to formulate the key question they want supervision to help them address.

There are many potential reasons for choosing a particular extract. Perhaps something specific happened within the session, or something about the session was unusual or distinctive. The therapist may have been left with a sense of puzzlement, frustration, worry or elation. Alternatively, a session may be chosen as representative of a course of therapy, or of the therapist's experience that repeats across sessions with different clients. Sometimes therapists report going through a phase of feeling uncomfortable, ineffective or unmotivated in their practice. In such instances, they are encouraged to bring an example of an occasion where this is most palpably felt, indexing it beforehand and considering how this reflects the issue they are struggling with in the form of a question.

This preparation for supervision not only ensures best use of supervision time, but also guards against supervision becoming seen as 'time with the expert'. The power differential is minimised and the therapist's capacity for independent reflection is strengthened because it is expected that the supervisee comes to the supervision not only with experiential memory of the session, but also with analytic and reflective knowledge from the indexing process. By spending time attending to the minutiae of the session in order to index it, the therapist becomes an 'expert' in the session and brings this expertise with them to supervision. This is manifested in their formulation of questions, the accuracy of their description of what happens, and their readiness to think and workshop creatively with the supervisor and the group.

LISTENING AND RE-LISTENING TOGETHER TO WHAT IS HAPPENING

As we start listening, I am struck that Jean's description of Zeb's drumming being chaotic is not how I'm hearing it. Rather, I hear three things. First, Zeb is playing irregular short bursts of un-pulsed drum beating, with varied articulation at the beginnings and ends of phrases and occasional accents. Second, Jean is accompanying this with more pulsed, regular piano playing, perhaps intending to lend some form and flow, but this isn't reflecting the specifics of Zeb's articulation or the timing within his phrases. Third, this discrepancy of articulation and timing between the therapist and the client seems to be resulting in reduced connection between them.

I ask Jean to replay a shorter section of the recording (about 20 seconds). I ask her to describe the detail of what she hears, encouraging her to differentiate between Zeb's input (focusing on how he is playing – the detail of articulation, accent and timing) and the therapist's input (focusing on the same elements). Jean initially struggles with the description, so I suggest she imagines that the client's input is part of a musical score that she has to notate. This seems to help.

Within the Nordoff Robbins approach, the cultivation of precise moment-by-moment listening is key since it enables us to attend to and respect each individual's uniqueness. Sometimes it can be challenging for the therapist to hear what the client is doing as musically meaningful, so finding a frame that enables them to describe the musical detail accurately (in this case through imagining this as a notated score) can be helpful. Likewise, intense collaborative listening is the cornerstone of supervision, lending a disciplined rigour by ensuring that ensuing insights are grounded in the reality of what has happened.

To enable this, the supervisor has a responsibility, where necessary, to share discrepancies between their hearing of the musical detail in the extract and that of the therapist. Direct challenge is not always necessary: sometimes it is enough for the therapist to re-encounter the extract in the supervisory setting for them to query their own initial hearing of it.

DESCRIBING WHAT IS HAPPENING

As Jean starts describing what is happening in the chosen 20 seconds, and the musical 'score' performed by the two players becomes vivid, she feels her premature labelling of his playing as 'chaotic' may have led to her missing the opportunity to hear Zeb's musical input as carrying clear musical meaning and direction. With occasional prompting from me and other group members, Jean is able to describe with some precision what Zeb is offering her – something she struggled to perceive in the session.

By listening again to Zeb's music in such detail in this analytic setting, Jean realises that the pulse that she intended as a means of 'offering structure' or 'combatting fragmentation' may in fact have been a way of appearing 'in control' in the eyes of the teaching assistant – a response to her own feelings of insecurity. Focusing on this meant she was distracted and not really listening to what Zeb was offering, resulting in lost opportunities for musical connection, invitation and development. We discuss how this may have impacted Zeb's experience.

This leads to consideration of the importance of any invitation for musical development being rooted in a precise connection with Zeb's offerings in each moment. Jean seems excited about this realisation, but also daunted by it, asking how she can do this differently next time.

Verbal description pins us down to precision within the discussion of what the therapist has been able to hear in the interaction, describing three elements separately: the client's musical 'self-portrait' – the way they present musically, as highlighted by Nordoff and Robbins (1971, pp.34, 52); the therapist's musical response and offering to the client; and the nature of the resulting interaction between them. Differentiating between these three aspects helps to disentangle the elements contributing to the musical relationship and cultivates discernment in the therapist's listening.

It becomes clear for Jean that her relating to the teaching assistant had impacted her ability to connect with Zeb. Verney and Ansdell (2010, pp.66–67) discuss the importance of being able to differentiate between the inner skin of the musical relationship (the detail of what happens inside a musical interaction) and the outer skin of the relationship (all the other aspects of the relationship, such as negotiation of boundaries, the experience of working within the setting, or of other people being present in sessions). Supervision offers an opportunity both to disentangle these two skins, enabling therapists to address them appropriately, and to consider the connections between them.

Verbal description is also a way of beginning to 'make sense', to get at something of what the client's experience may have been. Within the Nordoff Robbins approach there is a concern for the phenomenological, and this is reflected in the importance attached to first listening, then describing in detail, and only then trying to find meaning in what has been heard and described (or 'interpreting' it) as well as 'musically imagining' on from it. This ensures that pre-existing assumptions are re-examined, and any new interpretations (and 'imaginings') rooted in the reality of what actually has taken place. It also enables the therapist to investigate their own patterns and habits that lead to particular courses of action or interpretation. Being able to articulate the detail of what has happened in the session increases the therapist's ability to act with clarity and confidence in future sessions.

IMAGINING – WHAT MUSICAL WORLD IS THIS CLIENT LEADING US INTO?

I encourage the group to listen again to the same section, this time focusing specifically on the 'musical world' within the client's playing. Each group member contributes their creative ideas to this discussion – what musical style, genre or historical period does the playing remind them of? What musical picture comes to mind? What is the musical whole of which the client's music is a part? The group produces a few different images, with one thing in common, which I highlight to Jean – they were all a single line accompaniment to the drum (contrasting with the full harmonic accompaniment on the piano she had provided in the session). For example, one image is reminiscent of Britten's opera recitative, another an ostinato atonal violin motif. I suggest we move to workshopping to experience and experiment with these ideas.

Here we see the transition from working together to describe what *has been* happening to working together to imagine what *might be* possible and how. How is the therapist hearing the client? How *could* the therapist be hearing the client? And what possibilities for personal musical development does this suggest? Within this transition, a precise focus needs to be maintained on what has already been learned about the nature of the client's participation (and, based as rigorously as possible on this, a shared subjective conception of their potential musical experience) at the same time as imagining what might be possible as therapeutic ways forward. This ongoing focus anchors the transition, acting as a source of inspiration for musically imaginative work while guarding it from being swept away by a tide of assumption or habit. Within this process, the supervisor holds both the needs of the therapist and the needs of the client in focus. Navigating the complexity of such a dual focus is an important element of supervision in many therapeutic disciplines (Ladany, Friedlander & Nelson 2005).

This step of awakening musical imagination relies on the supervisee's and the other group members' musical artistry and creativity in hearing the client's musical offering as a part of a larger musical whole. The components of these imagined musical 'worlds' must be carefully considered to ascertain what needs to be added by the therapist in order for the bigger, collaboratively created musical meaning to come to life, drawing the client into closer musical connection and further into possibilities for development. In this case, an element contributed by the client (a rhythmic gesture), when framed by the single atonal melodic line contributed by the therapist, opens up a new potential opportunity for musical connection between them. When the therapist enters the musical 'world' led by the client's contribution it creates a potential for a thriving musical collaboration in which the expressive and aesthetic meaning of the client's contribution is recognised, valued and encouraged. Supervision also serves as a reminder to music therapists of the importance of nurturing their musical creativity and imagination via ongoing exposure to new and diverse musical worlds as well as active practical engagement with these as a musician.

The therapist's way of connecting with their client's music and the client's potential musical experience are further addressed via workshopping – an opportunity for the therapist, supported by the supervisor and supervision group, to have an embodied experience of a musical interaction and then, building on this embodied experience, to experiment with imagined ways forward.

The movement from verbal discussion to musical exploration in workshopping requires courage from the supervisor, who must initiate the shift at an appropriate moment, usually accompanied by physical action (getting up from the sitting position, moving to a specific instrument, rearranging the room and the participants' positions for role-play, etc.). The supervisor's conviction about the value of workshopping supports them in this. Beginner supervisors often need support in this area through investigation of their own experience of supervision and the role workshopping plays in it.

WORKSHOPPING – HAVING A GO AND LEARNING FROM DOING

To deepen Jean's insight into Zeb's experience, I suggest Jean role-plays Zeb, focusing in particular on embodying his movements and playing musically as closely as possible to how he did in the session. Group members take turns in the therapist role, trying out the ideas they had imagined earlier. This is an opportunity for Jean to come a little closer to Zeb's world and his potential experience of this musical interaction. It's also an opportunity to experience alternative ideas for musical accompanying given her desire for greater flow in her playing with Zeb.

After each turn, Jean describes her experience in the role of Zeb. To one group member who, as therapist, has used an atonal ostinato pattern, flexible in time and articulation but with a repeated melodic shape, she comments that this provided her with a much-needed sense of recognisability and order at the same time as being adjustable.

I then ask Jean to revert to her own role as Zeb's music therapist, and another group member takes on the role of Zeb. Jean says she wants to work further with the melodic ostinato idea she has just experienced in the client role, and we make a start. However, a few seconds in I feel impelled to intervene. Jean is meeting the music of the 'client' precisely, but as soon as a sense of regularity is established, she latches on to this, apparently not noticing the ever-changing nature of the client's response. It becomes apparent that it is the unpredictability of the metre in the client's playing that needs to be continuously attended to in order to retain the connection and engagement with them.

This leads to another episode of role-reversal as I briefly assume the therapist's role (with Jean playing Zeb again). I want her to experience the impact of my ceasing to listen closely to her. I then offer an alternative where the metre remains flexible while the shape of the melodic ostinato motif is retained. Having discussed her experience of these two ways of listening and interacting, we switch roles again so that Jean is again in the role of therapist. She works on sustaining both her listening and the flexibility of the metre in her playing.

Workshopping as an integral part of supervision is intended as inductive rather than deductive learning (Minuchin, Reiter & Borda 2014). In line with our understanding that musical development is personal development (Aigen 2014), the supervision process of growing personally in awareness, insight and confidence is intrinsically linked with the musical process of experimenting with and experiencing musical companionship in action. Workshopping is therefore a crucial element of music therapy supervision, linking the musical and the personal in action.

Our concern for enabling, embodied, active musical experience within Nordoff Robbins supervision practice has parallels with action methods used in supervision within systemic family therapy and psychodrama. For example, family therapist and psychodramatist Ochs (2021) appeals to supervisors not to overlook action methods in supervision. She sees these as crucial in helping a supervisee 'to overcome clinical impasse with their clients...deepening her understanding of the client's points of view...and exploring *through action* alternatives to what she is doing that is contributing to the impasse (p.264)'. With this in mind, Ochs invites supervisors to shift from 'talk supervisor' to 'action supervisor (p.258)'.

From systemic psychotherapy, Sherbersky & Gill (2020) suggest that 'by moving into action, we can change how supervisees think and act "on their feet" rather than what they say they do' (p.80). They discuss key supervision 'action techniques' such as mirroring, role-reversal and doubling, concluding that experiencing 'the action' and reflecting on it 'can mobilize insight and understanding that moves the work to a new level' (p.84).

Likewise in music therapy supervision, workshopping generates new levels of insight. It offers potential for increasing empathy and insight into the *client's needs* and their human experience, both within and beyond the music. Simultaneously, it offers perspectives on the *supervisee's actions* as a therapist. In this process, the musical habits and comfort zones of the therapist as well as potential new strategies for musical relating can be safely explored, enabling the subsequent growth of the therapist's awareness and confidence.

Kellerman (1992, p.85) discusses visceral learning in psychodrama supervision, suggesting that insights from action in supervision offer 'integration of emotional, cognitive, imaginative, behavioural and inter-personal learning experiences ... they are gained through a concurrence of inner and outer learning and cannot be given to the supervisee by the supervisor in the form of an interpretation'. On a practical level, as described above, this embodied experience supports the building of the supervisee's confidence when they find themselves back in the ther-apy room. In addition, it enables the supervisee to practise the courage required for staying present and working with the unknown, both of which are essential for empowering clients to lead musical collabora-tions. These elements of their therapeutic stance are prerequisites for facilitating clients to lead musical collaborations.

Musical meaning, in music therapy as elsewhere, is inherently embodied, framed in time and space, and physically relational (Havi-land 2011). Investing real effort into attempting to come a little closer to the experience of the client through embodiment (albeit inevitably imperfectly) and focusing on one's own experience of alternative musical ways of being with the client promotes active, respectful, physical and critical learning on the part of the supervisee. In role-playing we seek not to mimic the client but to support the supervisee in their efforts to understand the client's experience better so that they will be better able to serve them. As with all aspects of supervision, it must be rooted in both respect and acute awareness of the limitations of our subjective experience and done out of a powerful sense of the need to honour the client and their potential.

A few practical role-play options are listed in Table 5.1. How many options the supervisor uses and in which order will depend on what has been previously observed in the extract and the outcome of the discus-sion. It also depends on moment-by-moment developments within the workshopping and the supervisor's judgement of personal, musical and relational elements. The supervisee's learning style, individual musi-cal creativity and skills also shape the direction of the workshopping.

Finally, the insights of the participants of the role-play and the observing members of the group inform the further evolution of the process. Each of these options has different affordances and limitations and each therapist's way of experiencing them will inform the supervisor's choice of direction.

Table 5.1: Examples of different role-play options in workshopping

DRAWING CONCLUSIONS FROM THE INSIGHTS STEMMING FROM OUR MUSICAL EXPERIENCES, ARCHING BACK TO THE SUPERVISION QUESTION

As time is running out, I invite Jean and the group to summarise what has been experienced and learned. There is brief discussion of how we deal with metrical unpredictability and how pulse can sometimes give us a false sense of stability which can remove us from connection with clients. Jean observes that metrical regularity is only one way of structuring musical time: Zeb is inviting her to be open to the many different ways it can be organised. I amplify this, noting that by staying connected with the unpredictability in the client's playing, we are able to highlight and reinforce the meaning in their timing, shapes of phrasing, articulation and accents, thus recognising and celebrating the unique meaning and beauty inherent in what they are offering musically. Not connecting with this uniqueness impacts our ability to move forward together, leading to Jean's initial experience of inefficacy. We reflect on the importance of cultivating sustained listening as the principal route towards facilitating connection with our clients, which is crucial for any therapeutic change.

Jean resolves to try to share her awareness of the importance of connection and listening with the teaching assistant, which will help their understanding of music therapy practice and increase potential for multidisciplinary collaboration.

Here, the supervisor pulls the threads of the supervision together, encouraging Jean to reflect on her embodied experiences during workshopping so that she is clear about the links between this and her initial question. Wherever possible, it is important for the supervisee themselves to be able to identify this connection and the learning points they are going to work on in their own musical practice and draw on in subsequent sessions.

As in Nordoff Robbins music therapy practice, the direction of this supervision process has emerged from attention to musical detail, both within the recorded extracts of music therapy practice brought to supervision and within the workshopping. The discrepancy in the hearings of Zeb's musical presentation (identified in the initial listening to the extract) provided a valuable direction at the outset of the supervision. In addition, the observation of Jean's tendency to lose precision in her listening after the initial connection within the workshopping provided additional insight about her need to continue engaging with the ongoing unpredictability of Zeb's music, something she could pursue through the cultivation of sustained listening.

CONCLUSION – LINKING BACK TO THE APPROACH

Supervision within the Nordoff Robbins approach manifests many of the key features of the approach itself. Here we focus on just three: listening, imagination and courage.

Listening is something that many therapists, not only music therapists, would regard as foundational to their work. Within the music-centred Nordoff Robbins approach there is a particular concern for continuous and embodied listening with acuity, especially to the musical detail of what is happening moment-by-moment within the interaction.

This provides potential directions for the therapeutic process. Likewise, within supervision, first, collaborative retrospective listening in detail to what has happened in the session, and second, in-the-moment listening and experimenting in workshopping, together provide insights from which the supervision process can evolve.

Imagination (musical and hence personal) is key to development in music therapy. Much of a Nordoff Robbins music therapist's training is founded on learning to ask oneself, 'What kind of musical worlds could this be part of?' Likewise, in supervision, the supervisor is required to be thoroughly attentive to the musical detail that is being observed and heard. Rigorously grounded in this, they must then be creatively imaginative in terms of how to connect with it meaningfully and considering what kinds of development might be possible. This responsibility is shared with the supervisee and the group, who are all encouraged to exercise and develop their own musical-personal imagination as well as their ability to put this imagination into action. Supervision thus provides a safe space for the kind of imaginative and informed embodied experimentation that then enables a therapist to offer meaningful experiences of musical companionship and development to their clients.

Courage is required of both supervisor and supervisee for the necessary taking of risks in the supervisory environment: both must engage wholeheartedly with the unknown, just as in music therapy. Honesty and openness are prerequisites. Listening with precision uncovers assumptions made while listening. This requires considerable personal discipline and courage. Role-play within workshopping can be daunting: courage to go beyond our own comfort zones is required if we are to translate our insights into action rather than simply applying prelearned theory or techniques. For the supervisor, courage is needed to encourage ongoing precision in listening as well as to move from verbally discussing the therapeutic process to active and embodied exploration of practical potential ways forward. This courage is underpinned not only by a shared faith in music's potential to offer and expand opportunities for our clients to thrive, but also by an understanding of our responsibility to keep developing our ability to enable music to do its work.

Within the Nordoff Robbins approach, the notion of the client as collaborator rather than recipient of an intervention is crucial. They are our partner in the process of their music therapy, a co-musician with the capacity for complex, multi-modal ways of co-creating, experiencing and developing what happens. As music therapists, to serve our clients well, we must put our full selves – and hence our full musicianship – at their service. Supervision provides a regular space where we can rehearse this by critically reviewing our work in focused analytic company. In particular, we can consider the client's possible experience and what we can do – musically, and hence also personally – to honour and enhance this. This musically person-centred discipline of supervision is fundamental to our striving to be as useful as possible for the people we work with.

REFERENCES

Aigen, K. (1998) *Paths of Development in Nordoff-Robbins Music Therapy*. Gilsum, NH: Barcelona Publishers.

Aigen, K. (2014) Music-centered dimensions of Nordoff-Robbins music therapy. *Music Therapy Perspectives*, 32(1), pp.18–29.

Brown, S. (2009) 'Supervision in Context: A Balancing Act.' In H. Odell-Miller & E. Richards (eds) *Supervision of Music Therapy: A Theoretical and Practical Handbook* (pp.119–134). London: Routledge.

Haviland, J. B. (2011) 'Musical Spaces.' In J. Streeck, C. Goodwin & C. LeBaron (eds) *Embodied Interaction: Language and Body in the Material World* (pp.289–304). New York, NY: Cambridge University Press.

Kellerman, P. (1992) *Focus on Psychodrama*. London: Jessica Kingsley Publishers.

Ladany, N., Friedlander, M. L. & Nelson, M. L. (2005) *Critical Events in Psychotherapy Supervision: An Interpersonal Approach*. Washington, DC: American Psychological Association.

Minuchin, S., Reiter, M. & Borda, C. (2014). *The Craft of Family Therapy*. New York, NY: Routledge.

Nordoff, P. & Robbins, C. (1971) *Therapy in Music for Handicapped Children*. London: Gollancz.

Nordoff, P. & Robbins, C. (2007) *Creative Music Therapy: A Guide to Fostering Clinical Musicianship* (second edition). Gilsum, NH: Barcelona Publishers.

Norwegian Television (1971) *Øyvind Kan Slå På Tromme* [Oyvind Can Beat the Drum] Documentary film. Oslo: Norwegian Television. Available at: www.youtube.com/watch?v=81f8Wt7S_38 (Accessed 6 January 2024).

Ochs, P. (2021) Using action methods in clinical supervision: A journey from talk to action. *Social Work with Groups*, 44(3), pp.258–272.

Sherbersky, H. & Gill, M (2020) Creative action techniques in supervision. *Journal of Family Psychotherapy*, 31(3–4), pp.79–95.

Turry, A. (2001) 'Supervision in Nordoff-Robbins Music Therapy Training Program.' In M. Forinash (ed.) *Music Therapy Supervision*, pp.335-362. Gilsum, NH: Barcelona Publishers.

Verney, R. & Ansdell, A. (2010) *Conversations on Nordoff-Robbins Music Therapy*. Gilsum, NH: Barcelona Publishers.

CHAPTER 6

In Search of the Little Blue Girl

A Creative Exploration into the Supervisory
Relationship Between a Music Therapist Supervisee
and a Dramatherapist Supervisor

SOPHIE RIGA DE SPINOZA AND MANDY CARR

It was an evening late in October, and I distinctly remember peering down at a 'sculpture' I, Sophie, had just created, using various objects that my creative arts supervisor, Mandy, had provided. Having recently completed the Creative Arts Supervision Training (CAST) at the Royal Central School of Speech and Drama in London, I had been seeing Mandy for six months. This was our review session in which she invited me to use any of the objects laid out to build a visual representation of how I felt our supervision had been progressing. If this had been a talking session, my rational self would have politely and verbally reflected on what I felt had been a very rich and enjoyable first few months. However, instead I was gazing down on a Communicube (www.communicube.co.uk), a three-dimensional grid with five levels, made of transparent plastic, familiar in dramatherapy, but new to me. I tried to unpick the meaning of the various levels of objects I had laid out: a strange 'family' of items ranging from smooth stones and coloured material through to a figure of a little blue girl lying down on the very bottom level of the cube. In retelling this scene, I am reminded of the initial discomfort of trying to choose and place the objects, followed by the 30 minutes of looking at and exploring from every angle what I had recreated. And finally, together with Mandy, trying to make sense of it all. Who was that little blue girl, and what did she represent?

This chapter is written from the point of view of the music therapist supervisee, Sophie; however, it was co-created by both Sophie and Mandy, and Mandy's reflective words appear in parts. Mandy, as supervisor, is interested in the potential of creative supervision to support professionals in educational contexts, in co-creating supportive relationships within supervision in order to draw on unfamiliar modalities or art forms through which to increase awareness and vision.

INTRODUCTION

The significance of supervision in a music therapist's professional, and some might argue personal, development cannot be understated. A therapist might have many supervisors during their career to support their practice as it grows and changes over time. Pedersen identifies two different stages of supervision: that of the student and newly qualified versus that of the advanced music therapist (Pedersen 2009). She argues that the supervisor of the former should stay within one musical approach, moving towards multiple musical approaches when supervising a more experienced practitioner. This need for specific music expertise in the early years after graduating certainly resonates with my own experience of supervision when practising as a newly qualified therapist. As my practice has grown and developed, and over time I too have trained as a supervisor, my needs as a supervisee have also evolved. In the revision of her 1997 paper, Supervision in Context: A Balancing Act, Brown identifies this shift in need when reflecting on her own practice with a very experienced colleague, which she describes as being:

> much more 'level' and interactive between us... I have wondered for some time if as a profession we need to redefine and refocus the term 'supervision' itself – the clinical needs of newly beginning student therapists are not the same as those of very experienced therapists. On this basis, I would now propose 'consultation with colleagues' as a mutually beneficial and bidirectional further stage. (Brown 2009, p.130)

Here, Brown is describing a facet of collegiate supervision between two music therapists, but this 'mutually beneficial and bidirectional further stage' perhaps best describes the way in which Mandy and I have come together in our supervisory relationship. Since graduating I have worked closely with dramatherapists, both clinically as well as co-collaborating in written research. This has meant that my clinical practice has been greatly influenced by this modality, and drama elements of story, movement and symbolism are very present in my therapeutic approach.

Similarly, Mandy too straddles the two disciplines, and has a long and established relationship with music therapy. As a senior lecturer on the MA dramatherapy training at Anglia Ruskin University, Mandy became increasingly committed to partnerships between modalities and specifically between music and drama. While the MA maintained separate trainings for each modality, particular aspects of improvisation and psychology were taught to both groups together. As a result, Mandy has been fascinated by exploring whether cross-modality supervision can also provide further opportunities for enhanced learning, creativity and insight.

The purpose of this chapter is to consider the impact of using creativity in the supervision room, while taking into account our cross-modalities, and as such it is divided into two parts.

In the first part, the use of creativity, and how it differs to that of interventions that are purely language based, will be discussed in relation to brain function. This is further explored within the context of supervision, and the way in which creative techniques can be used to support the supervisee and their client material. In the second part of the chapter, through the use of creative techniques, the supervisory relationship will be explored, as well as the profound effect that using creativity has had, and continues to have, on this. We will examine the effect that our different modalities have on this relationship, and the challenges, advantages and disadvantages that this creates. We will reflect on what happens when there is resistance to using creativity in our supervision together, and why this might be. Finally, we will suggest that it is this very discomfort, enhanced by our creative differences, that is integral to the growth that takes place within our supervisory relationship.

SEVEN-EYED-MODEL AND THE CAST APPROACH

In order to contextualise the discussion of creative supervision in this chapter, it may be helpful to first give a brief background of the supervision training that Mandy and I have undertaken. Established in 1998, CAST uses the Seven-Eyed Model of supervision (Hawkins & Shohet 2012) as its theoretical underpinning. This model focuses on the relationships between client, therapist and supervisor, which are categorised across seven different areas, defined as modes:

- Mode 1: Focusing on the client and what and how they present
- Mode 2: Exploring the strategies and interventions used by the supervisee
- Mode 3: Focusing on the relationship between the client and the supervisee
- Mode 4: Focusing on the supervisee
- Mode 5: Focusing on the supervisory relationship
- Mode 6: The supervisor focusing on their own process
- Mode 7: Focusing on the wider contexts in which the work happens.

Hawkins writes that the model:

> is both relational and systemic in that it looks closely at what happens in both the relationship with the clients, what is happening within the supervisory relationship, and considers the interplay of both within the wider systemic contexts of clients, practitioners and supervisor. (Hawkins & Shohet 2012, p.86)

The CAST approach to supervision takes the Hawkins and Shohet model and overlays it with creative techniques such as art, sculpture, music, movement, object work and role-play. With the help and guidance of the supervisor, the supervisee is invited to use these various creative media as a method of gaining insight into the client material that they bring to sessions. Creativity, therefore, is pivotal to the supervisory relationship being explored.

AN EXPLORATION OF CREATIVITY AND ITS USE IN THE BRAIN
Creativity and the brain

Tempest (2020, p.107) writes, 'My creativity enables me to access other worlds that exist parallel to this one.' The concept of creativity is central to the practice of music therapy, given that the therapist and client communicate through a musical language. In his book *Music Instinct*, Ball (2011) writes, 'Music can trigger physiological processes... It can, for example, affect the immune system, boosting levels of proteins that combat microbial infection. Both performing and listening can also regulate the body's production of mood-influencing hormones such as cortisol' (p.245). It feels important, then, to consider the neuroscience of the brain when exploring how creativity and arts-based techniques might differ from verbal language-based techniques.

Historically the right- and left-brain hemispheres were ascribed as attending to different processes, with the left side focusing on logic and speech, and the right on emotion and visual/motor skills. It was erroneously believed that dominance of the use of the left or right brain could determine personality (e.g. left associated with being logical, right with being creative). However, as science has progressed, and ways of investigating the brain have become more sophisticated, research has revealed that, although the left and right hemispheres do have their own specific domains, in a healthy brain they do not function in isolation from one another. Instead, they are in continual communication when an activity is carried out (Siegel 1999).

In addition to these specific domains, McGilchrist (2019) highlights the different thinking styles of the right- and left-brain hemispheres, where the left is more able to process the individual elements, and the right tends to make a bigger picture by searching for more generalised patterns. This is particularly relevant when considering music-making as, according to McGilchrist:

> Music consists entirely of relations, 'betweenness'... Actually the music is not *just* in the gaps any more than it is *just* in the notes: it is in the whole that the silence makes together. Each note becomes transformed by the context in which it lies. (2019, p.72)

In an amateur (or non) musician, McGilchrist identifies the act of creating music as a right-hemisphere 'language'.

This also applies when considering other creative media such as art, story, drama and movement, along with their inherent symbolism. Here the non-verbal story that is constructed in the right hemisphere of the brain is often of greater emotional magnitude than the verbal narrative created by the left hemisphere (McNamee 2004; Wood & Pignatelli 2019). The creative act therefore can potentially offer a visual or auditory experience 'greater' than the spoken language used to describe it.

Creativity in the supervision room

Given the rich emotional non-verbal language that the creative act activates, the use of creativity in a supervisory setting can potentially amplify the client material that the supervisee brings in verbal form. It can also enhance insight into client needs and the client – therapist relationship, as well as shedding new light on psychodynamic issues such as transference and countertransference. Further, it can be a powerful form of self-care, providing creative opportunities for therapists' self-expression and reflection (Hinz 2018).

In their development of a specific art-based supervision tool, called the Scribble Story Technique, Wood and Pignatelli place emphasis on the visual and storytelling element of supervision, which combines the symbolic and the visual, thereby allowing the supervisee two chances to interpret the same picture. They write of their own visual technique, 'these types of changes can, of course, come about through just verbal processing, however, the use of the Scribble Story Technique provides another unique avenue of discovery, partnering with the wisdom of the unconscious and the value of symbolic representation' (Wood & Pignatelli 2019, p.241).

When relating this to my six-month review described earlier, the visual sculpture that I had created with the objects on the Communicube was, in effect, a second visual narrative alongside my more measured verbal response of 'everything is fine'. The three-dimensional nature of the sculpture meant that Mandy and I were able to look down over it from a height, and Mandy openly wondered what the model of the little blue girl might represent, observing that I had placed her at the bottom of the structure, where it was hard to see, and might also feel hard to access. An uncomfortable knot began to form in my stomach, and as I paid silent attention to this, I became aware of the emerging feelings of sadness, unease and discomfort associated with this somatic response, and how incongruent these felt to my initial verbal response of everything being fine. And so began the journey of exploration into this feeling of disconnection, and what the little blue girl might represent.

AN EXPERIENTIAL EXPLORATION OF THE CO-AUTHOR'S SUPERVISOR/SUPERVISEE RELATIONSHIP
Creative conversations

When Mandy and I met to think about how we were going to explore our supervisory relationship for this chapter, inevitably our discussion turned to this early review with the Communicube. I remarked how useful I had found this activity and how disconcerting, and yet also empowering, it had felt at the time to be able to explore and start a dialogue about what I needed in my supervision. In light of this we decided to revisit this medium of three-dimensional sculpture and object work in order to explore our professional relationship. Armed with arts materials in our respective Zoom offices, we each set about creating a three-dimensional picture/sculpt that represented our viewpoint of our supervisee/supervisor relationship. Object work such as this is an example of a creative activity that might be suggested by a creative arts supervisor. The supervisee is invited to use objects to create a tableau to represent the scenario that they are bringing to supervision. This is used as a starting point for discussion and exploration.

Once we had completed our sculpts, we revealed them on screen and briefly discussed how the process felt. Following this, we each wrote a piece reflecting our interpretation of our own sculpts.

Sophie's sculpt – her description and reflection

Description: I put my sculpture together very quickly, not thinking too hard, but feeling confident in my choice of object, and the placement thereof.

Reflection: *Initially, I viewed the scene from the front, but it feels important to view this from the side, with the light streaming in from the left, creating long shadows to the right.*

The central focus of the scene is the juxtaposition of the carved stone between the kazoo and the figure with pointed ears.

Reflection: *The lighting and low viewpoint make me think of an urban New York skyline and this resonates somehow with the navigation of mine and Mandy's relationship, winding through streets, both craning our heads up to the top of the buildings, trying to find our way.*

And then, juxtaposed against this urban backdrop are the purple unicorn and the figure with pointed ears with enough space between them to allow a breath (in contrast to the cluster of objects behind them).

Reflection: *Perhaps there is something about our difference in approach, and the way in which we work, which allows that necessary space for us to think about the work that I am bringing to the supervision room?*

The disturbing dinosaur skeletal toy (which is very much hidden behind the unicorn) and then the grater and the two gold coins also behind the unicorn are pivotal to the scenario.

Reflection: *The proximity of the grater to the gold hints at some of the discomfort that the creative process can cause. This immediately brings to mind the resistance that I often feel in supervision when being invited to engage in the art forms on offer; the dinosaur skeleton is a nod to the unprocessed, and often difficult, client (or supervisee) material that I bring to my supervision. The gold coins allude to those moments of clarity, when the 'penny drops' or I discover something about myself as a therapist/supervisor that I did not know before.*

To the left of this is an open castanet which is 'eating' a long piece of knotted string.

Reflection: *This perhaps reflects my slightly gnarly relationship to using music within supervision.*

In contrast, and on the other side of the picture, is the placement of a pebble and fish.

Reflection: *I remember choosing the stone as it felt warm to the touch, and somehow protected and offered shade to the fish (again, perhaps the fish*

*representing an aspect of myself/sessions that I brought to our supervision).
My overall feeling about these two elements is that they create a sense of
balance, and again are slightly displaced to the central bunching of objects.*

Mandy's sculpt – her reflection

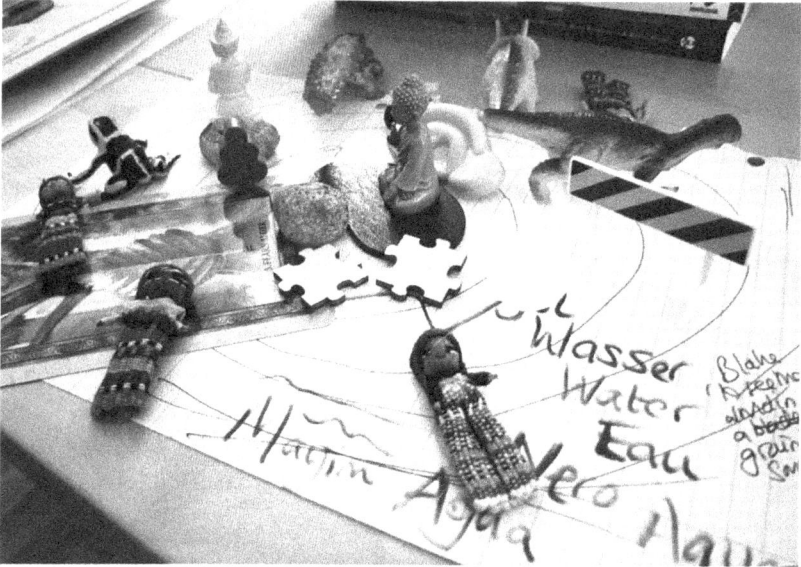

I am initially struck by the warm, rich texture of the sculpt. The spirals
drawn on the paper reflect the spirals in the shell. And the different
words for water remind me of my visit to a Hindu temple, fronted by a
calming pond, with the inscription: 'So many different words for water.
Yet it is the same water. And so it is with God.' In orthodox Jewish traditions, the word 'God' is seen as too sacred to name or to write. Are there
things in our supervision that feel too sacred or too painful to name?

Reflection: *I notice the diversity of the living creatures – different shapes,
sizes, textures. Mammals and reptiles. A human and an amphibian. Living
and extinct. Needing the right environment in order to thrive. What kind of
environment are we co-creating in the supervisory space? Does this reflect
the environment that the supervisee and her clients work in? I am aware
of the paucity of musical instruments I can offer, a few meagre pieces of
percussion. Sophie has brought her own instruments on occasions. Maybe
we could revisit that idea.*
   And in the centre a giant ear. Insert line drawing of ear. [PQ]*I can almost*

hear the ripples and rhythms of the water. So many different ways of listening. How do I listen in the supervision space? And now the picture of the tree seems to rise up from the water, although the grey stone blocks it from fully inhabiting the 'lake'. Insert line drawing of picture card with the stone on top of it I find myself wanting to relate musical terms to the supervision: rhythm, melody, tone, silence. I admire the musical expertise of music therapists. I start sinking into 'not-good-enough-ness', which I go on to process within my own supervision. A shared theme for both of us and the clients we discuss. Perhaps our different modalities help us name our own experiences of not being good enough. Perhaps curiosity, a quality important in this work, can be more easily accessed, because of the differences between our professional backgrounds as well as the similarities.

DISCUSSION

After performing this creative activity and coming together once more to reflect on what we have written, Mandy and I are both struck by the similar themes that emerge: the supervisory space, listening, not-knowing and not being good enough, as well as the difference in our modalities and what this brings to the relationship, particularly when resistance to creativity is felt.

The supervisory space

On first comparison, Mandy and my choice of setting appear very different; while I compare my landscape to that of a New York skyline, Mandy's sculpture is set in nature. My picture is taken specifically from the side, with lighting that casts long shadows across the objects; the setting depicts a journey of the two of us, exploring a collection of jagged objects and their shadows. Mandy's picture, however, is taken directly from above, giving a sense of symmetry and balance over the main background of water, which in both literature and art is often considered as a symbol for change. Similarly, her careful placement of the picture of the leaf is a reminder of fertility and growth. These contrasting scenes could be representative of the fact that we are trained in different modalities (which will be discussed later), but also may lean towards the different roles that we inhabit in the supervisee/supervisor relationship. The supervisor offers an outsider's perspective, which can bring balance to the supervisee, who is located 'inside' the issue being considered.

Despite this difference in scenery and viewpoint, the symbolism that we each ascribe to certain elements within our sculpts is similar. While I identify the placement of a pebble as something that provides protection and shade, Mandy remarks on the 'warm, rich texture' of her sculpt, writing, 'The spirals drawn on the paper reflect the spirals in the shell. And the different words for water remind me of my visit to a Hindu temple, fronted by a calming pond.' In the exploration of her own sculpt, Mandy questions the notion of 'needing the right environment to thrive'. Davies and Sloboda identify that the supervisee needs an environment in which they feel their material is confidential and they are taken seriously. 'By maintaining a secure frame, the supervisor makes it possible for supervisees to open up and share their vulnerabilities, doubts, lack of skills or competencies and, of course, the difficulties presented by the clients' (2009, p.160). Mandy's imagery, filled with such balance and symmetry, appears to capture this secure frame metaphorically in her three-dimensional scene.

Cross-modality

One of the most striking areas of similarity in our sculpts is our consideration of the different modalities. Collaborations across arts therapies, in particular music therapy and dramatherapy, have been explored in *Collaborations Within and Between Dramatherapy and Music Therapy* (Oldfield & Carr 2016). This looks at the link between the two disciplines and their potential synergy. It was partly inspired by students' experiences of training with others from a different creative modality. A dramatherapy student, for instance, commented that the *affect attunement* (Stern 1985) she had learned through the musical content of the course had helped her attune to the different emotions of the therapy group in her work placement (Oldfield & Carr 2016,). Similarly, the music therapists were also inspired by the dramatherapy techniques which helped them engage in play and reconnect to their inner child, enabling them to become even more communicative and playful in their music-making.

Cross-modality within the arts therapies in the supervisory space has also been documented to a certain extent. Sherbersky (2014) writes about the value added by using psychodrama techniques in family therapy supervision, and the art therapist Wakeman (2014) explores her work as a creative arts supervisor with a trainee play therapist. Much of the research here focuses on the collaborative effect of using creative techniques across the different arts modalities, rather than looking at the implication of the difference in modality *between* supervisee and supervisor. Moreover, at the time of writing this chapter, very little could be found that looked at the specific cross-modalities of music and drama together in the supervision room.

When I undertook my creative supervisor training, I was one of only two music therapists among 12 other dramatherapists. This shaped my experience of the training; on the one hand I had a creative skill that I could offer the group that most did not have, but on the other hand I was thrown into a world of drama-based interventions that often felt alien and scary. Edward Said talks about the merits of being in a minority or on the margins: 'I actually prefer not being quite right and being out of place' (Said 2000, p.295). It was this being-out-of-placeness that added discomfort on one hand, but potential growth on the other. The training showed me that taking creative risks could present me with an insight into my own practice, as well as the role of supervisor, accompanying a supervisee on their own journey of insight.

Not knowing and not-good-enough-ness

When describing our response to the object sculptures, we both identify different aspects that our cross-modality brings to our relationship. I identify a physical gap in the sculpt objects and contemplate whether this gap between us (and our approaches) allows for space – a space that is needed in order to process and 'wonder'. Of the client/patient relationship, Patrick Casement writes:

> therapeutic skill does not depend upon knowledge, as opposed to ignorance. Rather, there is an important difference between the attempt to understand something from a position of not-knowing and the tendency to prompt, or to direct, which goes with knowing too well. (Casement 1990, p.10)

When applied to the supervisor/supervisee relationship, I would argue that the different modalities encourage the former, rather than the latter.

Interestingly, from her supervisory viewpoint, Mandy holds a different interpretation, with the plethora of different objects causing her to question the supervisory space and environment and what she observes as a 'paucity of musical instruments I can offer, a few meagre pieces of percussion'. Reflecting further' she writes, 'I admire the musical expertise of music therapists. I start sinking into "not-good-enough-ness"... A shared theme for both us and the clients we discuss. Perhaps our different modalities help us name our own experiences of not being good enough.' This has echoes of my own out-of-placeness in supervision training, further developing the idea that difference can potentially offer insight, both into our own understanding, and also that of our clients (or supervisees).

What happens when the creativity doesn't flow

Despite our landscapes being described using different sets of objects, and taken from different viewpoints, both identify a painful aspect of the supervisory process. In response to her exploration of water, and reflection on spiritual associations therewith, Mandy asks the question 'Are there things in our supervision that feel too painful to name?' Similarly, I note the small grater, assigning it to 'the discomfort the creative process can cause', which 'brings to mind the resistance that I often feel in supervision when being invited to engage in the art forms on offer'.

Davies and Sloboda refer to 'invisible boundaries', and using Yalom's (2002) theory of 'here and now' (Davies & Sloboda 2009, p.159), distinguish between the interactions inside the therapy room and those that occur outside.

> It is more risky to address the present 'here and now' because of the personal feelings and interactions it evokes... It is our understanding that if something in the 'here and now' boundary feels too difficult to say, then this is a clear indication that it needs to be said. Finding ways of addressing the difficulty, however uncomfortable, might be the only way to further the understanding of the work. (p.165)

As Davies and Sloboda point out, this not only applies to the client work being presented in supervision, but also the feelings present between supervisee and supervisor. Perhaps the invitation from the supervisor for me to move from the 'there and then' verbal narrative to doing something creative in the 'here and now' shifts my supervisee lens. This change of viewpoint potentially causes initial feelings of resistance, hence my hesitation before engaging in something creative. At times, I choose to stay in the verbal mode, but often I will accept the invitation, trusting that the process will support what I perhaps have not been able to verbalise up to that point.

In our analysis of our creative activity for this chapter, however, I notice in particular my resistance to exploring creatively through music. This is highlighted in my sculpture, where I comment on the placement of a castanet and 'gnarly bit of string', which I believe signifies my 'slightly gnarly relationship to using music within supervision'. We reflected on this in our discussion of the sculptures.

M: I am aware that we haven't harnessed many musical elements in our supervision.

S: Do you mean the music?

M: I mean, yes, I mean using a mixture of music and drama.

S: But do you feel, and I feel this, that there is quite a lot of resistance from me to use music?

M: Yes.

Our subsequent discussion raises the question of why I am more willing to use other creative methods, rather than music. Perhaps a part of me wishes to get away from the pressure of expertise that I often feel as a music therapist with my client. We also wonder together whether this reluctance to use music in the supervision room highlights a wider disengagement with music, beyond that of our supervisee/supervisor relationship.

TAKING A CREATIVE RISK: A RETURN TO THE BLUE GIRL

To return to the review session described in the opening scene of this chapter, up to that point I had never been asked as a professional to review something in a creative way. In my experience, evaluations had usually been in writing, numbered on a sliding scale from 1 through to 5, with further questions asking you to rate what you like, what could be done better, and so on. When Mandy invited me to do this creatively, my immediate (internal) response was to decline, as I could not understand how a creative activity could facilitate what I felt was such a logical function. Sensing my hesitation, Mandy said, 'You don't have to, only if it is something you would like to do...' and in that moment I chose to take the creative risk. The offer of the Communicube as a way to explore our relationship – what I needed, what I wasn't getting in supervision – allowed me to inhabit an uncomfortable space that I perhaps would not have been able to access if evaluating in a more traditional verbal-only way. Mandy's open-ended questions enquiring what the little blue girl might mean, and the space she gave me to wonder and reflect (as opposed to rushing to attach a definite meaning to the scene) enabled me to look beyond the social politeness I had up to that point experienced in supervision, and instead turn my gaze towards a more authentic appraisal of the immediate here and now. And here again, four years later, the question of the little blue girl's significance still inhabits the space between us. Sometimes we wonder together if it might be something musical in supervision that is missing. At other times I have identified the lack of music with my own clients, and indeed in my own personal music-making. Over time, it has become the metaphor of 'that which is not being attended to', and the meaning of this metaphor shifts from session to session.

As Mandy and I pack away our objects, I am aware that the creative process we have just undertaken has added further insight into our supervisory relationship. This is not only in terms of the evaluation of my own needs and whether they are being met in supervision, but also in using creativity to reflect on the needs of my supervisees and their clients.

FINAL REFLECTIONS

For Mandy and me, the process of writing this chapter has reinforced for us the importance of the authenticity and trust needed in the supervisory relationship. It is our belief that the use of creativity has enabled us to name and work with the elephant in the room, such as the inner critic, particularly as we are overtly choosing to work with discomfort, and by this we mean the 'other' modality. At times, this cross-modality has created an enjoyable synergy, but on other occasions it has led to dissonance within our dynamic. However, it is often through the exploration of this creative 'crunch' that valuable insight has been gained into the client. We are aware that this approach suits our own personal training and background, and that for some it may not feel useful or appropriate. However, for those to whom this does appeal, we whole-heartedly encourage the use of the creative act to start a conversation in the supervision room.

REFERENCES

Ball, P. (2011) *Music Instinct: How Music Works and Why We Can't Do Without It*. London: Vintage.

Brown, S. (2009) 'Supervision in Context: A Balancing Act.' In H. Odell-Miller & E. Richards (eds) *Supervision of Music Therapy*. London: Routledge.

Casement, P. (1990) *Further Learning from the Patient: The Analytic Space and Process*. London: Routledge.

Davies, A. & Sloboda, A. (2009) 'Turbulence at the Boundary.' In H. Odell-Miller & E. Richards (eds) *Supervision of Music Therapy*. London: Routledge.

Hawkins, P. & Shohet, R. ([1989] 2012) *Supervision in the Helping Professions* (fourth edition). Maidenhead: Open University Press.

Hinz, L. D. (2018) *Beyond Self-Care for Helping Professionals: The Expressive Therapies Continuum and the Life Enrichment Model*. New York, NY: Routledge.

McGilchrist, I. (2019) *The Master and His Emissary: The Divided Brain and the Making of the Western World*. London: Yale University Press.

McNamee, C. M. (2004). Using both sides of the brain: Experiences that integrate art and talk therapy through scribble drawings. *Art Therapy*, 21(3), pp.136–142.

Oldfield, A. & Carr, M. (2016) *Collaborations Within and Between Dramatherapy and Music Therapy*. London and Philadelphia, PA: Jessica Kingsley Publishers.

Pedersen, I. N. (2009) 'Music Therapy Supervision with Students and Professionals: The Use of Music and Analysis of Countertransference Experiences in the Triadic Field.' In H. Odell-Miller and E. Richards (eds) *Supervision of Music Therapy*. London: Routledge.

Said, E. W. (2000) *Out of Place: A Memoir*. London: Granta Books.

Sherbersky, H. (2014) 'Integrating Creative Approaches within Family Therapy Supervision.' In A. Chesner & L. Zografou (eds) *Creative Supervision across Modalities*. London: Jessica Kingsley Publishers.

Siegel, D. J. (1999) *The Developing Mind: How Relationships and the Brain Interact to Shape Who We Are*. London: Guilford Publications.

Stern, D. N. (1985) *The Interpersonal World of the Infant: A View from Psychoanalysis and Developmental Psychology*. London: Routledge.

Tempest, K. (2020) *On Connection*. London: Faber & Faber.

Wakeman, C. (2014) 'Building Imaginative Bridges: Creative Arts Supervision and Therapeutic Work.' In A. Chesner & L. Zografou (eds) *Creative Supervision Across Modalities*. London: Jessica Kingsley Publishers.

Wood, L. L. & Pignatelli, E. C. (2019) The Scribble Story Technique: An arts-based supervision process. *Journal of Creativity in Mental Health*, 14(2), pp.229–242. Available at: https://doi.org/10.1080/15401383.2019.1566041. (Accessed 3 December 2023).

Yalom, I. (2002). *The Gift of Therapy*. London: Piaktus Books.

CHAPTER 7

Group Supervision with the Ahonen Method

Origins and Applications

CATHERINE WARNER, ADAM KISHTAINY AND ABIGAIL WILLIAMS

INTRODUCTION

In this chapter, through discussion and writing together, we aim to explore the origins and development of a method of group music therapy supervision pioneered by Heidi Ahonen-Eerikainen (2003) and practised by all three of us.

As we are seeking to analyse our personal experience to understand the cultural experience of group music therapy supervision and are aiming to do this in a socially conscious way, the approach could be described as autoethnographic (Ellis, Adams & Bochner 2010). Furthermore, we see the approach as 'collaborative autoethnography' in that we are co-constructing our understanding together through our dialogue (Chang, Ngunjiri & Hernandez 2016).

The three of us are practising music therapists and are both supervisors and supervisees. We have worked together in different capacities for a number of years, so have managed at times complex working relationships. We welcome the opportunity to share with the reader our own thoughts and feelings about a practice that we all believe has so much promise in group supervision practice.

Catherine encountered the method first in a conference workshop facilitated by Eckhard Weymann, a German music therapist with substantial experience in forensic music therapy work (2016). He explained that this six-stage approach was influenced by Balint groups (Salinsky

2018) and group analytic therapy approaches. Here is a description of what happened.

Six music therapists sit in a circle surrounding a set of musical instruments. This group has chosen one person's work to explore in supervision after several members of the group briefly described what they might be able to talk about. The chosen music therapist presenter begins to speak. She talks about her therapeutic work with a woman who is afraid to leave her house and was referred to music therapy because of concerns about her mental health. The group members are attentive and do not speak or move much while she elaborates; it turns out the woman has experience of displacement from her home country. The presenter is eloquent at first in her speech, but as she tries to talk about how she has tried many times to invite a connection in the music with her client, her speaking falters. She says, 'I think there is trauma,' and then she falls silent.

The group waits and listens. Finally, gently, the facilitator in the circle suggests the presenter moves into musical expression. The presenter leans forward and picks up a small stirring drum; it is cylindrical, made of wooden slats and produces a thin sound rising in pitch, then falling back to the lowest pitch at every circular stirring motion. She makes a tiny noise with it, faltering. Then there is another silence. Again, the group of six music therapists waits. She starts again, and again, but always stops. It seems that this will never end. But then another person in the circle gently starts to play a small gong, and then someone else joins in with the low, hollow tones of a bass xylophone in gentle pulsed regularity. After a time, the facilitator plays low holding notes on the piano. Another person shakes a cabassa intermittently and rather urgently. The presenter is finally not alone in her sound, and she begins the stirring drum again as the whole group joins as if in in support, and the collective volume swells.

When the improvisation ends, in a slightly stuttering, fizzling out way, the group continues to attend silently to the presenter. She starts to talk about her embodied response: a pain in her shoulder, a feeling of sickness in her belly, and a fluttering sense of panic. But she felt different when the gong was played: a sense that she was not alone, and she felt somehow 'seen'. Her breathing steadied.

The facilitator invites the group members to share any of their own embodied responses. The gong player talks of his desperation to join the presenter in the music and not leave her alone in the silence, the bass xylophone player talks about a deep sadness she felt when hearing the stirring drum, and the cabassa player talks about bursts of anger they experienced when listening to the presenter's words.

The presenter is invited to make connections with anything that resonated with or makes sense to her. She is surprised about the anger, but then remembers that she has on occasion felt enormous anger when reading about the client's experiences in her case notes. She identifies too with a deep sadness, something that she feels every time she meets her client, and understands it as something that emanates from the client. Finally, desperation is something that she comes close to feeling when she cannot connect in the music with the client. It is as if the members of the group were each able to connect with and articulate different parts of the client, or more broadly, the work. She can start reframing her approach to the client, which presently often borders on an impatient response. She concludes that she will be able to continue the work, which she was considering stopping.

Finally, those of us sitting around the inner circle, who are called 'witnesses', are asked about our own experiences of the process. We notice how the inner circle moved in to surround the presenter during the music, and how the facilitator held everything together by his presence, despite playing very few notes on the piano and speaking few words. We also notice many different embodied responses to the music in ourselves.

This is a workshop designed to introduce the method of group supervision. When I leave the workshop, I immediately talk with a music therapy colleague I respect and admire who also attended. We reflect on how, if we could contain a group half as well as the facilitator, we would be happy. We both feel it was a 'masterclass' in group supervision.

Catherine: The workshop was called 'Improvisation as "Unthought Known": Creative Techniques in Music Therapy Supervision'. I found it impossible to forget the depth of my experience just from witnessing this event. I was struck by how challenging the process felt in an emotional and sensory way, and the strength of collective support and focus from the other group members.

The staged structure of the process allowed the presenter to talk uninterrupted, and she was free to make the links between the immediate group experiences and her remembered experience of the work with the refugee client. No one jumped in, making assumptions, or to clarify details; instead, there was a strong focus on flow. It seemed vital that creating music was central to the process of responding to the work and eliciting feelings. There was space for everyone to think and feel rather than becoming clouded with words. But the spoken words that did emerge were offered to help understand, make sense of or explore possibilities – exactly what I felt supervision needs to offer.

Christopher Bollas's idea of the *unthought known* was central to this approach: the method enabled knowledge about an individual's music therapy work that was not yet conscious, suppressed or denied coming to consciousness aided by group exploration and free association using musical improvisation (Bollas 2017). When I read Bollas's book it gave me some kind of thinking framework to understand what was happening in the group: the use of music improvisation and free association in talking as a group enabled the presenter to start to make connections with aspects of the work she hadn't been consciously aware of before, yet had somehow known. Some of this was uncomfortable (such as the feelings of rage the cabassa player felt), which might suggest why it could have been suppressed in some way or denied by the presenter previously. I was left with a conviction that the use of musical play in the group was crucial and it made me wonder why as a music therapist I spent so much time talking in supervision without fully attending to the music.

Since that day I have aimed to understand, pass on and promote this practice among the music therapy community where I can. Together with music therapy colleagues Leslie Bunt, Adam Kishtainy, Hilary Storer, Hazel Dennis and Robin Bates, I undertook a collaborative inquiry over six months designed to develop a supervision training specific to music therapists. As part of the inquiry, we considered how this group supervision method could be adapted into a peer supervision method, where each member was trained in the facilitation.

This supervision training has now run for nearly ten years as a continuing professional development course at the University of the West of England.

Graduates of this course have continued to develop this practice in various ways. A group of music therapists based around Brighton started a regular peer group using the method. Joy Rickwood and I introduced it to the supervision interest group of the British Association for Music Therapy. In the music therapy master's programme at the University of the West of England, we teach the practice to final-year students for their peer groups, and some of these peer groups have continued to use it beyond their training. When I have taught as a guest abroad, music therapists have embraced this practice with enthusiasm and respect, quickly and intuitively understanding the depth it offered, even if my words have needed to be translated.

Ahonen requires the facilitator of the group to be an experienced music therapist supervisor, and often in the practices listed above, this has been the case; not, however, in student peer practice. Yet when we as a staff team monitor the student supervision groups, it appears to remain emotionally safe and useful without a skilled supervisor at the helm. I was interested to understand why this might be.

TALKING WITH ADAM

Returning to one of Ahonen's original influences, the Balint method, the obvious person to explore this with was Adam Kishtainy, a colleague, music therapist and accredited Balint group leader.

Adam explained that psychoanalysts Michael and Enid Balint had developed the model as a supervision group for general practitioner doctors (GPs) in the 1950s in London. This is well documented elsewhere (Otten 2017). There is a Balint Society in the UK and in many other countries – China, the Americas, Russia, Australia and much of Europe – and it has increasingly become part of medical training. The approach can also be used by other healthcare practitioners.

Adam: The Balints brought psychoanalytic thinking into the medical model with the intention of recapturing the importance of the doctor – patient relationship. Drawing on Winnicott's idea that there can be no baby without a mother, similarly, there can be no patient without a doctor. Balint (1964) suggests that before the dominance of the medical model, the doctor is the medicine; and perhaps more specifically, the relationship itself is at the core of the healing process. For psychoanalysts or arts therapists, this is a familiar concept and we are trained to notice and to be curious about the feelings that emerge in our work as well as to develop understanding of how our own experiences may relate to them. But this practice is neither part of how we train doctors in the UK, nor built into the ongoing support systems available to doctors as standard. As a result, the Balint model was created to give doctors permission to explore this aspect of their work and promote a healthier, more sustainable career path.

The process is based on free association, and there is no expertise needed to take part. Somebody with no psychological training can be part of a group, hear the story that the presenter tells and then share how they responded to the story, perhaps what it reminded them of or how it made them feel. You could have a group with a trainee nurse, a senior consultant, a healthcare assistant and a clinical psychologist; each will hear the same story – their free associations will be very different but equally valid in unpacking the underlying patterns that might be present in the relationship between the presenter and the patient.

Catherine: Adam, what are you doing in your own Balint group practice?

Adam: Over the past four years I have led a weekly group for foundation-stage doctors and psychiatry trainees; a group of up to ten, typically six or seven, people attend each week. When I was working on the wards in a psychiatric service, I ran a multidisciplinary group where the doctors made up the majority of the group but I also invited the whole staff team, and we would regularly have nurses, occupational therapists, physiotherapists, psychologists and other therapists attending over a period of around six months. I co-run a monthly group for GPs and psychiatrists who are dotted around the country and I have run groups for church leaders and music/dance/art/drama therapists. Essentially, any profession where there is a strong relational component to the work could make good use of the Balint group model.

Catherine: Can you tell me about the structure of a Balint group?

Adam: There are four main stages:

- An uninterrupted presentation of a case (typically around ten minutes).
- Brief questions of fact (two minutes maximum, although often we omit this stage).
- Group discussion without the presenter (20–25 minutes).
- Continued group discussion with the presenter (a further ten minutes).

Catherine: I'm interested in how inclusive this approach is and how it doesn't require psychological training to take part. Can you tell me how the session starts?

Adam: I start by asking, 'Who would like to bring a case today?' The person who volunteers to bring the case is referred to as 'the presenter'. They then tell the story of either an individual interaction with a patient or a series of interactions. The material is not prepared in advance, it's a spontaneous telling of the story; no notes are allowed and we're not expecting a complete case study. Sometimes people come to a Balint group with the intention of bringing a specific client, but it's usually whatever comes to mind at that particular moment in that particular group. They then speak uninterrupted for around ten minutes until they've said what they need to say.

Catherine: This lack of interruption is also found in the Ahonen supervision group practice. However, the 'questions of fact' stage seems more specific to Balint groups.

Adam: Yes, sometimes we have a 'questions of fact' stage where other people in the group can ask questions of the presenter. It's about clarification of certain details, such as how long the presenter has known the patient, or who else was in the room at the time. But if someone asks a question like 'How did you feel when the patient said that?' I would step in and suggest we keep that question for the discussion stage. It's important to allow the telling of the story to be preserved – the elements that the presenter can't recall or chooses not to share, the confusing or contradictory aspects, the ambiguities – these are important things to be curious about. For example, if the presenter hasn't mentioned how old the patient is, what are the fantasies we develop around this? Having the question answered shuts down this possibility. I increasingly skip this stage of the process!

Catherine: That part isn't present generally in our practice of the Ahonen method, although I can see it could be. How does the discussion work?

Adam: It's very levelling when you get to the third stage of the group. At this point the presenter removes themselves from the group; we call it 'push back'. If you're in a room together sitting in a circle, the presenter will literally slide their chair out of the circle, externalising themselves. With online meetings, the presenter usually mutes or turns off their camera. And then the group shares their experiences of hearing the story. We don't use the presenter's name in the discussion; we refer to them as 'the presenter'. This serves to depersonalise the story, allowing the group to put themselves in the place of the presenter and engage with free association.

There's something really powerful about telling your story and then listening to other people's responses and interpretations without being allowed to speak. If the presenter were part of the discussion, they could disagree or close off an avenue of discussion. But if they're muted and the group is exploring an aspect of the case to which the presenter is resistant or blind to, hearing the discussion can help them move to a place that potentially they wouldn't have been able to go. It can feel uncomfortable to be the muted presenter and very hard not to jump in mid-discussion!

Catherine: Do you ever ask people about their physical sensations?

Adam: Yes, I think particularly with the trainee doctors I try to encourage that more. If there is a particularly distressing case the physical sensations can be unavoidable, such as nausea or tightness in the chest, but it can be easy to ignore or dismiss more subtle sensations. I often find myself modelling the kinds of things that it's okay to share in the hope that the group will become more sensitive to their own responses.

Catherine: Facilitators also participate actively in the Ahonen group. I wonder what the kind of free associative talking is like?

Adam: As well as physical sensations or emotions it can simply be a discussion about the material within the case. Sometimes people get images in their mind of something that seems quite unrelated. People can talk about films, books or pieces of music. I often find myself contributing something slightly unusual compared to what others might say, particularly with a group of professionals who are working firmly within the medical model. I think that as a music therapist, familiar with group improvisations, offering something unusual is what I might do musically to prompt something new or deeper. I see verbal conversations as an extension of a musical exchange – interweaving themes, development, cadence, form, and so on. We want participants to have the freedom to say the 'wrong' thing, speak about taboos, respond in an 'unprofessional' way.

Catherine: What happens after this?

Adam: I invite the presenter to rejoin the discussion in whichever way they choose. Most commonly, the presenter will comment on what they have heard and answer some of the questions that the group may have been struggling with. The discussion continues until the end of the allotted time. Typically, a case takes 40–45 minutes. A normal session would involve two cases, a total of 90 minutes, including a little bit of housekeeping at the beginning and the end and then the transition between the two cases. Unlike the Ahonen method, there's no creative musical play or improvisation as standard, except possibly in the telling of the story – the presenter can use whatever they like to convey it, including music.

Here is an example of what emerged in a Balint group that highlights the effectiveness of skipping stage two (the questions of fact).

The presenter spoke about a consultation with a patient in the community which took place at 16:45 on a Friday evening. The patient was expressing suicidal ideation and in the course of the consultation the doctor had been going through all the standard questions you would be expected to ask in assessing and managing the risk. And it was red flags all the way down. They were incredibly concerned for this person and identified an imminent suicide risk. The doctor said, 'But my consultant had already left for the weekend. There weren't any other doctors that I could talk to about it on the Friday night and I had to make a decision.' All the support systems that would normally be around them weren't available. The presenter was thinking they would have to wait until Monday to know what to do beyond the consultation or to have any kind of resolution. That was where they stopped the presentation. The story ended.

At this point we all wanted to ask the question 'Well, were they okay on Monday?' or 'What happened?' But it felt important not to allow questions at that point because, for whatever reason, that's where the presenter decided to stop. I invited them to push back out of the circle and the group moved into the discussion stage, feeling incredibly anxious and desperate to know what had happened. During the whole of the discussion section, we had to sit with the feelings that the presenter had had all weekend; it was powerful.

And then when the presenter rejoined the group for the final stage, the first thing they said was 'I'm so sorry. I forgot to say that everything was okay on Monday, and it all sorted itself out.' But if they had said that at the start, the discussion wouldn't have had the same level of intensity in terms of recreating the presenter's experience.

Catherine: That sounds uncomfortable for all concerned but leads me to reflect on the pressures and burdens doctors carry, and evokes in me a strong compassionate response for them, as well as a concern for a patient who may risk less support if they feel suicidal over a weekend.

So given the widespread dissemination of the Balint model, this suggests both a cultural adaptability and a psychological safety, otherwise it wouldn't be used. From what you have said, it seems that for practitioners in the Balint group, exploring a presenter's work collectively promotes and sustains a potential 'ripple effect' of being able to apply the learning in some way to each group member's clinical experience.

Adam: Yes, I agree. And the practice seems to have become so widespread across the world; I wonder where there are places which could benefit from the approach. It does raise interesting questions about how culturally adaptable it is, and how it might evolve.

Catherine: After talking with Adam, I reflected on the importance of the 'ripple effect' with the Ahonen group supervision method, wondering how the Balint method could evolve into a process using music, much as Adam was doing naturally. This would mean specifically adapting the Balint approach to include musical improvisation as part of how the presenter brought the case. The presenter would describe their dilemma in words at first, as in the Balint group, but would then start making music freely, before others in the group joined her in music. This point where the group joined her allows all participants to express their own response to the case material wordlessly, and in musical free association. From Ahonen-Eerikainen's writing, she applied group analytic thinking to this process.

Group analytic thinking shares a common psychoanalytic root with the Balint group origins and was developed by S. M. Foulkes in the 20th century. It was also influenced by social psychology. Foulkes's idea of the group 'matrix' forms a key part of this. He described the matrix as being the network of relationship connections between group members and called it the 'dynamic matrix'. However, he also included the 'foundation matrix', which was a huge network of all past and current relationships that group members would be drawing on from their history. He likened this to a brain which has many millions of connections. So, developing this analogy further, thinking about the supervision group as representing a giant brain, all sensations, thoughts, emotions brought up by the case material can be pooled and shared.

In Ahonen's method, it is for the therapist presenter to make the connections first. To me and Adam, this feels empowering: rather than having interpretations forced on the therapist, the group plays with the experience of the music, and offers the opportunity for the therapist to make sense of it. With such an array of different responses, it is hardly surprising that the therapist can gain access to new and deeper understandings, particularly if they respond intuitively to whatever seems to make sense to them.

From a cultural and social perspective, it makes sense to do this. Group members harness their own cultural resonances, suggesting that a diverse cultural group may bring richness which can be used. And the task of the supervision group is clear; everyone is responding to help the presenting therapist understand more about the work, and in doing so they are enriched themselves. Dissonant or disruptive perspectives can be offered from the group and accommodated and assimilated if the presenter is able to do this. So, the Ahonen method offers to supervision process a chance to work with deeply hidden feelings: what Bollas terms the 'unthought known'. I found that reading an article by Dieter Nitzgen about Foulkes's writing helped clarify the idea of the matrix, if the reader wishes to explore this further (Nitzgen 2015).

There seems to be another important difference from Balint group practice: presenters in an Ahonen group are likely to be music therapists, or music therapists in training, with the psychotherapeutic support and understanding to make much of the depth of the encounter. This may make it more possible for other experienced members of the group to take the role of facilitator in the Ahonen group, and thus transform it into a peer supervision practice, as described at the University of the West of England.

TALKING WITH ABBY

So how can the Ahonen practice be developed further creatively, beyond music as a medium? The next step in exploring this model is in conversation with Abigail Williams, a lead creative therapist in a multidisciplinary team. She tells the story of when she introduced the Ahonen method as part of regular supervisory practice within the team.

Abby: At the time I was working at a specialist college for young adults with disabilities, and arts therapies were embedded within the college's emotional wellbeing service. Initially, the team consisted of three music therapists, two dramatherapists and a music therapy trainee. Later, the team expanded to include another dramatherapist and a dance and movement psychotherapist. We'd had the desire to have group supervision for a long time and when I was introduced to the Ahonen method during the supervision training, it gave me the incentive and motivation to try it with my colleagues. The team was receptive and willing to try it. As in-house supervision became more established, we began to meet as a group on a monthly basis.

As people became used to the Ahonen method, it allowed us to adapt it and use it when we thought it would be helpful, depending on what people were bringing to supervision. There were a variety of dilemmas brought to supervision. The work encompassed people with a wide range of disabilities, including profound and multiple learning disabilities, autism, acquired brain injury and life-limiting conditions. The age range was from 16 to 25 years old, and we were often working with themes related to entering adulthood. Other experiences might include being away from family for the first time, bereavement and forming and sustaining new relationships.

One of the hardest parts for me as the facilitator was deciding who was chosen to present. When each team member creates their own sentences about their practice dilemma, the sentences are like little teasers and each option could take you down such a unique and amazing path. Which door shall we open today?

Catherine: So, were you concerned about the democracy of this? That some people might get left out?

Abby: Well, even if you weren't the one presenting you could still learn and gain so much from being part of the experience, as the themes often resonated with your own work. It was a beneficial process for everybody.

Catherine: As the team is mixed in terms of the creative modalities, I'm curious about how the musical experiential parts of the method might have come to be adapted.

Abby: I've recently discussed that with my colleagues, in preparation for this conversation, and have valued their reflections. In the first few groups I facilitated, the experiential part was very much based in music and sound. I had only recently been introduced to the model and I wasn't sure how to adapt it to include other creative modalities. I remember the first time we tried it, one of the dramatherapists presented. I don't know if they were chosen because I as facilitator wanted to be as inclusive as possible to make the dramatherapists feel comfortable, or if they were really good at making their supervisory dilemma sound intriguing. But nonetheless, the group went with that.

The dramatherapist later reflected that they felt anxious to improvise in front of music therapists. But as soon as they began to play and the group joined in, their anxiety began to be alleviated, and they were able to think more within their own modality: 'Yes, I'm playing music, but I'm thinking about roles here.' They used the cluster drum (a five-headed drum) to think about the different people involved with the person they were working with. This enabled the group to understand more about dramatherapy thinking, particularly in terms of being able to envisage the dynamics of the social system surrounding the person. I think the music and different instruments gave the dramatherapist a different perspective of the case, especially in the reflective, free-associative discussion following the music-making. This was where everybody could share what it felt like to be in the music and the witness could share their experience and observations.

As the supervision sessions progressed, the group began to think about adapting it to include other means of creative expression. We wondered what it would add and what the risks might be if we adapted Ahonen's method. We began to introduce different props, sensory items, masks and fabrics and we also started to explore space and movement a lot more. It felt nerve-racking at first as both a facilitator and a music therapist, but gradually it felt liberating as it opened more opportunities to explore the work. I think traditionally as music therapists, we tend to sit in a circle, and we don't necessarily get up and move around. It felt invigorating to have permission to do this, as is common in drama-therapy practice.

There was very little sound at all during one group, although people were moving around. The experiential part was over within about 20 seconds. As the facilitator I thought, 'What am I going to do now? What is going on here?' I felt panicked. But then I noticed that people were still hiding behind mats and some people were in poses. Some were just very still. I thought, 'How do we come out of this?' It felt different from coming out of a musical improvisation. But as the group began to feed back their experiences, it became clear that what was being represented was the loss of voice for the person in therapy; they were not being heard. Being able to use other creative ways as well as silence to express this meant we were able to explore an aspect of the work which we might not necessarily have reached in the same way had we kept it just within the music.

Dramatherapy and dance and movement practices also helped us think about the use of space in the room. There was another example where the presenter's supervisory dilemma involved the symbolism of a 'murky swamp'. When I thought the group had come to a natural end, I motioned to get up and leave, but the dramatherapist said, 'What are you doing? We haven't finished!' And I thought, 'Oh no, what have I forgotten? How have I not ended this safely?' They said, 'We haven't de-roled! The swamp is still very much here!' As we hadn't put the stools away or put the instruments back in the box, the space itself still represented the swamp. I reflected a lot on that as it was such a powerful response from the presenter.

Over time, my colleagues reflected that during the verbal sharing and feedback, they felt as if they were back to being grounded in their own modality. So even though we could learn from each other and step out of our comfort zone during the creativity, we felt centred within our individual modalities when it came to processing the material verbally.

Catherine: I wonder why that is? It makes me think about training experiences and how we construct a verbal narrative about our practices within our separate modalities and how we understand them. This might be different in another modality. So, when we talking in words, we've got the language and concepts to explain therapy processes, but when we are in creative play, is it easier to move across to dramatherapy thinking?

Abby: I think it can be easier. It seems as if there's more of an immediacy to be able to embody our responses during creative play.

Catherine: The Ahonen method uses the creative medium first with the group and then moves to talking. How does that affect how the processing happens?

Abby: I thought the method was very prescriptive at first, as group members are not allowed to respond creatively or verbally until the presenter has finished talking. I was intrigued by that. But interjecting or responding verbally can pose many risks, for example jumping to conclusions or wanting to problem solve. Holding back and embodying the feelings first helps to open up everyone's ability to process. There was such a richness to the eventual talking, as so much had already been processed and experienced during the creativity.

Catherine: This has echoes with what Adam was saying earlier about the principle and result of not being interrupted in Balint group supervision.

Abby: There is something really powerful about being heard in this way. It supports the presenter to feel listened to unconditionally and there is a freedom to offloading. The process is the opposite for the witness, as they cannot speak until the end. On reflection, some witnesses shared that they felt pressure to share something quite profound, but this was difficult after so much had already been reflected on by the participating group members. But inevitably there was so much to be taken from the witness role in terms of what they observed and experienced. It's not always an easy position to take, especially when you're a creative person and the only one not playing.

Catherine: Talking of the witness or observer role reminds me that this can be a safer place to participate in this deep-process supervision if you as participant are feeling vulnerable. When we were trying out this method in Porto Alegre, Brazil, the presenter brought a very sad situation with a young child who was terminally ill in music therapy. As the presenter set out the story, one group participant, an experienced therapist, found that she was beginning to feel emotionally vulnerable, due to a recent significant bereavement. Moving to the outer circle to become a witness allowed her to remain involved, but not so directly in terms of the embodied experience. It is helpful if the facilitator can offer this so that participants can exercise self-care if needed.

CONCLUSION

In conclusion, our conversations have raised several questions in general about music therapy supervision we believe are useful to ask.

The first relates to interruption of flow in a supervision space. What might be learned from allowing supervisees to talk and play freely about their experiences in their work, while supervisors hold back a need or tendency to ask for clarification or steer the narrative early on? Can a little more patience while listening, and the space to attend to our feelings and associations, allow deeper understanding rather than a constant dialogic interchange?

The power of the collective experience of making music together in response to hearing about music therapy work does come across strongly in this exploration. To us, this power raises questions about whether we might spend more time meeting in groups for supervision, to harness the foundational matrix of our collective lives and histories when thinking about the situation of a client in a difficult place. In Chapter 10, the authors explore how it might be possible to adapt the Ahonen method for a supervision workshop online, and to involve larger numbers of people in this exploration of music therapy practice. This might open the possibility of greater access to group supervision in the future.

Abby talked about anxiety evoked when crossing to another creative medium such as dramatherapy. However, she and her colleagues were able to feel that allowing creative fluidity and moving outside the boundaries of the medium of music into drama and movement enabled a breadth of insight not necessarily afforded just with music. This also raises questions for me about the scope of this book: why concentrate primarily on music therapy supervision when other creative therapies offer so much? Openness to Abby's experience of transmodal working, and the transprofessional working that Adam experiences in his Balint supervision groups, is surely something to be encouraged rather than avoided.

The cultural adaptability that the Balint and Ahonen approaches afford shows ways to tap into collective experiences and explore what it is to be human. As Foulkes aimed to explain though the foundational matrix idea, we all bring intergenerational and immediate relational and cultural experiences to all we do. These are expressed not only in thoughts but also in sensations and emotions. In order to work against a sense of being overwhelmed by this complexity, structured methods like the Ahonen and Balint methods give a diverse supervision group some boundaries and structure within which they are freer to play, and therefore access more deeply what can be known intuitively or unconsciously.

Writing this chapter together through our creative conversations has enabled new understandings for us about what an ethnographic encounter offers when exploring supervision practices. This inquiry has challenged us to recognise how important it is to allow for musical flow and emotional processing during supervision, and about the importance of collective experience in supervision. Rather than routinely following traditional practices, it seems useful to learn more about the roots of these practices through conversations about perceived differences between approaches, thus bringing about new ways to be creative and social.

REFERENCES

Ahonen-Eerikainen, H. (2003) Using group-analytic supervision approach when supervising music therapists. *Nordic Journal of Music Therapy*, 12(2), pp.173–182. https://doi.org/10.1080/08098130309478088

Balint, M. (1964) *The Doctor, His Patient and the Illness* (second edition). London: Churchill Livingstone.

Bollas, C. ([1987] 2017) *The Shadow of the Object: Psychoanalysis and the Unthought Known* (30th anniversary edition). London: Routledge. https://doi.org/10.4324/9781315437613

Chang, H., Ngunjiri, F. & Hernandez, K. (2016) *Collaborative Autoethnography*. New York, NY: Routledge.

Ellis, C., Adams, T. E. & Bochner, A. P. (2010) Autoethnography: An overview. *Forum Qualitative Sozialforschung/Forum: Qualitative Social Research*, 12(1), 10. http://nbn-resolving.de/urn:nbn:de:0114-fqs1101108

Foulkes, S. H. (1975) *Group-Analytic Psychotherapy. Method & Principles.* London: Gordon and Breach. Later: reprint Karnac Books.

Nitzgen, D. (2015) Group psychotherapy: The psychoanalytic approach by S.H. Foulkes and E.J. Anthony. From the first to the second edition. *Group Analysis*, 48(2), pp.126-136. https://doi.org/10.1177/0533316415580500

Otten, H. (2017) *The Theory and Practice of Balint Group Work: Analysing Professional Relationships.* London: Routledge.

Salinsky, J. (2018) Balint under the microscope: What really happens in Balint groups? *International Journal of Psychiatry in Medicine*, 53(1-2), pp.7-14. https://doi.org/10.1177/0091217417745287

Weymann, E. (2016) Improvisation as "unthought known": creative techniques in music therapy supervision. *Nordic Journal of Music Therapy* 25: 114-15. DO - 10.1080/08098131.2016.1180133

SUPERVISION DURING THE PANDEMIC

CHAPTER 8

Approaching a New Threshold

Integrating Learning From Supervision Pre and Post Pandemic

MARIA RADOJE AND SALLY PESTELL

INTRODUCTION

This chapter reflects on a publication in the journal *Approaches: An Interdisciplinary Journal of Music Therapy*, 'Thresholds: Skype supervision and the liminal with in a "journey of two", about online clinical supervision, which was written before the Covid-19 pandemic (Radoje & Pestell 2022). It is written from the dual perspectives of the supervisor Maria Radoje and supervisee Sally Pestell. At the time that article was written, Sally was a newly qualified music therapist, working in a care home for older adults and with a child in a mainstream school; Maria was an experienced music therapist and trainee supervisor, on the first clinical supervision training for music therapists in the UK, at the University of the West of England.

When we were invited to write this chapter, we revisited the period during which we had clinical supervision together, and also the resulting publication and presentations which were the outcomes of our work. We had several meetings online as well as communications via email over a six-month period, to explore and reflect more deeply on that time. This period of revisiting the work revealed how important our online supervisions had been in shaping our individual responses during the pandemic, and how our experiences in the virtual supervisions continue to influence our practices long after we have ceased working together.

REFLECTIONS
Maria

The very few books we have on clinical supervision of music therapy by Forinash (2019), and Odell-Miller & Richards (2009) tend to be written from the perspective of the supervisor. As the music therapy profession has begun to question its approach to social justice, voices have emerged which speak from a variety of perspectives and lived experiences. It now seems timely to consider the impact on clinical supervision, and 'Thresholds' touched on an important theme which presents itself throughout this book, namely the inclusion of dual perspectives and unheard voices within the supervisory relationship. If clinical supervision can be said to be a type of 'super' vision that truly encompasses a 'journey of two' (Amir 2001), then the perspectives of the supervisee and their presence in the work must be of equal importance to our understanding of the impact on the client. If we do not include these voices then our vision may only encompass one lens, leaving us squinting at part of the picture.

Sally

For the voice of the supervisee to be heard, they might need to feel safe in the knowledge that they will not be judged and will be listened to with unconditional positive regard (Rogers 2003) for the work they are doing. This is particularly important in the early days after qualifying, as they step out into the unknown without the nurturing support and guidance of university tutors who have been alongside them for the duration of the course.

It took me some time to trust that a supervisor was able to give non-judgemental support because of my previous Ofsted experiences in teaching. Ofsted (Office for Standards in Education) is a non-ministerial department of His Majesty's Government in the UK, responsible for inspecting a range of educational institutions and reporting back to Parliament. During these kinds of inspections, skills and outcomes are judged not from a holistic perspective over time, where one's voice can be heard in a dialogue, but in a small snapshot in which an observer cannot see and understand the whole 'picture'. Knowing that my voice was in concert with the voice of my supervisor helped me to work through this barrier in music therapy supervision. As my trust grew, so did my confidence, and I was able to express myself with more transparency and authenticity. Two single voices became equal voices. Ryde suggests that learning from the supervisory relationship 'ricochets down the levels of supervision' (Ryde 2011, p.140). A parallel might be made here with this process cascading down to clients, helping them to trust, take risks and feel safe in an altruistic relationship with the therapist.

In our original paper, we wrote, 'undertaking this journey of learning together, this supervisor and supervisee...dared to risk the exposure of external and internal landscapes, and the interface of their physical and dream worlds' (Radoje & Pestell 2022, p.20). When the pandemic struck and we went into lockdown, our inner and outer landscapes changed. The sense of normality disappeared, and the world seemed smaller. We were standing collectively on another threshold trying to cope with the uncertainty, fear and anxiety of what might lie before us. I became acutely aware of how the world outside fell silent as lockdown rules were observed but also noticed how the beauty of nature seemed to emerge in great clarity, providing me with much-needed reassurance that the infinite bounty of the natural world would continue. However, although my relationship with nature had become more apparent, I felt that our human and communal nurturing had become more compromised.

Maria

Prior to the pandemic, working in the same space as our clients and supervisees/supervisors had been the most common way of practising. Online services may have been seen as 'second best' or somehow not as adequate as in-person work, until they became the lifeline we all needed to connect with each other and survive the lockdowns and isolation of Covid. Many more people in the profession could access online training and have supervision that may have been out of reach before, due to economic or logistical issues. These opportunities also seem to have contributed to the journey we are now undergoing as a profession towards change and the democratisation of music therapy.

My previous learning from the Skype supervision was invaluable as it helped me adapt quickly to the new parameters of my clinical work during the pandemic and develop the resilience I needed to move forward in my new role. In February 2020, I began working in a community mental health team for older adults. I arrived without instruments or referrals, wondering what might lie ahead. Within a few weeks I found myself working exclusively online and mainly from home. I now had referrals, but only my personal instruments such as cello, keyboard and a small amount of hand percussion. Zoom and telephone calls became the spaces in which the clinical sessions now took place. I do not believe I could have managed to build up a caseload and offer the sessions that I did without those previous online experiences. Incredibly, I was to work in this way for a whole year before I met any of my clients in person.

As well as my online supervision experiences, I also believe that my learning in Guided Imagery and Music (GIM) training opened new avenues and understanding in my practice relating to receptive music therapy. GIM is a music-centred therapy that supports the exploration of issues in a non-ordinary state of consciousness, through a process of deep relaxation and music listening (Bruscia 2013). It was important to develop what might be described as 'blind trust' in the listening process, when it was so difficult to practise clinical improvisation as I had previously known it. This enabled me to understand that I could also use the music as a co-therapist, facilitating my work with clients who were now only figures on a screen, or a disembodied voice coming through a phone.

During that first year of the pandemic, I was able to facilitate a therapeutic songwriting process for one client on the telephone, which helped them process feelings about their mortality and resulted in a song cycle about the end of life. With another, we worked with a grieving process, and developing the client's confidence after the loss of their partner of 50 years. Listening to pre-recorded music with me on the Zoom platform was especially helpful, as she was able to share Hindu chants in a way that may have been very different if we were using active, in-person music-making. Another client shared a rich musical, cultural heritage, as well as her experiences of loss, which were also facilitated by music listening.

Sally

My earlier experience of participating in supervision online with Maria also helped me to engage in some online training. This training enabled me to prepare and record my own material, which I sent to the care home I worked as a music therapist via YouTube, opening a link to them during lockdown. My initial reticence of 'being seen' on screen during pre-pandemic Skype supervision had decreased because of the support I was receiving from Maria. As I prepared my YouTube material it was the thought of the residents receiving support from *me* that helped overcome similar feelings. The introjection of a 'good object' from Kleinian theory comes to mind here. The ego needs identification with and introjection of a stable good object in order to integrate experience (Klein 1958).

My self-consciousness took second place as I realised that for the residents to see a familiar face and hear familiar music in the isolated space they found themselves in was more important. Although this was a one-way communication, it then developed into a live Zoom session that held the potential of being a two-way interaction; but in reality, there were technical difficulties. I appeared to be reaching through to them, but their responses were distorted by the time delay and the poor sound quality. The helpful intermediary here was the care worker (J), who provided the human connection to cross this threshold by coming close to the computer microphone and linking us together with positive feedback on both sides. This was especially important when my perceptions of the interactions were impaired.

Reflecting further on the role of J, I became aware of how her physical presence in the care home provided a link in other ways. During this time of Covid, she and the care team were a link to the outside world as no visitors were permitted, including relatives. Following the ethos of the care home, J intuitively prepared residents at lunchtime, sitting with them and initiating conversation to remind them about the music therapy session which was to follow. This helped to maintain a sense of routine and offer an opportunity to look forward to a shared activity because apart from mealtimes this was the only occasion that residents gathered together. Thus, sharing lunch and conversation moved into the experience of sharing music. During the music therapy session, J was able to support individuals well because of the relationship that had developed between us over a period of nine years. She had become aware of the importance of observing, reflecting, reassuring and encouraging and the beauty of facilitating people to express themselves however they wished during a music therapy session.

Following this, J offered a time to help process the music by serving tea and being sensitive to emotions that may have arisen. Her knowledge of people's histories was another valuable link of support here. Later in the day, some of the same songs from the session were revisited on an individual basis to help motivate personal tasks such as getting ready for bed, taking medication or to soothe and comfort as an aid to relaxation. Singing with the residents also spontaneously arose during the week, which the whole team of carers were keen to encourage as this helped underscore the rhythm and flow of the daily routine. The presence of music in the care home seemed to now take on the form of an infinity loop or a grounding musical ostinato as a source of nurture and nourishment. As J said, 'We kept it going when everything around us was changing.'

Drawing in the voice of the care worker in this situation was invaluable, and I also found myself drawing on my inner resources to find a new way of working that fully embraced this partnership so that the work resonated with optimum mutual respect and understanding. It was helpful to reflect on Gro Trondalen's words here. She suggests, 'As *homo comminicans* we are seeking each other through different dimensions, while striving towards meaning and fulfilment in daily encounters – not least through music therapy practice' (Strange *et al.* 2017, p.9).

Maria

The layers experienced in online supervision and clinical work allow us to view each other simultaneously but be present and rooted in our own spaces. There is something about this third space or shared dimension that is important to be aware of when working online. As Sally has described, sometimes we might need an intermediary or someone who can cross the threshold for us to help facilitate clinical work, such as the carers of my older clients who would open the link to the Zoom sessions and set up the technology so that we could be present together. Sometimes, this intermediary function might be a part of ourselves, and if we can utilise this part, clients who are brought to supervision may be present in a different way than we have been used to before.

Concepts of time and presence are changed when we are simultaneously together and apart. Kroeker (2019, p.58) states that 'Music exists mostly in a non-physical way, within the realm of time and sound perception.' He considers Einstein's ideas of spacetime in which 'three dimensions of space are combined interdependently with one dimension of time into a conceptualised continuum' and suggests that music could be a 'sound time continuum'.

Could we, perhaps, begin to think of online music therapy and clinical supervision with its non-physical, virtual element as a continuum of presence within the dimensions of space, sound and time? I document a moment in 'Thresholds' in which I prepared to get into this space with Sally before supervision four. There had been no communication between us prior to our meeting, but something compelled me to light the candles in the room I was working in. Even though I questioned myself, I listened to the part of me that could act as the intermediary function: 'as the supervision unfolded, I began to understand, as Sally talked about the death of four residents at the care home over the Christmas period' (Radoje & Pestell 2022, p.17). Something of the clients' experience had been picked up on in this continuum of presence and the symbolic act of lighting candles had connected me to what was about to come into the space between us.

Lawlor discusses the power of the symbol in his preface to Schwaller de Lubicz's seminal work, *Symbol and the Symbolic*:

> A method of viewing is required comparable to our hearing faculty: one must learn to listen to the symbolic image, allowing it to enter into and pervade one's consciousness, as would a musical tone which directly resonates with the inner being, unimpeded by the surface mentality. In this moment of inner identity between the intellect and the aspect of the tangible world evoked by the symbol, we have the opportunity to live this knowledge. (Lubicz 1981, p.11)

I documented another symbolic act in 'Thresholds', when the dreaming part of myself compensated for the inability to respond to Sally with music when she discussed these deaths. This was a time before there were online platforms where we could easily share sound, and the scope for playing or listening to music with Skype was very limited. It made it difficult to respond with my habitual musical self, the part of me that was used to live improvisation or performance. Countertransference feelings of being stuck or frozen also had a part to play in this inability to provide or suggest music to help with processing the situation. However, following this session, I dreamt of a rehearsal of Elgar's *Dream of Gerontius* in which I took the role of the angel – the figure that accompanies the souls of the dead as they transition to another place – and it seems as if my dreaming, creative psyche was also linking me with the clients, post-supervision. The liminality of the online experience, the dream world, and the transition of so many souls were amplifying each other. This quote from Bunt and Hosykns feels especially relevant to my understanding of liminality, not only in online music therapy and supervision, but also in my GIM practice and experiences of the pandemic:

> A threshold can...be a doorway or gateway to new understanding and awareness... The Roman god Janus was the first god of all doorways...he

was represented as looking in different directions simultaneously with a double-faced head. He could observe both the entrances and exits of public buildings and the interiors and exteriors of private houses. He was the god of beginnings and endings, of representing transitions between outside and inside, between the worlds of the country and the city. (Bunt & Hoskyns 2002, cited in Radoje & Pestell 2022, p.16)

Sally

As the pandemic spread, so did the feeling of uncertainty about our world. This led me to search deeply inside myself to find some sense of connection with what we still had to help us feel safe and secure. I felt frozen and couldn't move forward, but like Janus I was able to look back. I took comfort in thinking about my parents, grandparents and other ancestors and the challenges they had come through while the same wonderful cycle of nature and the seasons continued. This rotational pattern may have helped them to look forward too.

My paternal ancestors had lived in a rural setting as I do now, and this is where my thoughts lay as I wondered what had helped them to cope with the hardships of life and build resilience. I needed to know more, so eagerly I read Flora Thompson's *Lark Rise to Candleford* (Thompson 1945), the trilogy of semi-autobiographical works which describes village life in Oxfordshire at the end of the 19th century. She started to write this in 1939, with the complete set being published in 1945. The timing of this literary work seems significant as this period might also be seen as a threshold looking out towards World War 2, with the experience of having lived through the devastation and trauma of World War 1. As I read about the village celebrations that accompanied the seasons of the year, it became apparent how a simpler way of life was valued and enjoyed by the community through music. This was particularly so in May when the natural world was just beginning to bring forth its wonderful bounty. Traditional instrumental folk music was predictable, comforting, had a strong structure and was a good companion to dancing and singing.

During the pandemic I, and presumably many others, gradually experienced a certain simplicity about the structure of our own lives because we were losing so much, withdrawing into a smaller landscape that contained an element of fear and instability, much like the person with dementia, whose memories are significantly diminished as the disease progresses. My intention was to facilitate a positive and valuable experience for the residents, working in the 'here and now' with subtle reminiscence of the past. I decided to adopt a simpler structure in my online sessions, choosing music for the residents that promoted positivity in a calm way and encouraged the release of stress through physical engagement, followed by music that facilitated relaxation, comfort and opportunity for quiet reflection.

As well as using traditional folk tunes I used songs from the two world wars, knowing that for many residents this was a musical link with their ancestors and the regular, steady beat, predictable tonality and structure might provide reassurance and courage. I was also careful to use songs that were particular favourites of individual residents, hoping that a sense of recognition and inclusion would be experienced. Uppermost in my mind, though, was providing a safe, 'holding space' that promoted feelings of meaningful human connection, uniting and supporting the care home family. To reflect back seems to illuminate the present, and if the future seems precarious then surely the virtue of living life to the full is to concentrate on the here and now, taking strength from the past.

Maria

Reflecting on some of the drawbacks we discussed in the previous publication:

> not being in the same room can be seen as a barrier to connectedness because it is harder to 'read' the other person to pick up on those non-verbal cues, and there can be a distinct lack of flow if there is a technical problem. (Radoje & Pestell 2022, p.13)

Today, those of us who work online generally have fewer issues with the technicalities of sharing sound, which have been resolved by various platform providers, allowing us to be much more fluent in the use of online spaces for clinical and recreational use. For instance, if I were supervising Sally on this material today, I would feel more confident to share a piece of live or recorded music and have the facility to easily do this in a way that we were not able to do during those early Skype supervisions. However, despite the lack of music available at the time of the supervision discussed, it is significant that the symbolic act of lighting the candles was continuing to resonate within Sally's psyche several years later. It had transformed and matured into a connection with a treasured story linking her back to her ancestors, supporting the development of her inner resources, and allowing her to draw on the internalised 'good objects' rooted deep within.

Reflecting on my relationships with my own supervisors, I realise how important they have been to my development, and during the period I mention when I was starting out in a new team, especially so. I have been challenged to work at becoming a better therapist and supervisor, and it is important to recognise how they have been introjected and utilised in my own work, supporting the development of my internal resources. For newly qualified therapists, it is important that specialised clinical supervision is available that recognises the extra support needed when leaving training and starting their professional life. It is a positive step forward that the British Association for Music Therapy has developed a mentoring scheme that provides broad support around aspects of career development which lie outside the scope of clinical supervision for these newly qualified therapists. This may go some way to helping the professionals of the future establish themselves (BAMT 2022).

Some final thoughts on the pandemic lead me to mandala theory. Mandalas are frequently used as a processing tool in GIM. Kellogg's theory of the Twelve Archetypal Stages of the Great Round of the Mandala (1984) suggests that Stage One, also named 'The Void', can be a terrifyingly empty place, but also a place in which seeds are silently germinating in the fertile darkness. When we experience The Void, the world is slowed down, time almost suspended. Seeds planted here begin to appear as the possibilities of a new cycle of development, as we progress and journey through the stages of the Great Round.

We could think of the pandemic as a void, and for most of us in the UK, our world was narrowed by the lockdowns and then expanded by the later return to 'normal' life, following which many of us questioned our roles in society and our professions, creating conditions for change. Collectively and individually, we learned much about ourselves and the ways we can be together and separate in a 'continuum of presence'. As we have emerged from the collective chaos, there is potential for the development of a more diverse profession and the growth of new ideas and practices. Online music therapy and supervision can offer broader opportunities for learning and development, as well as for clients who may not be able, or wish, to access in-person therapy.

Significantly, 'Thresholds' was written in 2019, published in February 2020 and then republished in 2022, both at the beginning and the end of the pandemic lockdowns. This was something we had no control over, reminding me of a new seed emerging out of The Void, unbidden, when it is ready to grow. Strong roots are needed, which require watering and tending to help individual therapists and the profession to thrive. I strongly believe that the possibilities afforded by online supervision within the container of a 'continuum of presence' can provide some of the necessary conditions for growth.

Sally

My concluding thoughts centre around the importance of connections. When I qualified as a music therapist the seeds of a potentially rewarding career helping others through the medium of music had been sown, and the care and nurturing I had received in my training were the motivation to branch out and expand on that growth. Although initially struggling with feelings of isolation and loss, I looked inwards to weave together the strands of my own resources and personal development, taking on risks and challenges. By doing so I believed I might attain a deeper awareness of the intrinsic qualities inherent in music therapy. Accessing supervision was important in helping me to do this.

In March 2020, when the pandemic arrived, some of the same feelings of loss and isolation returned again, only this time it was on both a personal and collective level. The need to connect with others became paramount but the barriers were difficult to break through, and this is where our own creativity emerged to find a way forward. By using our unique creative skills in our own way and working with the latest technology, we were able to slowly reconnect step by step to reinstate some semblance of normality and learn much about ourselves in the process.

Using online tools in the music therapy profession has now become customary and an ongoing area of development. However, we must be careful not to lose the qualities that are present when we work in the same room with clients. A way forward seems to be an embracing of all that we had, combined with an openness to accept what the future might hold for us both personally and professionally. If we are able to access our inner and outer landscapes with more understanding, courage and a sense of hope, then we may be able to live even more rewarding lives and help others to do the same. I believe music will take us there.

REFERENCES

Amir, D. (2001) 'The Journey of Two: Supervision for the New Music Therapist Working in an Educational Setting.' In M. Forinash (ed.) *Music Therapy Supervision* (pp.195–210). Gilsum, NH: Barcelona Publishers.

BAMT (2022) BAMT launches the fully funded development scheme for newly qualified music therapists. Available at: www.bamt.org/DB/news-view/bamt-launches-the-fully-funded-development-scheme-for-newly-qualified-music (Accessed 3 September 2023).

Bruscia, K. E. (2013) *Defining Music Therapy* (third edition). Gilsum, NH: Barcelona Publishers.

Bunt, L. & Hoskyns, S. (2002) *The Handbook of Music Therapy*. Hove: Brunner/Routledge.

Forinash, M. (ed.) (2019) *Music Therapy Supervision*. Gilsum, NH: Barcelona Publishers.

Kellogg, J. (1984) *Mandala, Path of Beauty*. Williamsburg, VA: Graphic Publishers of Williamsburg.

Klein, M. (1958) On the development of mental functioning. *International Journal of Psychoanalysis*, 39(2–4), pp.84–90.

Kroeker, J. (2019) *Jungian Music Psychotherapy*. New York, NY: Routledge.

Lubicz, S. (1981) *Symbol and the Symbolic: Ancient Egypt, Science, and the Evolution of Consciousness*. Rochester, VT: Inner Traditions.

Odell-Miller, H. & Richards, E. (2009) *Supervision of Music Therapy*. London: Routledge.

Radoje, M. & Pestell, S. (2022) Thresholds: Skype supervision and the liminal within a 'journey of two'. *Approaches: An Interdisciplinary Journal of Music Therapy* [online], 14(1), pp.9–21. Available at: https://journals.qmu.ac.uk/approaches/article/view/122 (Accessed 21 January 2023).

Rogers, C. R. (2003) *Client-Centered Therapy: Its Current Practice, Implications and Theory*. London: Constable.

Ryde, J. (2011) 'Supervising Psychotherapists Who Work with Asylum Seekers and Refugees'. In R. Shohet (ed.) *Supervision as Transformation: A Passion for Learning* (pp.124–144). London and Philadelphia: Jessica Kingsley Publishers.

Strange, J., Odell-Miller, H., Richards, E. & Trondalen, G. (2017) *Collaboration and Assistance in Music Therapy Practice: Roles, Relationships, Challenges*. London: Jessica Kingsley Publishers.

Thompson, F. (1945) *Lark Rise to Candleford*. London: Penguin.

CHAPTER 9

Music Therapy Group Supervision in a Brazilian Clinic

Difficulties, Challenges and Learning Experiences

GUSTAVO SCHULZ GATTINO, JOYCE RIBEIRO, JEMIMA
RODRIGUES, GABRIELA SANTOS SILVA DE ALMEIDA,
SARAH CAROLINE JERONIMO DA SILVA, TATIANA HARUMI
KOMI AND JÚLIO CESAR RAMON OLIVEIRA

INTRODUCTION

This chapter aims to present the details of a supervision practice for a group of six music therapists in Brazil within a multidisciplinary clinic that mainly supports children on the autism spectrum. The clinic is located in a municipality in the metropolitan region of São Paulo. The population of São Paulo, added to the neighbouring cities, is 22,807,000 inhabitants (Britannica 2024). The reason for exploring this particular practice is that it involves a unique combination of the difficulties, challenges and learning experiences during the supervision process between the six music therapists and the supervising music therapist. The supervision approach was based on pragmatism, problem-solving and a compassionate focus on the wellbeing of the supervisees. Before describing the supervision process with this group in detail, it is worth looking at some aspects of music therapy in Brazil and its supervision practices.

MUSIC THERAPY IN BRAZIL AND THE SUPERVISION PRACTICES IN THIS COUNTRY

Music therapy began formally in Brazil in the 1960s and had its first undergraduate course in 1972 at the Brazilian Conservatory of Music in Rio de Janeiro (Barcellos & Santos 2021). The entity responsible for the organisation of professional music therapists is the Brazilian Union of Music Therapy Associations (UBAM). Given the continental size of the country, there are 17 regional associations which act in a coordinated way together with the national association (UBAM 2023a). Brazil currently has seven bachelor degree training courses in music therapy and specialisation courses (also responsible for training music therapists who already have a degree in another area) (UBAM 2023b).

One of Brazil's primary music therapy practices is music therapy for autistic people, as pointed out by the census of music therapy students and professionals carried out by UBAM in 2020. One of the peculiar characteristics of this practice is the large number of music therapists who work in clinics and institutions with a behavioural orientation, specifically applied behaviour analysis (ABA). According to the Association of Professional Behavior Analysts (n.d), ABA involves using scientific principles and procedures discovered through basic and applied research to improve socially significant behaviour to a meaningful degree. Curiously, none of Brazil's music therapy training courses has a behavioural orientation, and, therefore, professionals end up seeking continuing education courses on ABA and behavioural music therapy. Only one of Brazil's undergraduate music therapy courses, the Faculdades EST in the city of São Leopoldo (Gattino 2020), had specific content on behaviourism in music therapy in its early years. This was where the supervisor of the supervision practice described in this chapter carried out his training and had a learning base within behavioural music therapy.

Supervision in music therapy is an established practice in Brazil, and recently a specific seminar on the subject was organised by UBAM (2022). This seminar discussed the different nuances of supervision and how these practices occur in the country. No particular guidelines define the characteristics of supervision in Brazil for either group or individual formats, or the characteristics of a supervisor in music therapy (e.g. minimum time of experience, training in supervision). Similarly, no official documents explain the different supervision practices concerning the supervision of students and professionals and academic supervision in music therapy. Supervision is essential within the country and has existed for many years. However, there are no clear guidelines on how to carry it out. Furthermore, the topic of supervision is not a common theme within the music therapy literature of Brazil, which has a critical tradition in the creation of models and theoretical guidelines, as well as for conducting ethnographic, psychometric and randomised controlled studies.

THE METHOD USED TO DESCRIBE THE SUPERVISION CASE

The practice described reports on the lived experiences of the six music therapists and their supervisor. Therefore, it is likely structured based on previous research findings. The description below inspires the qualitative research paradigm mainly due to its subjective character, focus on experience, and different possible interpretations to describe an inevitable reality (Hiller 2016). Specifically, the narrative is inspired by the interpretative case study (Murphy 2016), particularly within a descriptive proposal and with an intrinsic design. An intrinsic design occurs when the authors are interested in learning about a particular phenomenon but do not seek to create theories or generalise their results.

For the development of this chapter, a WhatsApp group was created to enable the authors to exchange text messages. In this group, the supervisees wrote from their perspective what they felt was most significant within the supervision process. Each person had the opportunity to write what they thought about the topic and, at the same time, had the chance to read the words of their colleagues. The supervisor withheld his views as he believed that the voice of the supervisees had a more critical role in this process. In addition to the message exchange via WhatsApp, the supervisor organised an online meeting via Zoom so that each music therapist could see, hear and talk with their colleagues about their experiences with supervision. This was after all the supervisees had already put their considerations into the WhatsApp messages. This virtual meeting aimed to promote listening to each person after writing and reading the reflections of the other colleagues. This process was necessary so that every person could voice their views on the subject as well as listen to the opinions of others. As was the case for the written text, the supervisor left the space only for the supervisees. The reflections carried out by text on WhatsApp and in the Zoom meeting were gathered by the supervisor and summarised, and are presented below, with quotations from the data.

The following paragraphs present a detailed description of the supervision process, starting with the practice context, describing the main challenges and difficulties and finally detailing the main learnings within the process. The voices of the supervisees (and authors of this chapter) can be heard through the quotes from Joyce, Jemima, Gabriela, Sarah, Tatiana and Júlio.

PRESENTATION OF THE PRACTICE AND SUPERVISION CONTEXT

The six music therapists who received supervision in music therapy carried out all their training in music therapy in the state of São Paulo. They had different professional experiences, both in terms of places of work and the timing of the professional practice of each. These professionals worked in the same clinic, but not all worked in the same institution unit. In other words, due to the size of the city and the number of people who needed assistance, the clinic had different centres to facilitate the displacement of families. The music therapists were thus scattered in different places in the city where the institution offered music therapy.

For this reason, some music therapists only got to know each other during supervision meetings. Four of these six music therapists attended and participated in the sessions in the same physical space and the others in another physical area. It is worth pointing out that the supervisees were in Brazil during the supervision, and the supervisor was in Portugal. The supervision sessions lasted an hour, mainly at the end of the working day or after the lunch break. When the supervision sessions occurred after lunchtime, the music therapists needed to leave a few minutes earlier to prepare their rooms for care. Even though the meetings were online, the places where the music therapists met to perform their supervision presented some problems that hindered their participation in the meetings, particularly a lack of privacy for the meetings, a high noise level in the different units of the clinic and a low quality of internet connection in these spaces.

The case supervisor carried out his training as a music therapist in Brazil. However, during the period of supervision, he also carried out his practice in Portugal, and activities as a teacher in Denmark. From the supervisor's perspective, the cultural and practice differences between the supervisees and the supervisor turned out to be crucial in opening up the possibility of a departure from the reality and options faced by the supervisees in some situations, mainly due to the experiences lived by the supervisor in these other countries.

The approach used during problem-solving supervisions was based on four steps: listening to the needs of the supervisees, suggesting possible ways of dealing with the problem, listening to the supervisees to see if what was proposed made sense, and finally asking the supervisees to reflect on how they could deal with the said problem. In the first stage, the supervisees usually brought concerns experienced in the clinic or internal conflicts hindering their work in the institution. The supervisor usually presented some theoretical or practical reflections on the different issues, showing ways to understand the problem and possible solutions within the moment. The supervisor always made it clear that there were ideal and real solutions to deal with the problems. Therefore, the supervisees needed to check what was possible within their reality. In asking if the supervisor's suggestions made sense, the main idea was to hear how the supervisees were receiving and 'digesting' what was proposed. Finally, the time came to discuss what solutions would be taken for a given situation. Only a few things were solved within the same supervision. When the theme was the protocols of assessment in music therapy within the clinic, various meetings were necessary to establish the main points from different assessment instruments.

It is important to note that the supervision practices with this group occurred during the first two years of the Covid-19 pandemic (2020 and 2021). For this reason, this first meeting of some of the music therapists took place online. An important feature is that the music therapists held the sessions at a specific time made available within the institution. In most cases, the music therapists were wearing face masks. The supervisor only got to know their faces after many encounters, when they were without a mask or had the mask down, making this unique to all concerned in the supervision practice.

The music therapists in the different institutions had an average of eight sessions per day and 28 sessions per week (each). In addition, they had one hour of weekly supervision, during which they all met via the Zoom platform. The themes of the supervision meetings covered many topics. The first was how to adapt assessments and intervention practices to the applied behaviour analysis (ABA) context in music therapy. Behavioural learning within ABA is based on reinforcement, punishment and repetition (Mohammadzaheri *et al.* 2014) and has been linked with traumatic childhood experience (McGill & Robinson 2021).

The approach contrasted strongly with the more client-led theoretical framework in music therapy the therapists were used to. Other themes included how to deal with institutional changes and demands, how to develop musical resources, how to deal with burnout as a music therapist, perspectives on professional development and how to create theoretical resources in music therapy (coming from different perspectives in music therapy). Another complication was a time zone difference between the supervisor and supervisees throughout all supervision sessions.

One of the curiosities of this supervision process is that until the writing of this chapter, some of music therapists and the supervisor did not know each other personally. This situation demonstrates how supervision processes in Brazil have changed since the Covid-19 pandemic, as there are now opportunities to seek a supervisor based not on where they live, but on their interests and what they can offer.

MAIN DIFFICULTIES AND CHALLENGES ENCOUNTERED BY THE SUPERVISEES DURING SUPERVISION SESSIONS

Although the previous section detailed the broad themes of the supervision, the main difficulties and challenges experienced were largely focused on three areas: how to deal with burnout as a music therapist, how to adapt the assessments and intervention practices to the ABA context in music therapy and how to deal with institutional changes and demands. A detailed account of these three areas of difficulties and challenges follows, including quotations from the supervisees.

HOW TO DEAL WITH BURNOUT AS A MUSIC THERAPIST

One of the recurring themes from the supervisees was their difficulties and challenges in coping with the burnout and fatigue that was building up with each week of care. This burnout was worsened by the pressure of the institution for particular demands to be met, as well as sudden changes in institutional dynamics, which directly affected the music therapists in the clinic. Moreover, the Covid-19 pandemic had a tremendous impact on professionals' physical and mental health:

- The pandemic affected most people on the planet in different ways. It also specifically affected the practice of these professionals in general at constant risk of infection; most were infected with the Covid-19 virus (Adhikari *et al.* 2020).

- The pandemic required several precautions for therapists regarding hygiene care and protective materials.
- Many had to change their practices to a remote format, conducting sessions online or calling clients to know how they performed the recommended activities when they could not receive face-to-face sessions.

Within this theme, Gabriela reported that they had many hours of work and were increasingly less able to perform their professional practices with the quality they wished. The significant number of clients meant that the music therapists had little time to talk to each other and to plan and evaluate the different cases. Despite highlighting this to those responsible for the clinic, the level of attention and demands remained the same for the professionals.

As Gabriela explained:

The activities and attributions began to overload our work, directly affecting the quality of our work and, in particular, our quality of life. The work overwhelmed us. The agendas were filled with patients. What seemed very positive began to add up in adverse effects: the music therapy team was overloaded, demotivated and sickened by the signs and symptoms of burnout inside the institution where the doors were opened to them but they were limited by not having the voice and space to show the quality and positive results of their work.

According to Jemima, after completing five months of work at the institution, she worked eight hours a day, and her body started to send signals such as tachycardia and fatigue, due to the stress of fulfilling her work obligations. When she started to have these burnout symptoms, she did not know how to deal with the situation. Meanwhile, she was also excited to learn and apply different kinds of knowledge to her music therapy practice.

As the clinic had no solution to reduce the burnout of these professionals, the music therapists used the space of supervision to report their main difficulties, and the supervisor provided some suggestions to diminish these demands. One of the solutions adopted was to optimise the evaluation of the therapeutic process, distilling the documentation of the overall process and each music therapy session. The professionals adopted forms where they needed to write far less information and only include what was essential for the process.

Another of the supervisor's solutions was to use the supervision space for each supervisee to think about how they cared for their physical and mental health outside their work as a music therapist. Thus, the supervisor recommended that the supervisee think more about this self-care time and try to increase it to preserve their health. It was fascinating to hear what each person liked to do outside the context of music therapy to take care of themselves. For example, Gabriela and Sarah liked to play and sing at the church, Júlio liked football, Tatiana liked to make origami and Jemima liked to wear wigs. This situation allowed each to learn other characteristics and details about their colleagues. These exchanges strengthened the group, despite their difficulties in dealing with burnout.

Júlio reported that he often wondered if his reality within the clinic was normal and reasonable or something out of the ordinary. Within supervision, the supervisor clarified that this was not ordinary or fair, and that fighting for institutional change was necessary. Joyce reported that she never knew whether she could say what she thought to the other professionals or if she should avoid confrontation to maintain a better quality of life at work. In the supervisor's view, it was essential to clarify what needed to be improved for the other professionals at the institution. Otherwise, the music therapist would get sick. Jemima raised this point first, but then the other supervisees started to reflect on this and realised that something needed to change in their workplace. Jemima said that she was starting to have burnout symptoms, and she did not know how to handle the situation. According to her, the supervisor was open to discussing these points with the supervisees. Tatiana said that in 2021, she felt embraced by the supervision approach because, in many meetings, burnout, the number of work hours and the strategies to take care of mental health were the main topics.

Even though it was not an option expected by those supervisees, one of the themes discussed was the possibility of the professionals either leaving the clinic for a period or resigning to improve their physical and mental health. In many meetings, the supervisor opened up the idea of looking for other places to work and other opportunities to work in music therapy, including privately or opening their own clinic, for example. According to Joyce, at first, it seemed strange and even impossible to think about, given the commitment of the different professionals to their work and because the clinic work was an essential source of income for all of them. These conversations significantly influenced the music therapists in the long run, as they all moved away from the clinic to work in other places that offered better professional conditions.

HOW TO ADAPT ASSESSMENTS AND INTERVENTION PRACTICES TO THE ABA CONTEXT IN MUSIC THERAPY

One of the central themes of the supervision was how to adapt the ABA ideology and principles within the context of music therapy for clients on the autism spectrum. As explained earlier, music therapy within the ABA context needs to be taught in training courses in Brazil as it is such a widespread practice in education. Furthermore, the music therapists in the group needed more experience in ABA, including its methods and theoretical basis. Given that the supervisor had experience of working in an ABA context in music therapy practice, teaching and supervision, a first action was to facilitate a theoretical grounding on behavioural music therapy and music therapy in the ABA context (which is a more training-focused branch of behavioural music therapy).

Even though the theoretical background helped the supervisees, they did not see themselves as ABA music therapists. They tried to adapt the ABA concepts to their practice in music therapy, which included other approaches such as improvisational music therapy and interactive music therapy (Barcellos 2021). In other words, it was difficult to move away from the theoretical and philosophical basis of the various music therapists. This situation caused anguish for the music therapists, as they knew that they needed to follow the principles of ABA, even though they were not convinced about them, since this was an institutional demand.

Sarah felt alone, with little clinical experience in the context of ABA and with professionals from other disciplines querying the work developed by the music therapy professionals at the institution. She found this challenging. For her, the main challenge was using the ABA terminology, techniques and approaches and translating them to music therapy in a way the other professionals could understand. One action encouraged by the supervisor was for them to divide the music therapy sessions into moments more centred on ABA and others within the theoretical/philosophical perspective with which they were more familiar and most identified with. This generated a positive result in the group, as they realised that they could 'act as themselves' and still meet the demands and philosophy of the institution. Júlio mentioned that his previous experience with supervision based on ABA required using a timer for the music therapy sessions for turn-taking and to count how many times the client maintained eye contact.

The supervisor tried to contain and modify the group anxieties about this situation and then used the supervision to empower the music therapists in the field of music therapy. According to Júlio, it was essential to build trust regarding music therapy among the supervisees in the first moment and then to use the time to work on more pragmatic topics like assessment in music therapy. He said this learning process helped him be more confident using the music therapy vocabulary with other professionals.

Besides needing to adapt the objectives and the way of attending centred on ABA, they still needed to adjust their assessments, mainly focusing on the two assessment instruments commonly used in ABA within the context of autism: the Assessment of Basic Language and Learning Skills (ABLLS-R) (Partington, Bailey & Partington 2018) and the Verbal Behaviour Milestones Assessment and Placement Program (VB-MAPP) (Sundberg 2008). These two instruments assessed the clients seen in the institution right at the triage, and the data from these evaluations was used by the music therapists so that they could establish the goals and objectives of music therapy, as well as possible interventions for the clients. The institution required the music therapy team to create a music therapy-specific assessment connected to the basic principles and contents of the ABLLS-R and the VB-MAPP. To deal with this significant challenge, the supervisor suggested using the Individualised Music Therapy Assessment Profile (IMTAP) (Baxter *et al.* 2007) for the main topics of the two instruments used by the institution. Some subsequent supervision meetings were used to compare the similarities and differences of the IMTAP with the two instruments and see how it could bring these different universes closer together. One solution was to relate the aspects of verbal behaviours and language of the two instruments to the domains of the IMTAP, which is more focused on communication and musical behaviours (musicality).

Besides the IMTAP, the tool Music in Everyday Life (MEL) (Gottfried *et al.* 2018) was used in the supervision as a possible way to assess the family musical context, which was absent in the primary screening assessments of the institution. This tool was adopted and incorporated into their music therapy assessment protocol within the clinic.

HOW TO DEAL WITH INSTITUTIONAL CHANGES AND DEMANDS

One of the main characteristics of the supervision process was the sudden changes experienced by the music therapists within the institution. According to Sarah, the beginning of the Covid-19 pandemic drastically changed the music therapy practice in the clinic. The in-person music therapy sessions were prioritised only to cases with a significant need of support, and the other cases were referred to the online modality. She mentioned that in 2021 the clinic made other changes, especially related to opening new clinics in other parts of the city. This process spread the group of music therapists differently, so that three music therapists were permanently working in the main clinic, two in the new clinic and the other two splitting their work hours between two clinics.

Another example was the change of professionals in the clinic responsible for the music therapy service. The institution had never given the opportunity to one of the music therapists to coordinate the music therapy service. Professionals from other fields always did this. The institution also demanded a different function from the music therapists in their last year. Besides their work as clinicians at the institution, they were required to receive new music therapists and music therapy students and provide some specific training and supervision to them. Another important change was the modification of the format of the music therapy sessions. All the individual sessions needed to be changed to the group format, with an entertainment focus.

All these changes happened at different times, but at least challenge was present in each supervision meeting, which hindered the possibility of the supervisees focusing on the demands of their therapeutic work. For each situation, the supervisor sought to encourage the music therapists to fight for their rights and to try to prevent some of the changes from being implemented. These struggles for their rights made the group more and more united, and empowered the voice of each one within their needs. This empowerment gave an even greater sense of trust and security offered by the supervision space. Sarah stated that being part of a team of music therapists in a supervision context helped the whole group to grow in themselves, with the feeling that they could carry out big projects.

LEARNINGS WITHIN THE SUPERVISION PROCESS

From the supervisees' verbal and written accounts, it is clear that they considered the supervision experience in their practice context to be extraordinarily positive and enriching. For them, supervision was an essential space for professional growth that continues to bear fruit today. It is important to mention that some of the supervisees still work together in other institutions. During the meeting on Zoom, all of them agreed that the supervision process they participated in together was vital for their professional 'maturation'. According to Joyce, the supervision process was a mix of safe space and conflict. She identified the 'safe space' because it was a safe space to share all the challenges, to ask about specific doubts, to search for a clear direction in their music therapy practice and to feel, with the other music therapists, embraced and oriented in how to deal with the many challenges. It was also a space for conflict because it was a space to set new ideas against previous ideas to improve the quality of the music therapy sessions.

Supervision made a significant difference for some and because they had already had structured supervision as part of being a new graduate, they were more open to the learning this supervision provided. The challenges and difficulties uniquely shaped them because, given the experiences mediated by supervision, they are now more prepared to work in any practice context. After all, they believe it will be easier than they experienced in that practice.

Júlio was able to summarise the learning process they experienced during the supervision period. He said, 'Supervision worked so effectively that none of the six music therapists works in this practice any more.' Even though supervision is a teaching and learning process, it is possible to perceive a therapeutic outcome. Everybody left the institution with similar perceptions about the need for change and the importance of seeking other paths for professional practice. Júlio also said that 'supervision cures institutionalisation'. One of the significant challenges for music therapists working in a specific organisation is to prevent the institutional demands from taking away the space, the voice and the actions of the music therapist and increasing the chances for personal and professional illness. In this way, it is possible to understand that supervision can 'cure' some institutional blockages in the search for greater empowerment of the music therapist within their practice.

FINAL CONSIDERATIONS

The process described here in this chapter may reflect some different perspectives. One may be that what is described here represents an atypical reality and happens only in a few institutions. This perspective represents the feeling of professionals who practise in the private modality or work in institutions that value their professionals. In contrast, some professionals will identify with what has been reported, for this is the reality of many music therapists in different institutions. Only sometimes do they have the opportunity to participate in supervision practices and consider their demands and needs.

From this experience, the authors would encourage other music therapists to report their experiences of group supervision, particularly in the context of behavioural institutions that today are a vital reality in Brazil and Latin America. This very current and specific situation needs to be discussed further.

The chapter also points to some subjects explored in the current music therapy literature, such as supervision in music therapy (Hahna & Forinash 2019), assessment in music therapy (Gattino 2021), the adaptation of models, approaches and orientations in music therapy (Gattino 2022), and burnout in music therapists (Meier-Nielsen 2022). These issues are likely to be increasingly discussed in the literature so that supervisors and supervisees will have a more detailed view of them from the practical and research experiences of other professionals in music therapy. This chapter is also an incentive for the promotion of more publications about supervision in music therapy in Brazil, since it is an area that still needs more attention in the country.

The supervision process can be essential for developing music therapists in different situations, from various difficulties and challenges. In the group context, supervision strengthens the relationships between the supervisees, promoting trust, respect and learning collectively. In conclusion, group supervision is the maximum representation of unity and trust.

There is an expression we use in Brazil to say that a group is united and is fighting for the same purpose. The expression does not have a clear origin, but it mainly refers to the protection, care and defence of rights and causes vital to a group of people. This came up during the writing of this chapter, but it is not easy to define how or how much it came up. Thus, we end this chapter with this expression summarising this whole supervision process in Portuguese and English: *ninguém Solta a mão de ninguém* (nobody let go of anybody's hand).

REFERENCES

Adhikari, S. P., Meng, S., Wu, Y. J., Mao, Y. P. *et al.* (2020) Epidemiology, causes, clinical manifestation and diagnosis, prevention and control of coronavirus disease (Covid-19) during the early outbreak period: A scoping review. *Infectious Diseases of Poverty*, 9(1), pp.1–12.

Association of Professional Behavior Analysts (n.d.). *About Behavior Analysis*. www. apbahome.net/page/aboutba (Accessed 6 January 2024).

Barcellos, L. R. M. (2021) 'Musicoterapia Interativa.' In G. Gattino (ed.) *Perspectivas Práticas e Teóricas da Musicoterapia do Brasil* (pp.27–60). Gilsum, NH: Barcelona Publishers.

Barcellos, L. R. M. & Santos, M. A. C. (2021) A musicoterapia no Brasil. *Brazilian Journal of Music Therapy*, 23(32), pp.4–35. Available at: https://doi.org/10.51914/brjmt.32.2021.378 (Accessed 6 January 2024).

Baxter, H., Berghofer, J., MacEwan, L., Nelson, J., Peters, K. & Roberts, P. (2007) *The Individualized Musical Assessment Profile: IMTAP*. London: Jessica Kingsley Publishers.

Britannica, T. Editors of Encyclopaedia (2022) São Paulo summary. *Encyclopedia Britannica*. Available at: www.britannica.com/summary/Sao-Paulo-Brazil (Accessed 6 January 2024).

Hahna, N. & Forinash, M. (2019) 'Feminist Approaches to Supervision.' In M. Forinash (ed.) *Music Therapy Supervision* (second edition, pp.59–74). Gilsum, NH: Barcelona Publishers.

Gattino, G. (2020) *Music Therapy for Groups* [virtual seminar presentation]. Heart Beat Music Therapy Project, 17 May.

Gattino, G. S. (2021) *Essentials of Music Therapy Assessment. Forma e Conteúdo Comunicação Integrada*. Florianópolis, Santa Catarina, Brasil. Available at: https://vbn.aau. dk/files/455876666/Essentials_of_Music_Therapy_Assessment_141221.pdf (Accessed 6 January 2024).

Gattino, G. S. (2022) *Music Therapy and the Autism Spectrum: An Integrative Overview*. Gilsum, NH: Barcelona Publishers.

Gottfried, T., Thompson, G., Elefant, C. & Gold, C. (2018) Reliability of the Music in Everyday Life (MEL) Scale: A parent-report assessment for children on the autism spectrum. *Journal of Music Therapy*, 55(2), pp.133–155.

Hiller, J. (2016) 'Epistemological Foundations of Objectivist and Interpretivist Research.' In B. L. Wheeler & K. Murphy (eds) *Music Therapy Research* (third edition, pp.236–268). Gilsum, NH: Barcelona Publishers.

McGill, O. & Robinson, A. (2021) 'Recalling hidden harms': Autistic experiences of childhood applied behavioural analysis (ABA). *Advances in Autism*, 7(4) [online]. Available at: www.emerald.com/insight/content/doi/10.1108/AIA-04-2020-0025/full/html (Accessed 2 January 2024).

Meier-Nielsen, A. A. (2022) Understanding Burnout in Danish Music Therapists – A Phenomenological Study Based on Two Semi-Structured Interviews [master's thesis]. Aalborg University: Project Library. Available at: https://projekter.aau.dk/projekter/ en/studentthesis/den-forsvundne-lyd--et-faenomenologisk-studie-om-forstaaelsenaf-to-danske-musikterapeuters-udbraendthed-baseret-paa-to-semistrukturerede-interviews(c7b850d2-3a1b-4dcb-ae52-a8e7adf31041).html (Accessed 6 January 2024).

Mohammadzaheri, F., Koegel, L. K., Rezaee, M. & Rafiee, S. M. (2014) A randomized clinical trial comparison between pivotal response treatment (PRT) and structured applied behavior analysis (ABA) intervention for children with autism. *Journal of Autism and Developmental Disorders*, 44(11), pp.2769–2777.

Murphy, K. (2016) 'Interpretivist Case Study Research.' In I. K. Murphy & B. Wheeler (eds) *Music Therapy Research* (pp.1135–1146). Gilsum, NH: Barcelona Publishers.

Partington, J. W., Bailey, A. & Partington, S. W. (2018) A pilot study examining the test-retest and internal consistency reliability of the ABLLS-R. *Journal of Psychoeducational Assessment*, 36(4), pp.405–410.

Sundberg, M. L. (2008) VB-MAPP Verbal Behavior Milestones Assessment and Placement Program: A Language and Social Skills Assessment Program for Children with Autism or Other Developmental Disabilities: Guide. Available at: https://marksundberg. com/vb-mapp (Accessed 6 January 2024).

União Brasileira de Associações de Musicoterapia (UBAM) (2022) *Supervision in Music Therapy*. Seminar organized by the Brazilian Union of Music Therapy Associations. 21 May.

União Brasileira de Associações de Musicoterapia (UBAM) (2023a) Associações de Musicoterapia no Brasil [Music Therapy Associations in Brazil]. Available at: https:// ubammusicoterapia.com.br/institucional/associacao-de-musicoterapia-no-brasil (Accessed 6 January 2024).

União Brasileira de Associações de Musicoterapia (UBAM) (2023b) Cursos de Formação [Training Courses]. Available at: https://ubammusicoterapia.com.br/formacao-em-musicoterapia/cursos-de-formacao (Accessed 6 January 2024).

CHAPTER 10

Large Group Peer Supervision

Working Online with the Unthought Known

JOY RICKWOOD, HILARY STORER AND CATHERINE WARNER

INTRODUCTION

What happens when an experiential embodied group supervision method is translated online?

This chapter explores our joint process of developing a music therapy conference online supervision workshop, which was attended by 80 people during the Covid-19 pandemic in 2020. Originally conceived as an in-person workshop for a maximum of 30 participants, we needed to adapt and plan the workshop as we could not meet in person. This raised interesting questions about how embodied experiences can be translated online, and how both private and collective responses to case material can be captured and shared in a way that contributes to a deeper understanding of the work. We focus on an explanation of the adapted method, interspersed with reflections on the choices made.

The workshop was based on what we call the Ahonen supervision method, explored in Chapter 7 (Ahonen-Eerikainen 2003). This group supervision approach is derived from an application of Balint peer group supervision structure (Salinsky 2018) and influenced by musical group analytic approaches. Theoretically, Bollas's idea of the 'unthought known' underpins the approach (Bollas 2018), where the staged process of group exploration of a case reveals knowledge that was until now unconsciously held by the music therapist who presents the case.

JOY

I am a music therapist and supervisor working with adults with a learning disability in NHS Wales. In 2016 I set up a supervision network within the British Association for Music Therapy (BAMT), creating a forum for music therapists to reflect on and develop the supervisory relationship, whether giving or receiving supervision. When attending the training for music therapy supervisors based at University of the West of England (UWE) I made links with Catherine and experienced the Ahonen method. This method was explored further in a CPD day for the BAMT Supervision Network, and a dialogue with Catherine remained open as to the possibilities of sharing the model more widely within the UK.

The opportunity arose to present the Ahonen model at the BAMT Conference in 2020. It was originally due to be in person in spring 2020 in Northern Ireland, but the Covid-19 pandemic halted this, and it was moved to an online conference in April 2021.

Catherine and I had planned an in-person workshop. We wondered if we could find a way to present this method online that could still allow the use of shared improvisation – and whether the material could still be processed in a 'felt' sense. We aimed to be faithful to the initial ideas and underpinning. Given the gravity of the Covid experience and the necessity of online contact for work to continue, I wondered if passing on the method could allow for a safe contained space for the ongoing work of music therapists. Furthermore, we had a sense of the very strong need for music therapists to have opportunities to gain support in groups with peers and reflect on their changing work. There were many unusual clinical challenges; for example, music therapists required to go on furlough immediately in the UK were not at liberty to engage in any of the appropriate ending work with their clients that music therapy models of good practice promote (Office for National Statistics: UK 2021).

I was curious as to how this might be put into practice. I had started to provide online music therapy sessions myself and ran an online community choir. These experiences gave me the confidence to rethink the presentation, allowing for the direct creative engagement of those attending.

When we were planning for the in-person workshop, we were aware of the boundaries involved in potentially 'live' music therapy cases being explored in the experiential realm, and the impact this could have on the participants. We decided it would probably be safer to have a prepared participant bringing a less complex case, anonymised, with consent from the client. It was considered ideal to avoid trauma work to give a secure example of the model and keep participants psychologically safe. We were due to co-facilitate this as the original model suggests, with Catherine as facilitator and Joy as a witness, planning to limit the number of active participants to around 12, with up to 18 more people attending in an observational role. Working online requires more safety protocols when it is not possible to be physically present with the client or supervisee and we were mindful of this (Agres, Foubert & Sridhar 2021).

At first, it seemed logical simply to present the model without the experiential component. On reflection, this seemed less than satisfactory in terms of the essential learning that comes from experiencing the model in real time.

I had planned to take on a gatekeeper role, supporting Catherine in her role as facilitator. To offer the workshop virtually, we realised this gatekeeper role had an additional function: focusing on the here and now by observing the chat and supporting participants to access virtual space. From our experiences of holding virtual therapeutic and supervisory spaces for groups early in the pandemic, the importance of having supporting roles to hold the virtual boundaries, keep the work safe and look after technical 'housekeeping' for participants was clear. There were also clear boundaries around each stage in the Ahonen process, and I was able to mind these stages as Catherine set out the structure.

Catherine and I could not bring a case, given our facilitative roles. Rather than inviting a workshop participant to bring a clinical dilemma to the workshop, we needed to prepare a clinical case in advance. This is where Hilary came in. We initially thought that Hilary would present a clinical case and improvise live, with the group joining the improvisation with their audio muted, giving feedback after the improvisation had taken place.

There were several dilemmas to consider. The thought of the presenter improvising live with no audible feedback seemed exposing and unsupported in a way the model would not intend. We were keen to reduce the risk of audio issues with live music online, due to latency and sound filtering settings on online video platforms. We concluded it would be most secure to record the improvisation in advance, with at the same time a supporting musician taking on the role of the participating group. Hilary and I met to record; first Hilary giving a short description of the clinical dilemma, then improvising. I joined the improvisation in the role of the group. This recording then formed the basis of Hilary's presentation musically in the workshop.

HILARY

I am a music therapist working mainly in the field of neuro-disability and I supervise students while on placement. In 2014, I took part in the pilot to develop the supervision training module with Catherine Warner and Leslie Bunt. We looked at creative ways of exploring the supervision process, including the Ahonen model. Joy and I already knew each other professionally. I was happy to be asked to present at the conference workshop as I felt confident in working with therapists I already knew well, despite the challenges of delivering the workshop online.

JOY

We needed to convey to attendees what the original model was, and the ways in which it had been adapted, so we put a poster together clearly showing the different stages in the model and the adaptations for online practice. It was made available to attendees as a resource via the digital platform. Key information from the poster is shown in Table 10.1, which takes you through the six method stages. The group in both cases consists of a presenting clinician, facilitator, participating (inner) group members and witnesses.

Table 10.1: The six method stages

Stages in group process	In person	Online adaptations
1. Case exploration	Each practitioner writes a single sentence about a dilemma from their work. The group collectively decides on the case presented. The presenter describes the dilemma and gives background, uninterrupted.	Case is pre-arranged. Other practitioners self-select their part in the process, either using instruments or voice in the small group or witnessing and creating artwork. More time is allowed for setting up.
2. Solo improvisation	When the presenter is ready, they move into solo improvisational playing; again, this is uninterrupted.	The music therapist presenter shares a pre-recorded improvisation which others listen to together. The pre-recorded improvisation has already been responded to by a second music therapist and recorded. Other online participants have their microphones muted.

3. Group improvisation	The facilitator indicates when the inner group can begin playing, or the group intuitively begins to join the presenter musically. They all improvise together.	Online, during the live session, participants who have chosen to be in the inner responding group start to improvise music with their microphones off. Witnesses, who do not actively participate, choose to create drawings or a mandala at home, or simply witness.
4. Presenter responds	The presenting music therapist describes their response to the group improvisation and their own experience first, starting with sensory responses.	The presenting music therapist will not have heard the music by online players but could respond to the visual impact of people playing. One option is that the group members could unmute in turn to play extracts of their responses.
5. Group discussion	Enabled by the facilitator, the group members slowly offer their sensory experiences and emotions – *without interpretation*. It is the presenting music therapist who begins to make links and concludes this section.	Group members express in the 'chat' function their sensory experiences and feelings; the facilitator may follow up verbally. Again, interpretation is avoided, so that the music therapist presenting the case themselves is free to make the links.
6. Witnesses respond	Witnesses, who have sat in an outside circle, and have not actively participated, provide feedback on their experiences. The session ends with closing comments by the facilitator.	Witnesses share their mandalas on camera and share their feedback either in 'chat' or verbally. The facilitator may need to manage this entire process: directing when not to use chat, for example, or following up on written comments by asking someone to come on microphone. The session ends with closing comments from the facilitator.

We now explore the step-by-step experience of delivering this online. Quotations from Heidi Ahonen-Eerikainen have been adapted to use 'they' pronouns.

1. CASE EXPLORATION

> The presenter (supervisee) describes their case without preparation (about 20 minutes). They can also tell their dreams about the situation. Free association and free flow in which the unconscious material becomes conscious. Usually, the presenter finds out that they know about their client more than they thought. (Ahonen-Eerikainen 2003, p.175)

In this first stage, there are three distinct processes: encapsulating the dilemma, role division of the group and uninterrupted description of the dilemma by the chosen practitioner.

1.1 Encapsulating the dilemma

Normally the facilitator in a face-to-face group introduces the session and explains the process. Each group member then prepares a 'dilemma' expressed in one phrase or sentence which encapsulates the main question they might want to bring to supervision. Examples of this might be something like 'What is happening in the silence between us?' The group chooses one dilemma. Sometimes a particular dilemma speaks to several people in the group for a reason, as there may be resonances with some of the questions they are facing in their work at present.

For the online workshop we felt that the process of collectively choosing a dilemma and then the chosen, possibly unprepared practitioner improvising spontaneously online might be difficult to manage and could take up a disproportionate amount of time. As part of the workshop role was to teach attendees about this method of group supervision, we were concerned to make the main aspects accessible. Inviting a music therapist with a pre-prepared dilemma would take the pressure off the beginning of the workshop and allow us to plan more carefully, freeing up more space later in the workshop for exploration of participant responses and how this could illuminate deeper understanding of Hilary's clinical dilemma. We approached Hilary to see if she would be interested in taking this role, which she agreed to.

Hilary

I identified the following dilemma: How do I keep the needs of my client at the centre of my focus?

1.2 Role division

Normally at this point the remaining group is asked which roles they wish to take in the process: the supporting 'inner' group of improvisors, or the outer group of witnesses. In small groups, there may only be one or two people in either circle. The inner circle of up to six people sits with the person bringing the dilemma (from this point called the 'presenter'). This circle has a selection of musical instruments available. Others can take the role of witness, sitting outside this circle. The group of witnesses can be larger or can just be confined to one witness.

For the online workshop, the virtual 'circle' needed to be transformed into a community of workshop attendees improvising on their own instruments or singing at home in response to, but not heard, online. Alternatively, attendees could choose to draw a mandala in response to the recorded music and this was explained to them. This practice of drawing mandalas while music is playing is a known therapeutic approach and is used in Guided Imagery and Music practices (Dimiceli-Mitran 2016). Attendees were asked to choose whether to take the role of witness or role of inner circle creative responders.

1.3 Describing uninterrupted

In the face-to-face version, the presenter talks about the dilemma they have brought, bringing in any background description or explanation of the person they are working with that they feel is necessary while maintaining anonymity and confidentiality. They will also describe in words how they are responding to that person in the work.

Hilary

The dilemma I brought to the online workshop concerned a young man, whom I will call B. Now in his twenties, he had sustained a severe traumatic brain injury aged 17. He was in full-time residential care. At the time, he had a disorder of consciousness, responding to sensory stimuli, but variable in his responses, non-verbal and with left-sided paresis. The multidisciplinary team members found it difficult to reach any agreement about him, but he responded well in music therapy sessions and often displayed good levels of attention and response.

B could hold a beater in his right hand and engage with playing various instruments, including a drum and cymbal on stands, and plucking the strings of a guitar placed across his lap, and was particularly engaged when playing the wind chimes, positioned on a stand to his right side.

His parents were sometimes present on the day of B's music therapy session; they visited separately, and both liked to attend his sessions as they felt they were seeing him 'at his best'. In more detail, my dilemma was how to balance the needs of my client by providing this window of expression and non-verbal communication for him, and keeping him as the primary focus, while supporting the involvement of his parents.

2. SOLO IMPROVISATION

> Anything that the presenter needs to improvise. The small group reflects themselves. The referential improvisation usually deals with the feelings, countertransference issues or needs of the presenter. (Ahonen-Eerikainen 2003, p.175)

For the online session, Hilary's improvisation took place several days earlier, together with Joy's initial musical response.

Joy
We wondered how it would be for Hilary to present, having recorded a solo earlier. We wondered if there would be a vacuum in the thinking in the time between recording and the supervision process at the workshop. We were mindful of potential technical issues with attendees responding with live music online, and the timing delays. We decided it was better to record in advance and play the recording within the workshop structure at the solo improvisation point, and have attendees respond to the recording.

Hilary
The improvisation for the supervision took place with my colleague, Joy, in a dedicated music therapy space. I was aware that if I were to play live, I would not be able to hear any of the musical responses from the 'inner circle', which seemed to be a fundamental part of the process. The decision to add a second player to the improvisation (Joy), standing for the 'inner circle', made the process feel more authentic.

I did, however, have concerns that pre-recording the music would detract from its spontaneity and that I might feel as though I was performing rather than it being a genuine, in-the-moment, emotional response. I described the case dilemma to Joy before we started to play so that we could both hold it in mind. We then selected instruments; I sat at the keyboard and also chose the wind chimes as they were an important instrument in B's music-making; Joy chose a shaker, a drum and a tongue drum.

I started to play a single melodic line on the piano, beginning on the same note in each of three phrases, which grew from three, to five, to ten notes, each time coming to a pause. Harmony was introduced by me gradually and the music began to move forward little by little, though still in the shape of falling phrases, each time coming to a point of rest. After about a minute and a half I played the wind chimes for the first time, which seemed to bring more energy, with the music shifting towards the lower register of the piano.

It was nearly three minutes into the improvisation before a shaker was quietly played by Joy. Still the music moved, then paused, in gentle waves. The subtle entry of her fingers quietly moving across the drum skin and then the sound of the tongue drum injected more energy and momentum, the music still repetitive, ebbing and flowing, but now there was more than one voice to be heard, the music had a greater sense of rhythm and a feeling of direction. As the music drew to a close, my piano returned to a single melodic line, accompanied by a pulse on the tongue drum and ending on a rising interval.

Joy

After the recording, we had a short discussion, checking that the recording had worked, but there was a reverence for the need to contain the material, and a sense that the recording was part of the wider supervisory process, in preparation for the workshop. We discussed whether we wanted to re-record, but both preferred to leave it as an authentic musical account of the work within the supervisory structure provided by Heidi Ahonen-Eerikainen.

3. GROUP IMPROVISATION

> Musical reflection of their feelings and images. (Ahonen-Eerikainen 2003, p.175)

The process Heidi Ahonen-Eerikainen describes has already been modified through the practice described in the previous chapter.

Ahonen-Eerikainen suggests that before the group improvises, there is discussion. However, in Echart Weymann's version, the supervisee's solo improvisation is immediately joined in music by the inner circle. The inner circle joins the solo improviser intuitively, or possibly directed by the facilitator. This can vary depending on circumstances. The group plays until the music stops naturally. The facilitator may steer the music towards an ending if it goes on for a particularly long time.

For the online version at this stage in the process, we invited people who were taking the role as musical responders in the 'inner circle' to listen to this recording live, and then respond individually at home with microphones turned off, aiming to retain a sense of being with Hilary and Joy. The choice was to improvise music with any instrument they had available, or sing, or move, or any combination of those.

4. PRESENTER RESPONDS

The practitioner describes their somatic, embodied and emotional reactions to the music. This is uninterrupted, and they must resist interpretation and analysis of what has just happened, focussing only on their body and their feelings. (Ahonen-Eerikainen 2003)

In this case, once we were sure that workshop participants had all stopped playing at home, Hilary, then Joy, described their responses.

Hilary
During the opening phrases of piano playing, I felt focused and absorbed in the process. After what seemed to be a few minutes, I felt a strong impulse to play the wind chimes, but it felt incongruous as I did so. I had a wish to try to fill the space; it felt uncomfortable to stop playing or to allow space or silence. When Joy joined the music later in the improvisation, playing the tongue drum, I immediately felt supported, and the musical underpinning seemed important; a relief from the ungrounded feeling in my own music.

Joy
In recording, and listening back, I was surprised at how long it took me to join Hilary in playing. I was aware of a sense of guilt in leaving her to play alone for so long, but desired to provide space to hear the material

unfold. When I did join the improvisation with hand-held percussion, I felt my sounds were not very musical at first, but then grew into a more collaborative, supportive musical offering.

5. GROUP DISCUSSION

> The expressions of the reflection group make the process richer and sometimes offer new points of view. Usually there is more objectivity and distance. Often the therapeutic relationship that became visible in the small group becomes stronger in the reflection group. It is like a double mirror. (Ahonen-Eerikainen 2003, p.175)

Online, we asked for feedback from the inner group through the 'chat' function during the workshop. However, unexpectedly, participants had responded more fluidly, using both music and drawing in some cases, and not staying with the distinction between inner and outer circle. Those who had improvised musically with the recording reflected on their music either by typing a description of their musical response in the chat or raising a hand to simply describe their music verbally. We started to get a written cascade of feedback from participants, some of which is reproduced here.

> I experienced a welling up with tears in my eyes initially.

> At the beginning I felt bleak. Stuck. Staring.

> While I was playing, I felt empty. I felt I needed to ground myself and find a way of using my cello that was authentic; it felt hard to do this. I felt 'speechless'.

> I felt a sinking feeling in my stomach.

> Despairing and lost.

> I closed my eyes and tried to 'sink' into my saxophone.

> I felt the heavy and poignant mood of the improvisation and I tried to match it with long deep pizzicatos on my double bass.

I started thinking I was going to draw but the initial sounds compelled me to play instead – something to do with wanting/needing to make a connection with the sounds.

I felt a sense of longing. I felt a need to 'break out' of the tonality, it felt unbearable to stay within it.

I felt a statement of presence and identity in the first notes, I felt so drowned by the music and decided to join with a few notes in the harp. Felt held and contained in my playing, also in moments where emotions were more intense, a sense of anger arising and impotence.

As the music continued, I found a more comfortable place in the outer registers of the piano, pentatonic 'gong-like' sounds.

I am left with a slightly sore left shoulder/neck.

I felt pulled into the heaviness and a sense of plodding on (parents?).

After the wind chimes there was more movement in the music, and I physically moved more.

Feeling of intrusion from the wind chimes.

I felt like wanting to move, dancing with a scarf while listening to the music Hilary was playing.

Following this discussion, the practitioner starts to make links between their dilemma and their own reactions. They also start to bring in links they can usefully make between what people of the inner circle have experienced and described. They do this without interruption or judgement from the inner circle.

What did they discover about the therapeutic relationship? What did they experience or feel? What is the client expecting from them? What could they offer and what could they not? (Ahonen-Eerikainen 2003, p.175)

Hilary

While playing, I felt as though I was asking a question, but on reflection the music felt static, stuck, lost. The tonality remained relatively constant and there was little dynamic contrast. There were echoes of a life unfulfilled and the sadness surrounding that, and of concern for this family unit. The mother's need to care for her adult child now permanently in a child-like state and of a father not knowing what his place or role was. The wind chimes, although feeling out of place at the time, seemed like a wake-up call, a reminder of the client's presence in all of this – his voice was still here at the centre of everything.

Joy

At first my intention was to attune to and support Hilary by harmonizing with her, then I felt moved at the end to have two voices harmonizing with her...client and family?

Hilary

In the event, it felt very important to the process that another musical voice joined mine. In the group's experience, many people noticed the change in mood at this point, and for me it was the moment when I felt supported and able to move forward in the music. When reflecting on the comments from the group I felt that however difficult the situation was for the rest of the family, my most important role was in supporting my client, with the hope that by doing so his parents would gain something positive too. The expression from the group of the sense of sadness and possibly anger conveyed in my improvisation helped me to recognise these feelings, but also the comments about the 'intrusion' of the wind chimes and its expression of 'hope' reminded me that B was there, able to respond through his music.

6. WITNESSES RESPOND

Only then are the witnesses invited to make their own observations and links to Hilary's clinical situation. Those who had drawn mandalas held these up to the camera on their device, creating a 'gallery' effect of the images created. One participant, R, had an empty space on the left side of her mandala.

In R's drawing, it looks to me like the left side of it is the emotional part in the brain.

Mandala response light grey single strand searching, ice blue, brown, disconnected strands, much space. Sadness and evaporation – somehow out of reach.

I wonder if the non-verbal state of the client and the work makes it hard to speak, but I had a sense that a lot was felt and stated musically by many.

The witness group made more links with trying to understand the client's parents within the dynamic.

Wondering about identification with each parent's experience as well and them being caught between action and a sense of denial.

I find myself left with strong feelings of potential parental grief and frustration.

Ending

The facilitator thanks the practitioner and invites any closing remarks. The session can then move on to another dilemma or question. Here, we only had time for one case. Instead, we asked workshop participants to write their final reflections, including thoughts on the value of the experience, into the 'chat' function.

Here are some of the participant reflections on the value of the approach explored in the workshop:

The use of musical improvisation within the clinical supervision process is such a valuable tool. I felt sad and stuck listening to Hilary's improvisation and as the music progressed a 'closing in' as if I was looking out onto 'another world'.

It's strengthened my belief that there is this part in us all that can be enhanced and developed, the 'unthought known'.

It felt very sad but I felt very connected musically as I was playing, which surprised me given we were working online. The music felt centred and contained.

This interesting process allows space for embodied experience and a free associative way of working.

I wonder how it feels for Hilary to be doing this exercise 'blind' – not able to feel or see the responders for most of the session?

In the chat there was a chain of comments about how powerful the experience had been: these were generated very quickly as though there was strong identification with this feeling that people wanted to express.

It was so very powerful – I still feel on the edge of tears.

It felt like a powerful experience to witness and also to be able to participate in. The shared embodied experiences were profoundly moving and interesting!

A very powerful experience. A real resonance was felt with others in this experience and similarities of felt experience. I imagine as the 'presenter' this is hugely validating and supportive.

This was a powerful and engaging way to process clinical material. It's a very useful structure and a strong way to bring in the embodied and felt experience.

Very powerful experience and such a shared resonance within the online group.

A second rapid chain related to the value of holding back interpretation and attending to physical embodied responses first.

I really appreciated being asked to stay with my feelings rather than interpret.

I found the collective step away from interpretation so powerful as it opened up a space to just 'be'.

It felt important to be asked to stay with our feelings as this is such a rich way of unlocking...

It is interesting to read these chains and get a sense of how particular words and thoughts appeared to create a cascade of collective agreement. Perhaps this is a phenomenon of online experiences of large groups that warrants further research, but it may also be a feature of this kind of reflective experience which promotes strong connections of resonance. Unlike the spoken word, some of the comments may have been written some time before they were posted, so they don't necessarily represent a linear sequence.

Some people reflected on the challenge of suspending interpretation:

Really hard to hold back on interpretation as I was unable to in my description of my drawing! But really valuable, and I will be using it with my colleagues at work.

I found it very hard to hold on to my interpretations, probably a defence for getting in touch with the emotions at the core, but eventually happens when there is holding from the supervisor.

Others had thoughts about the use of this approach with other arts therapies:

I wondered about how this could be expanded out to include all creative modalities?

I work with a dramatherapist at school and would be really interested to see how this modality could be incorporated.

Body moving could engage his parents too, this is what I felt, and a lot of expressions and feelings coming out of it.

I work in a multi-modality team, and I am going to try this!

Future potential of the method was explored:

I can imagine how powerful this method would be in trauma work.

Also working with clinical psychologists and vicarious trauma.

Some people were encouraged to think about their current clinical or supervision practice in a more innovative way:

> I could feel the value of Joy's music in supporting Hilary's improvisation, and it made me realise how valuable it would be to have a music therapist in the supervision room supporting *our* music as therapists.

> In the Continuum Model GIM supervision we listen, share mandalas. How would it be for parents to draw during sessions?

REFLECTIONS ON THE PROCESS
Hilary
I was really surprised at how intense and moving the whole experience was. I had feared that my music would feel separated from the group response as I was not playing live, but in the event, this did not seem to matter too much, and I felt a strong sense of connection and support from others' descriptions of their music and artwork.

Catherine
For the workshop, the facilitative roles were shared, as we had a sense that there was greater holding required. First, Katie Bycroft chaired the session, introducing the workshop facilitators and closing the workshop. Second, I took the facilitator role of explaining the method and guiding each process through the separate stages, creating space for responses from Hilary. Third, Joy facilitated the chat function and fed in participant responses throughout the stages that involved this. These three levels of containment allowed us to pace the workshop spaciously, and some participants commented on this at the end.

Initially I was overwhelmed to see that more than 80 people were attending: many more than I would feel it possible to involve in a face-to-face group. The boundary between the inner circle and witnesses was more blurred in the online method as some people took part in the inner circle, then drew mandalas and joined the witness group. We had two new kinds of space instead: the writing space (chat) with Joy responding to this in the here and now, and the video space where participants unmuted and talked about their experiences, and in some cases showed their drawings.

Did the virtual space mean that people were responding more privately? Perhaps, and perhaps this allowed people more creative freedom to express themselves away from collective gaze. Many people did not engage in the writing: out of 80 participants, about 40 wrote comments, so there was a silent contingent whose experience is unknown. However, from the 'chat' we can see that some people got caught up in a collective experience in their writing. It was particularly interesting that it was reinforced by repetition of key words like 'powerful'; it is interesting to speculate whether this kind of repetition might be less likely between those physically present together. Perhaps the separation between private and collective was more starkly observed online. I wonder whether some of the embodied experiences people reported were reduced in impact or lost online, despite some vivid descriptions, because we were not physically together. I also reflected that it seemed possible (but perhaps more difficult) for Hilary to make detailed and explicit links between the chat experiences and her new understanding of the work in the moment.

The phenomenon of oversharing or rapid sharing in large groups online is supported by the literature in teletherapy (Havlik *et al.* 2023; Wood, Wilson & Parry 2021). Havlik's study identified how facilitators might overshare if the participants were less forthcoming, and Wood found that the therapeutic alliance developed more rapidly because of the speed of sharing when the client was not seen. Certainly, in our workshop there were some very open comments made in the 'public' arena and we did try to allow a good time to debrief near the end of the workshop. However, it did seem that pre-selecting the case material avoided vulnerability for both Hilary's client, as Hilary had plenty of time to work on anonymising details and gaining permission, and Hilary herself, as she had already pre-recorded her solo music.

Joy

We wondered whether the therapists attending the workshop had a particularly strong need to connect with other practitioners because of the isolation they were experiencing. This forum involved opportunities to do this. It would have been interesting to consider some form of embodied debrief when possible.

FINAL COMMENTS

We aimed to be transparent about which stages had been altered. Writing this up as a chapter has helped the process of evaluating the impact of the workshop further. Keeping clarity between stages, even if modified, did stay largely true to the key principles of Balint and Ahonen practices: interpretation was put on hold, emotional and embodied responses were prioritised and people responded differently at different stages, according to their roles. Unconscious material was discussed and explored. We considered that the boundaries we put in place during the workshop were significant in the process, allowing the stages in the process to be separate and pure in themselves.

The aim of the workshop was to disseminate the practice more widely; instead, surprisingly, we ended up producing something new; a more public form of large group supervision. We wondered what there was in this experience to help us understand more about supervision processes. We believe that the collective phenomenon of cascading responses using the chat function has potential for future practice and research, and further exploration of curated and distinct role-shared facilitation online could also be useful to develop.

REFERENCES

Agres, K., Foubert, K. & Sridhar, S. (2021) Music therapy during COVID-19: Changes to the practice, use of technology, and what to carry forward in the future. *Frontiers of Psychology*, 12. https://doi.org/10.3389/fpsyg.2021.647790

Ahonen-Eerikainen, H. (2003) Using group-analytic supervision approach when supervising music therapists. *Nordic Journal of Music Therapy* [online] 12(2), pp.173–182.

Bollas, C. (2018) *The Shadow of the Object: Psychoanalysis and the Unthought Known* (30th anniversary issue). London: Routledge.

Dimiceli-Mitran, L. (2016) 'Accessing Strength from Within: Music Imagery and Mandalas.' In J. K. Edwards, A. Young & H. Nikels (eds) *Handbook of Strengths-Based Clinical Practices: Finding Common Factors*. New York, NY: Routledge.

Foulkes, S. H., (1975) Group-Analytic Psychotherapy. Method & Principles. London: Gordon and Breach. Later: reprint Karnac Books.

Havlik, S., Malott, K.M., Gamerman, T. & Okonya, P. (2023) Working across differences while online: Examining the experience of facilitating a virtual group. *International Journal for the Advancement of Counselling*, 45(2), pp.291–309.

Office for National Statistics: UK (2021) An overview of workers who were furloughed in the UK: October 2021. www.ons.gov.uk/employmentandlabourmarket/peopleinwork/employmentandemployeetypes/articles/anoverviewofworkerswhowerefurloughedintheuk/october2021

Salinsky, J. (2018) Balint under the microscope: What really happens in Balint groups? *International Journal of Psychiatry in Medicine*, 53(1–2), pp.7–14. https://doi.org/10.1177/0091217417745287

Weymann, E. (2016) Improvisation as "unthought known": creative techniques in music therapy supervision. *Nordic Journal of Music Therapy* 25: 114-15. DO - 10.1080/08098131.2016.1180133

Wood, M. J., Wilson, H. M. & Parry, S. L. (2021) Exploring the development and maintenance of therapeutic relationships through e-health support: A narrative analysis of therapist experiences. *Medicine Access @ Point of Care*, 5. https://doi.org/10.1177/23992026211018087

PART 4

REFLECTIONS ON SUSTAINED EXPERIENCES OF SUPERVISION

CHAPTER 11

Now and Then

Reflections on Supervisee and Supervisor Perspectives in Early Career

ANN SLOBODA AND HILARY MOSS

INTRODUCTION

This chapter came about as a result of a keynote presentation that Hilary Moss gave at the 2021 BAMT conference in Belfast. Here she talked about working with people in a range of clinical contexts over the last 20 years, and her work at the intersection between arts therapies and arts and health. As part of her presentation, she noted and thanked Ann Sloboda for her clinical supervision and mentorship, especially in the early years following graduation from the Guildhall School of Music and Drama, where Ann had also taught her and been her placement supervisor. Ann was moved and pleased but also surprised that this experience remained such an important influence for Hilary, leading her to reflect anew on the significance of the supervisory relationship, particularly in one's early career, and she suggested that they collaborate to write about it. 'Now and Then' in the title refers to the Beatles song first written in by John Lennon in 1995 but released in 2023; this matches our timeframe neatly.

ANN

I learned the hard way how vital supervision is for music therapy practice, from my experience of starting off in a full-time NHS job as a newly qualified music therapist in the mid-1980s without any clinical supervision at all. This was at a time when the professional body, the APMT (Association of Professional Music Therapists, precursor of BAMT, British Association for Music Therapy), was seriously highlighting the need

181

for supervision, but it was not yet built into working structures or seen as essential. I was the first, and only, music therapist working in the service. I was balancing a large caseload with the task of establishing, promoting, and explaining music therapy to colleagues. There was management supervision and general support, but nobody to help me think about what I was doing in my sessions. I was very isolated clinically and professionally. The situation quickly unravelled: I couldn't switch off from work at all, became very over-identified with some of my clients, and got close to burnout after only 18 months.

It was only then that I was encouraged to get supervision with music therapist John Woodcock, tutor on the Roehampton music therapy training course at that time. The experience of talking to another music therapist who understood the musical content of the work was a transformational experience. I realised this was necessary for me and joined the APMT Committee to spend more time with other music therapists. I also began taking music therapy students on placement, which helped me to feel part of the music therapy community.

This supervision experience highlighted my need for my own personal psychotherapy, which had neither been mandatory nor even recommended when I was training, so I then began this.

This helped me develop a theoretical base to my work and led me into further training in psychotherapy, at the Portman Clinic in the 1990s and as a psychoanalyst from 2006 to 2012.

One early development in the late 1980s/early 1990s was the formation of a supervision group of music and art therapists working in learning disabilities led by Valerie Sinason, psychoanalyst and author of the pioneering book *Mental Handicap and the Human Condition* (Sinason 2010). She recognised the value of music therapists' work in their efforts to engage with the internal world of people with learning disabilities and little or no verbal language. This group was extremely valuable in helping to combat my isolation, through hearing other therapists share their work, and building confidence in my own practice. It was soon after this that the APMT set up a system for approving supervisors, and I began offering supervision to newly or recently qualified music therapists myself. Hilary was working in two part-time jobs in the south of England, travelling to London for evening supervision.

At that time, the qualifying training programmes in music therapy were only one year long, and while it was widely acknowledged that this was not long enough, it was not until 2006 that a two-year master's programme became a requirement.

HILARY

I was supervised by Ann from 1995 to 1999. From 1995 to 1996 I was a student on the Postgraduate Diploma in Music Therapy at GSMD (Guildhall School of Music & Drama), receiving weekly group clinical seminar and placement supervision from Ann. After qualifying until 1999, I received fortnightly supervision from Ann while I set up and worked as a newly qualified music therapist. I chose Ann to be my supervisor and hoped she would say yes. I admired her approach to music therapy work. As my teacher at Guildhall, I noticed the psychodynamic and reflective perspective she brought to reflecting on my student clinical cases, while also being very practical in how to tackle management and organizational issues. I felt that she brought a humanistic and psychodynamic perspective but also was very experienced in working as part of a mental health clinical team and setting up new posts. I knew she would both challenge me and be clear in her advice. Supervision took place normally at my supervisor's home, often with refreshments. These were welcome following a day at work. This felt like a supportive place, and the time was boundaried without interruption. The home location and the relaxing atmosphere helped me to unwind and reflect on my work. As this supervision was external to my workplace, the supervision took place in the evening. This can add a burden to the professional therapist who must bring their work out with them in the evening. Nowadays I would hope to have supervision within working hours wherever possible, to recognise its centrality as part of doing the job.

I had two jobs as a newly graduated music therapist. For the first six months after qualification I established a new music therapy post three days per week at an NHS Trust in the mental health service. I was managed by an allied health professional and belonged within a large mental health team. At the same time, I was lucky to stay on for two days a week at my final placement site in West London, where Ann was also head of department.

After the first six months I moved to work there four days per week for the following two and a half years. After three years of this supervisory relationship, I moved to Ireland to build a life with my partner, where posts were fewer and difficult to establish. At that time, the supervision with Ann also came to a natural conclusion.

ANN

It's interesting to reflect from the perspective of 2023 that any sort of remote supervision would have been very difficult in those days. We were not yet using the internet or mobile phones and had to communicate with phone landlines, answerphones and paper letters. Had it been possible, we would have organised some remote supervision – or at least mentoring sessions in the early stages of that move – but with communications as they were in those days, this wasn't really considered. The recent rise of online supervision is a great addition to the range of clinical supervision opportunities available and affords one the opportunity to seek out a clinical specialist even if living far away.

Given my work experience ten years earlier, I strongly identified with Hilary in the new post where she was pioneering music therapy in a new area and I wanted to help her manage the situation. I felt her employment conditions were in many ways worse and more precarious than mine had been. My salary at least had been secure, and the contract was permanent.

Nevertheless, there were some parallels in our experience:

- The burden of responsibility of establishing a new service.
- The pressure of being an ambassador for music therapy, and indeed at times, fighting for it as a newly qualified therapist while still developing a sense of a therapeutic identity.
- The isolation of the position and the tendency to take setbacks personally (e.g if a colleague was dismissive, critical or undermining to music therapy, it would feel as if I was being ignored or attacked).

I remembered all too well how stressful and demoralizing these aspects could be and wanted to support Hilary from another music therapist's perspective.

HILARY

The two roles I held were both in mental health work but had contrasting cultures and settings.

In my first post I was one of a team of 12 arts therapists, with an arts therapies manager, three other music therapists, and drama and art therapists, and I had the experience of working within a team where arts therapists were accepted.

Like any other entry grade clinician, I was working with appropriate supervision, supported by senior therapists and entering an established service. In both settings, as a newly qualified music therapist, I found that clinical supervision from an experienced music therapist was critical in terms of ensuring my professional competence and duty of care to clients, as well as maintaining my own wellbeing in a challenging environment. Clinical supervision exists as part of a suite of support to new therapists. These include clinical managers in health services (non-music therapy) such as the occupational therapy manager; colleagues in occupational, speech and language, nursing and psychology departments; personal therapy (continuing to develop self-awareness so that I can be a better therapist) and other activities that support work/life balance.

In this context, my supervisor was also my manager in one post and previously my university tutor. These dual relationships worked well in this instance because the supervisor was clear, an excellent communicator and had safe boundaries around various aspects of the work. In other instances, I have experienced being a supervisor who is entirely separate from the organization, and this makes a clear demarcation between supervisor and manager. However, in my first role, it made sense that the organization funded clinical supervision from within the existing arts therapies team, and I received monthly clinical supervision for that work from another senior music therapist.

Hawkins and Shohet comment that:

> The supervisor must integrate the role of educator with that of being the provider of support to the worker and, in most cases, managerial oversight of the supervisee's clients. These three functions do not always sit comfortably together, and many supervisors can retreat from attempting this integration to just one of the roles. (Hawkins & Shohet 2000, p.4)

In the second part-time post I was the sole music therapist, pioneering a new service within an NHS Trust that had no other music therapists. This new post involved setting up music therapy sessions in five areas of the large mental health institution. I ran a group in the forensic psychiatry ward and the acute women's ward, individual sessions in the day hospital for adults in the community and on a ward for people with dementia, and one group a week in the child and adolescent mental health services (CAMHS). This was a complex juggle of clinical scenarios, sites and clinical teams. The variety of clients was an amazing experience for a newly qualified therapist.

While I found it extremely stimulating and interesting, and learned a great deal, it was a lot to take on and certainly not sustainable longer term. The organization paid for my clinical supervision, but I attended in my own time in the evening.

Clinical supervision from an external music therapist was a vital support in helping me develop confidence in establishing professional expectations, boundaries and resources.

It was also crucial in helping me to start to evaluate my work as a music therapist.

In establishing the new service, I was also required to carry out a six-month evaluation of the work to prove the value of music therapy, and to produce 'evidence' of benefit at the end of this period. My own salary was contingent on establishing the value of the service.

In this case, I initially felt very lost, wondering anxiously what evidence I could gather, who and where to get it from, and what questions to ask. I brought this to supervision, and together we spent one session designing an evaluation form which I could use during the first six months of my new post. This is an example of the supervisor planting a seed which can then be cultivated by the supervisee. From here, I was able to carry out the evaluation and afterwards I wrote up this work and had a paper published in the *British Journal of Music Therapy* (Moss 1999). Looking back now, as an experienced researcher with many more publications, I recognize Ann's instrumental role in helping me to get started and to think about evaluating the work. If I were publishing that paper now, I would add Ann as co-author, given her substantial input into this work.

It felt as if the job's success depended on me being successful, and I think as a young person I was less aware of this pressure than I am with hindsight. My supervisor was crucial on many levels during this period, particularly in naming difficult situations that she recognized from her experience (e.g. the large caseload and number of teams to engage with); clinical expertise to help me work with new client groups; service management experience to help me with evaluation and time management; and multidisciplinary team experience to advise me on how to manage staff relationships and gain appropriate referrals. There are numerous other ways in which the supervisor was crucial – for example, guiding my report writing, decision-making about prioritizing referrals and setting aims for clinical work, to name a few.

The supervision helped me to grow in confidence as a therapist and professional. However, I made mistakes in setting up the post, and after the six months I left as I found the funding uncertainty incredibly stressful. The continuation of the part-time post was renewed monthly. This felt very difficult, both in terms of working with clients (should I tell them I was finishing up or keep going and then risk suddenly having my contract terminated?) and also my own financial instability. My supervisor helped me to think about this. I arrived at one supervision session in tears. Ann offered to contact my line manager, as she was contracted by the organisation to provide external clinical supervision in this new post. This 'interference' was viewed very negatively by my manager. In effect, I was isolated and mistrusted for having discussed the situation externally. This was a very difficult time in my life, when my limited experience of working life, coupled with work stress, impacted me personally. The professional direction, objectivity and support from clinical supervision was extremely helpful and important. It highlighted for me how unsupported I felt by the manager, and my sense of being overwhelmed in dealing with them, and helped me to decide to leave the organization.

ANN

Reflecting on this incident, I have wondered whether I would act in that way now, and if I would make more efforts to help the supervisee find ways to assert themselves and negotiate with their manager rather than contacting them directly. However, I do think I needed to intervene in some way, as I was employed by the organisation to support the music therapist in establishing the service in a way that was both professionally and clinically safe. I considered that the expectations placed on Hilary to complete this sort of role with such minimal clinical support, as a lone and newly qualified therapist, were unreasonable.

At the time I was very influenced by the recently published book *The Unconscious at Work* (Roberts & Obholzer 1994) and its valuable insights into the dynamics of institutions, still widely used in organizational consultancy training. It still is a useful component to music therapy trainings in understanding the tasks, and unconscious processes of the organisations that music therapists work in, for example in institutional settings such as a mental health ward where a persecutory fear of danger, blame and litigation may lead hospital staff to spend a lot of time documenting that procedures have been followed correctly, thereby distancing themselves from direct patient care.

In this case it did appear that something neglectful and unfair was going on, albeit perhaps unconsciously, for both therapist and clients, which I was reluctant to collude with. It was clear that Hilary was in a rather powerless and very insecure position and needed an ally for support. I was shocked that she was expected to provide therapy for such a large caseload, while simultaneously experiencing so much anxiety herself about the survival of her position and livelihood. Unable to inform her clients whether she was staying or leaving, she thus passed the anxiety down to them.

In retrospect, I think we can both see this as a consequence of the internal market/target culture introduced into NHS services in the early 1990s, where clinical managers who are responsible became their targets, and staying within their budget would be expected to prove that therapeutic services are providing value for money. Hilary's experience seems a vivid example of the tendency described by Evans (2021, p.132) for 'management, filled with anxieties about survival, to turn a deaf ear to clinical staff's concern, and push their anxieties into frontline staff'.

I am aware that, at that time, the music therapy profession, although it did have a recognized pay scale within the NHS, did not yet have statutory registration by a regulatory body, as this happened in 1997. Currently, in order to stay registered, UK music therapists are expected to receive regular supervision, abide by the Health and Care Professions Council (HCPC) code of conduct, and provide a detailed record of their continuing professional development. The value of clinical supervision is specified under the standards set by HCPC, and clinical supervision is also an expected element of practice under the guidance on ethics and conduct for professional members of the BAMT. As such, all music therapists who are practising their profession are expected to receive clinical supervision as part of their work (BAMT 2023).

It would have been easier for someone in Hilary's position to make the case that her working conditions compromised her ability to maintain the HCPC Standards of Professional Practice, and for me as supervisor to support that.

It is still often the case that unrealistic expectations are placed on newly qualified therapists when setting up a new service, or indeed they may themselves sometimes have unrealistic expectations of what they can undertake. A good supervisor can help them to navigate the boundaries of their own professional and personal capacities, to prevent being pushed beyond them to clinically unsound work. For example, Hilary was asked to add music therapy delivery to a CAMHS unit with teenage girls with eating disorders to an already stretched workload. Discussing this proposal in supervision helped her recognize that the time allocated to this site was not sufficient or reasonable, as it was a long drive from the base hospital and allowed for no relationship-building with the team there.

HILARY

As I write this reflection, more than 25 years after the supervision experience, and with years of experience of supervision and supervising since, I reflect on how one never stops needing clinical supervision. There is still a need for me to learn, reflect, develop and adapt my work.

For example, after a break from working as a therapist, and teaching music therapy students instead, I still seek out clinical supervision as I return to clinical work, as I need to remind myself of key principles. If I embark on working with a new client group, I need to seek out specialists who can help me understand my role in this new context and adapt my skills for this client group. Supervision helped me to develop a person-centred outlook, to consider the whole person, including their journey from birth to the present day. For example, the social and economic context of people in secure mental health settings was something I was made aware of thanks to Ann's supervision, as well as learning that there were disproportionately high numbers of young black men in forensic psychiatry settings.

ANN

It is worth noting that at this time questions were being asked about this situation by psychiatrists in the forensic service, such as Boast and Chesterton (1995) and Coid *et al.* (2000). Seeking to understand the over-representation of African and Afro-Caribbean people in secure psychiatric hospitals, they called for further wide-ranging investigation of all the factors that influenced the provision of psychiatric services, including diagnostic practices and the role of stereotypes in modifying social judgements. Later studies have investigated this further (Barnett *et al.* 2019) and the conclusion has still been that more work needs to be done to understand the complex causes of this situation.

At the time of our supervision work together in the late 1990s, we understood to some extent that contributing factors were trauma and displacement, but there was less emphasis on the impact of colonisation. At the time of writing in 2023, there has been a great shift in the understanding of racial trauma and bias in general society as well as in the medical profession. Recent writings focus more on the experiences of black people within the system, such as Awokoya (2020) and Alleyne (2022), making the point that while trauma can play a part in the over-representation of black people in the British mental health system, so do cultural disconnection, racism and poverty. Alleyne (2009) also provides thought-provoking considerations for therapists working in this context that would have been helpful for us as supervisor and clinicians more than a decade earlier.

HILARY

Supervision has been defined as a process that is fundamental to learning music therapy skills, whether as a student or as a music therapist; the primary means to enhance and improve clinical skills; a safeguarding of the client, the therapist, the public and the profession; a container to hold the client and therapist safely; and a space to help the therapist to develop their own internal supervisor (Brown 2009; Forinash 2019). Ultimately, clinical supervision protects the client and puts their needs first and foremost. By encouraging me, as a new therapist, to reflect, challenge my assumptions and be honest about my lack of skills and knowledge, the supervisor was able to help me to be a more ethical, skilled therapist, which ultimately benefits the client.

A huge amount of trust is required to allow the supervisee to open up and share their difficulties or 'failures' with the supervisor and also to accept it if the supervisor needs to step in and criticise their work to protect the client's wellbeing. In my case, although I brought clinical material to supervision, I remember that I never brought detailed musical examples. I think I avoided bringing musical material or improvising in supervision as I perceived that this was my weak area. However, on reflection, I realize that this symbolized my lack of confidence and imposter syndrome. I feared that my supervisor, on hearing my improvisation in the sessions, would realize I was a fake and not up to the job. I leant into my areas of strength by describing sessions, bringing written material to review, or discussing organizational issues. In retrospect, I realize how useful it would have been to bring my *clients'* music to supervision, to reflect on the communication, but as a new therapist I was too wrapped up in my own performance and skills, or lack of, to think of this.

Ann accepted this, for which I am thankful, as I think the emphasis at that time needed to be on the challenges in setting up a new post. This was important as a new therapist, but I hope that if the sessions had continued this would have been addressed.

ANN

I did notice the absence of musical material in Hilary's early supervision, and it was not the only time where the music was neglected. I was certainly aware, and indeed have written that 'if a supervisee never brings any recorded material, the supervisor's ability to help reflect on musical interventions will be severely limited and may need addressing' (Davies & Sloboda 2009, p.155).

The distinct levels of supervision (labelled from A to E) described by Sandra Brown (2009) are useful to consider here. The work with Hilary in the first year concentrated on levels B (practical management in the therapy room and workplace) and D (interpersonal dynamics in the workplace), with some attention paid to level C (interpersonal dynamics in the therapy room). However, level A (the musical relationship in the therapy room) was being neglected or even actively avoided. This was quite different from Brown's observation that level A is usually the primary focus when supervising music therapists in their first year of work. However, my sense was that Hilary's position was so precarious, with the constant pressure to prove herself and keep her job, that level A could not be explored until level B had been more securely established. We only discussed it briefly, but it was clear that further pressure to scrutinize her musical interventions would have been experienced as persecutory rather than helpful. It helped that I had a good knowledge of Hilary's musical skills during training and knew that they were strong. At this crucial stage of uncertainty, it was important to trust her to manage this aspect independently in the initial stages, while establishing her professional identity.

I was impressed, however, that despite the difficulties of this experience she was able to use the experience of evaluating the service to write it up, publish it, undertake further research, and go on to make such a great contribution to music therapy literature, training and practice.

HILARY

There was always a sense of needing to bring too much to supervision and wondering how to choose which clinical issue or client to bring! It is so important to prepare for supervision and use the time well. As a newly qualified therapist, this larger client load is a shock after careful, limited student work.

Practical issues such as referral criteria, report writing, advertising the service and timetabling were a large part of early supervision. Some of the work of supervision, for me, in those early days, was learning to know whether the workplace was right for me, how to assert myself, how not to take everything personally around job creation and to gain both more confidence and a more global perspective.

As the months went on, I noticed that discussing one client in supervision fed into all my other work and increased my experience and wisdom as a therapist. By discussing one client in depth, I became aware of how I was relating to this client, and psychodynamically informed supervision was critically important in deepening my naive awareness to another level. For example, with one client I felt very tired every week in the sessions and lost for ideas of what to do musically. Describing and reflecting on this experience in supervision helped me to realise that this phenomenon could be countertransference of the client's own state of mind. Despite often working in a community music therapy approach these days, I still hold to the importance of psychodynamic reflection on clinical work as the most useful approach to supervision and am grateful for this grounding in psychodynamic ways of working.

It was extremely useful to go to a supervisor with extensive experience, who had encountered my problems and saw them as manageable rather than overwhelming, had a range of strategies and solutions, and provided a space where I didn't have to explain what music therapy is!

In my case, we thought about how to evaluate music therapy in the new service, and how to translate other allied health professional values and goals into music therapy language. It was important to realize what I could offer and when someone else might be better able to address the client's needs. The principles of supervision that I gained at that time, and have informed the work I am now doing, encompassed:

- clear boundaries, with a problem-solving approach
- practical solutions coupled with psychodynamic reflection
- advice and mentoring from someone with significantly more clinical experience than me
- a safe, kind space where I could discuss complex issues, and clarity about when this needs to be taken to therapy
- encouragement to continue and that I am doing okay as a new therapist!

CONCLUSION
Ann and Hilary

We both feel truly fortunate that our first clinical supervision experiences were so positive, and that they formed the inspiration for our work as therapists, supervisors and managers in years to come.

We considered Hawkins and Shohet's words on supervision highly relevant to our work. They highlight what a complex process it is, without tangible outcomes that can be measured for *effectiveness*.

One person brings to another a client, usually never seen by the supervisor, and reports very selectively on aspects of the work. Moreover, there may be all sorts of pressures on either or both from the profession, organisation, or society in which they both work. So, as well as dealing with the client in question, they must pay attention to their supervisory relationship and the wider systems in which they both operate. (Hawkins & Shohet 2000, p.5)

Winnicott's theory of the 'good enough mother' has been applied to supervision, whereby:

> the 'good enough' counsellor, psychotherapist or other helping professional can survive the negative attacks of the client through the strength of being held within and by the supervisory relationship. The supervisor's role is not just to reassure the worker, but to allow the emotional disturbance to be felt within the safer setting of the supervisory relationship, where it can be survived, reflected upon and learned from. Supervision thus provides a container that holds the helping relationship within the 'therapeutic triad'. (Hawkins & Shohet 2000, p.3)

This can be extended to the idea of the need for a paternal function (Britton 1989; Winnicott 1965), in which the supervisor can observe and discuss what is going on in the therapist's clinical and professional relationships from a third perspective. This can help the therapist to hold and develop a third space in their mind that attends to their own needs as well as those of their clients. Winnicott also stressed the necessity of a facilitating environment, which is necessary for a sense of authentic self to develop. The example given in this chapter shows Ann as supervisor exercising a paternal function, in stepping in to highlight and challenge a situation in which the 'mother's' (the music therapist) needs were not being met, making it difficult to give adequate care to her 'baby' (her patients or service users). This helped Hilary to recognise that if the work environment continued to be inadequate, she would need to leave that environment and find one that gave better support.

To this day, our own approach to managing others, supervising students and clinical supervision has adopted the basic principles outlined above. We also include improvisation and role-play in the sessions where possible, to recreate a scenario that a supervisee brings, to reflect and become aware of the client's experience. Currently, we both lead master's programmes where we aim to offer students a safe place to discuss work, and an approach that is kind and caring, but also able to challenge, trying to ensure that experienced clinicians are available to students to advise and guide them.

REFERENCES

Alleyne, A. (2009) 'Working Therapeutically with Hidden Dimensions of Racism.' In D. S. Fernando & F. Keating (eds) *Mental Health in a Multi-Ethnic Society: A Multidisciplinary Handbook* (second edition), pp.161-173. London: Routledge.

Alleyne, A. (2022) *The Burden of Heritage: Hauntings of Generational Trauma on Black Lives*. London: Confer.

Awokoya, A. (2020) Why are black people so overrepresented in the psychiatric system? *New Humanist*. London: The Rationalist Association.

Barnett, P., Macky, E., Matthews, H., Gate, R. *et al.* (2019) Ethnic variations in compulsory detention under the Mental Health Act: A systematic review and meta-analysis of international data. *Lancet Psychiatry*, 6, pp.305-317.

Boast, N. & Chesterton, P. (1995) Black people and secure psychiatric facilities: Patterns of processing and the role of stereotypes. *British Journal of Criminology*, 35 (2), pp.218-235.

British Association for Music Therapy (forthcoming) *Supervision Guidelines*.

Britton, R. (1989) 'The Missing Link: Parental Sexuality in the Oedipus Complex.' In R. Britton, M. Feldman & E. O'Shaughnessy (eds) *The Oedipus Complex Today: Clinical Implications* (pp.83-101). London: Routledge.

Brown, S. (2009) 'Supervision in Context: A Balancing Act.' In H. Odell-Miller & E. Richards (eds) *Supervision of Music Therapy: A Theoretical and Practical Handbook* (pp.119-134) London: Routledge.

Coid, J., Kathan, N., Gault, S. & Jarman, B. (2000) Ethnic differences in admissions to secure forensic psychiatry services. *British Journal of Psychiatry*, 177(3), pp.241-247.

Davies, A. & Sloboda, A. (2009) 'Turbulence at the Boundary.' In H. Odell-Miller & E. Richards (eds) *Supervision of Music Therapy: A Theoretical and Practical Handbook*, pp.153-172. London: Routledge.

Evans, M. (2021) *Psychoanalytic Thinking in Mental Health Settings*. New York, NY: Routledge.

Forinash, M. (ed.) (2019) *Music Therapy Supervision* (second edition). Gilsum, NH: Barcelona Publishers.

Hawkins, B. & Shohet, R. (2000) *Supervision in the Helping Professions: An Individual, Group and Organizational Approach* (second edition). Birmingham: Open University Press.

Moss, H. (1999) Creating a new music therapy post: An evidence-based research project. *British Journal of Music Therapy*, 13(2), pp.49-59.

Roberts, V. & Obholzer, A. (1994) *The Unconscious at Work: Individual and Organizational Stress in the Human Services*. London: Routledge.

Sinason, V. (2010) *Mental Handicap and the Human Condition: An Analytic Approach to Intellectual Disability* (revised edition). London: Free Association Books.

Winnicott, D. (1965) *The Maturational Process and the Facilitating Environment: Studies in the Theory of Emotional Development*. London: Routledge.

CHAPTER 12

Working with Unconscious Processes as Part of the Music Therapy Supervisor's Task

ROBIN WILTSHIRE

INTRODUCTION

My curiosity in working with unconscious processes developed during my music therapy training, which was psychodynamic in its approach. To broaden and further my clinical skills and practice, I trained as a clinical supervisor in psychoanalytic/psychodynamic supervision. It was during this training that my theoretical understanding of unconscious processes deepened, and I have continued to draw on these processes to guide and inform my practice as a music therapist and music therapy supervisor.

An aspect of the music therapy supervisor's task is to engage with their own emotional experiences emerging out of the supervisee's clinical material and the supervisory relationship. Searles (2015) termed this the *reflection process*. A consequence of this phenomenon is that unconscious processes and difficulties existing in the therapeutic relationship are reflected and permeated across the supervisory relationship. When the organisational context of the clinical work is also considered as part of this process, the unconscious dynamics of the organisation can impact on the supervisory process. This extends the supervisory triangle, of client, therapist and supervisor to form a four cornered rhombus shape. Ekstein and Wallerstein (1958) coined this the *clinical rhombus*. In this structure, each separate corner point represents the client, therapist, supervisor and an aspect of the organisational function and setting respectively.

A characteristic of this structure is that each point within the rhombus, apart from the supervisor and client, interface and interact with one another, creating a multiplicity of dynamic relationships, each having their own organisational history, unconscious process and defences which filter across the different parts of the rhombus. In music therapy supervision, clinical material can be brought into the supervisory encounter through a combination of words and music. This poses an interesting predicament in how we listen to the unconscious in the supervisory situation, given its relationship to music.

FREUD AND THE NATURE OF THE UNCONSCIOUS

Freud (1912) noticed that there are aspects of our psychological life which are hidden and remain out of awareness, yet somehow they impact on our conscious life. He considered that these concealed aspects were often manifested through symbolic communications, such as dreams, mistakes or slips of the tongue, which he regarded as representing an existence of an unconscious in our mind. Freud postulated that our mental functioning could have meaning at a conscious level while simultaneously hold an unconscious meaning, of which we are unaware. In his work of identifying and understanding the nature of our conscious and unconscious processes, Freud (1915) considered that the unconscious had its own structure and logic, where such conscious concepts of time and space became distorted. He categorised the unconscious as having five unique characteristics, which he identified as condensation, displacement, timelessness, absence of mutual contradiction and replacement of external by internal reality. All of these co-exist dynamically alongside each other and can become symmetrically linked. Therefore, for example, in the unconscious, objects, people or things can be dead and alive at the same time; what is experienced internally is also experienced externally; and the idea of a whole with its separate parts disappears as all space becomes the same.

This idea of unconscious anxieties and conflicts being symmetrically linked was developed further by Matte-Blanco. He reconfigured Freud's idea of the unconscious and considered the relationship between the unconscious and emotions, by applying mathematical set theory, and a system of unconscious logic founded on the principle of symmetry and asymmetry. Matte-Blanco (1998) regarded the interaction and entwining of these two processes, based on similarity and difference, as underpinning his theory of the unconscious and of our emotional experiences. I would like to explore this world of symmetry and asymmetry in the context of the unconscious and consider the implications of this concept for the supervisory process.

THE UNCONSCIOUS AS A WORLD OF SYMMETRICAL AND ASYMMETRICAL RELATIONSHIPS

Matte-Blanco postulated that the unconscious 'treats the converse of any relation as identical with the relation. It treats logically asymmetrical relations as if they were symmetrical' (Rayner 1995, p.25). The implication of this principle means that in the unconscious, all relationships are regarded as the same, and any difference is ignored, whether this is connected to gender, age, experience, knowledge or power. For example, an asymmetrical relationship, such as 'Tom is the father of John', is treated the same as it's inverse. Consequently, the relationship 'John is the father of Tom' and 'Tom is the father of John' are regarded as identical, even though logically in the conscious mind this relationship makes no sense at all. Rayner (1995, p.25) noted of Matte-Blanco's principle of symmetry that the unconscious 'selectively' treats asymmetrical relations as symmetrical, and aspects of the unconscious continue to behave asymmetrically. This interweaving of asymmetry and symmetry processes in which one becomes more salient in the way that it manifests was termed by Matte-Blanco (1998) as *bi-logic*. This process is relentlessly at work in the mind and functions on five different stratums. At the highest stratum, asymmetry is dominant; here the world and relationships are perceived with clarity and experienced consciously and concretely, without emotion. As feelings emerge, both consciously and unconsciously, the level of asymmetry and symmetry changes. At its deepest level, the fifth stratum, asymmetrical relations become diminished, everything is experienced as identical, and the capacity to think becomes impaired, as feelings predominate.

It is possible, I believe, that this phenomenon is experienced in music therapy practice. During musical improvisations between therapist and client, when the emotional connection becomes stronger and deepens, it can feel increasingly difficult to distinguish between the two separate musical parts, as the music between therapist and client is felt as one (Odell-Miller 2009). It is as if time and space have become blurred as we experience the sense of timelessness, condensation and an absence of mutual contradiction. Similarly, in my supervision practice, I have noticed that this interweaving of asymmetry and symmetry can often occur, particularly when supervisees present clinical work involving highly disturbed clients with histories of early trauma and deprivation. There are times when we can think coherently together, yet this capacity can diminish instantly, and we are both left feeling the same, unable to think or move between our feelings and thoughts.

Matte-Blanco (1959) viewed the mind as operating as a classifier that is continually discriminating one thing from another as it acquires knowledge of people, objects or things to form thoughts. As it continues in this moment-by-moment classificatory activity, the mind organises itself by putting things into collections or sets. He considered that unconscious processes actively looked for shared attributes of objects or things, and in doing so created larger and larger sets and sub-sets. To put this into a clinical context, when a client reflects on their relationship to their father in therapy and the different feelings this can evoke, the client's father can be identified as belonging to a set of paternal figures in their life which may share attributes with other paternal figures such as a teacher or their therapist. Due to the timelessness quality of the unconscious, when shared attributes from previously formed unconscious sets overlap with a present experience, this can create the misperception of regarding similarity as sameness, and leads to the phenomenon of transference; feelings from the past are transferred as if they are happening in the present (Casement 1985).

If we consider this framework of the unconscious, where relationships are treated as the same and become linked, and the symmetry relates to the feelings experienced, and we have the added factor of the music, then what are the implications for music therapy supervision when the supervisor engages with their own emotional experience?

ASYMMETRY AND SYMMETRY IN THE SUPERVISORY ENCOUNTER

I consider the music therapy supervisory relationship as one which is asymmetrical. Our differing qualities, whether these are regarded in relation to our professional roles, comparative clinical experiences, training backgrounds or, more often than not, our differences in seniority, all play a part in the asymmetry. This is particularly the case when supervising trainees or recently qualified therapists. However, when in my role as supervisor and I engage in the task of connecting with my emotional responses evolving from the supervisee's material and supervisee/supervisor relationship, my experience of this can change.

Searles (2015) termed this process of the supervisor engaging with their own emotional experience as the *reflection process*. He regarded the supervisor's emotion as 'a reflection of something which has been going on in the therapist-patient relationship, and in the final analysis in the patient' (2015, p.201).

The effect of this phenomenon is that unconscious processes and difficulties situated in the patient and existing in the therapeutic relationship between client and therapist become symmetrically linked and permeate across the supervisory relationship. This creates a supervisory triangle, consisting of client, supervisee and supervisor, with the link between the two relationships being the supervisee.

Searles viewed this process as being initiated when the therapy taps into parts of a client's suppressed or dissociated feelings which are near to awareness and are defended against. This in turn arouses anxiety in the therapist, who manages it by either unconsciously identifying with the client's defence or recourses to a defence which corresponds to one being used by the client. When the client material is brought to supervision, the therapist's anxiety or defences prevents the therapist/supervisee from consciously communicating to the supervisor, creating an intricate network of cross-identifications within the supervisory triangle (Berman 2000). The implications of this for music therapy are interesting, particularly when audio recordings of the shared client/therapist music-making are brought into the supervision relationship. This can sometimes be a source of anxiety and be defended against by the therapist/supervisee.

Before drawing on a clinical vignette to demonstrate this reflection process, I would like to consider the relationship between music and the unconscious in music therapy supervision, a relationship which continues to create much curiosity in my roles as a music therapy supervisor and as a supervisee in my own clinical practice.

A MUSIC THERAPY SUPERVISOR'S PREDICAMENT – WORKING WITH MUSIC AND WORDS

I find that working with unconscious processes in music therapy supervision raises an interesting predicament, as often a client's material is brought into the supervisory dynamic through a combination of words and music. This may either be via the supervisee playing audio or video recordings of sessions, recreating the music live in supervision, or the supervisee verbally describing the musical experience.

My understanding of this musical material in supervision has often been influenced by the wider psychoanalytic field. Several writers have reflected on the relationship between music and the unconscious. Nagel (2008) suggests that music, like dreams, can be a point of entry into the unconscious. She refers to Graf (1910), who considered that music made the unconscious conscious, and to Ehrenzweig (1953), who perceived music as a symbolic language of the unconscious. Others, such as Di Benedetto, propose that music can communicate indefinable parts of the unconscious and enables us to hear the voices that go unnoticed by suggesting that music can support us to 'listen to what we cannot say' (2001, p.175). Richards (2015) also notes its capacity to voice feelings and emotional experiences for which words cannot always be found, and John (1992) comments on the link music plays between unconscious and conscious processes. In the context of this relationship, it raises the question whether as music therapy supervisors we are listening to the unconscious directly in our client's musical improvisations or therapeutic musical dyad (Levinge 2002).

In psychoanalytic psychotherapy supervision, Martin (2005) considers that it is the task of the supervisor to help the supervisee to unfold and unveil the unconscious hidden material, and to find the words to convey it in a way that can be heard and processed by the client. Reflecting on Martin's (2005) view of the supervisor's task, I often speculate about the implication of this for music therapy supervision, considering the assumptions around the relationship between music and the unconscious. Di Benedetto (2001) describes an aspect of a psychoanalyst's work as being able to read the musical score of the patient's unconscious, and then interpret it into a listenable sound. This description resonates with me as a supervisor. I frequently notice my curiosity as to whether my task is to help the supervisee find the music to digest and contain the client's unconscious material being musically expressed, or to support the supervisee to translate the musical experience and find the words for this non-verbal material.

I would like to draw on a clinical reflection and discussion to demonstrate the way unconscious anxieties and conflicts can permeate across the different relationships in supervision, and the way Searles's and Matte-Blanco's concepts can offer a framework to give meaning and understanding.

CLINICAL REFLECTION

During my clinical supervision training, I recall in a supervision session questioning my skills and theoretical knowledge as a clinical supervisor. I was doubting my capacity to contain my supervisees, particularly those who were working with complex clients. I then started to focus on one case, where a supervisee had discussed their work supporting an adult client living with complex needs. The supervisee described their client as having profound learning and physical disabilities, as non-verbal and communicating through passive vocalisations, subtle facial gestures and restricted body movements.

I reflected on an audio extract the supervisee had shared, where the client's fragmented and passive vocal murmurs and hesitant exploring of the wind chimes could be heard. I shared how it appeared that the supervisee was finding it hard to remain open to their client's disjointed music and be alongside them, through their tentative use of guitar melody and voice. I noted my response to the supervisee, which was to encourage them to think about their musical responses by drawing on the mother/ infant dyad and how a mother mirrors, elaborates and facilitates an infant's non-verbal communications. As I reflected on this, it seemed as if by reminding the supervisee of these techniques, I was offering a framework to manage the interactions, rather than helping them to stay with the feelings being communicated.

While I continued to explore the case in my supervision of supervision, the word 'resources' seemed to resonate. The more I thought about my response to the supervisee and the fragmented quality of the music, themes surfaced which were resonating across the supervision triangle. These were associated with having limited resources and self-agency, and feelings of helplessness, self-doubt and increased anxiety this can educe.

DISCUSSION

It could be deemed that the unconscious anxieties relating to limited resources and a capacity to play and contain were emanating from the client, enacted in the therapeutic dyad and reflected in the supervisory relationship. It was as if the separate unconscious conflicts and anxieties of the client, supervisee and supervisor had become symmetrically linked, creating 'a kind of echo or harmonic' (Collens & Van Hout 2017, p.181) that could be heard across the different parts of the triangular relational structure.

My initial intervention seemed to be an avoidance of the feelings the supervisee and their client were experiencing. It appeared as if the supervisory relationship was mirroring aspects of the therapeutic dyad. Where I had heard the supervisee struggle to musically attune to the feelings of the client, I similarly offered an intervention which managed the feelings, rather than attuned and contained my supervisee. In my supervision of supervision, the increased emotional distance from the therapeutic dyad enabled my capacity to think more about the feelings evoked by the supervisee and their client. I was able to notice that my reassuring stance failed to contain my supervisee and together we had unconsciously identified with the feelings present, creating a symmetry across the different relationships.

By reflecting on the meaning of resources, I was able to deepen my insight into my supervisory stance and acknowledge that it is the supervisory relationship which helps further the work of the supervisee, not only my clinical skills and theoretical knowledge. As Mattinson (1975) suggests, while the reflection process may only take up a small proportion of supervision, it provides clues to the relational dynamics and difficulties encountered in the client – therapist relationship, and ultimately the client. It enables the supervisee to understand the client from a less defended position and use the new information to convey an alternative message to the client, one to which they may respond differently. From this shifted position, the supervisee and client can find a shared and conscious understanding of the issue being defended against.

Gradually, through acknowledging and containing the feelings of the supervisee and examining the 'here and now' within our supervisory relationship, the supervisee was able to notice their own feelings and instead of over-identifying with the client, was able to separate their own feelings. In turn, the supervisee was able to connect with their self-agency, draw on their therapeutic musical resources, and steadily find ways to attune to and contain their client's musical communication.

REFLECTION PROCESS: FROM SUPERVISORY TRIANGLE TO CLINICAL RHOMBUS

An additional aspect of the reflection process occurs when unconscious dynamics of the organisation impact on the supervisory relationship and clinical work. In my experience as supervisor, the organisational context of the music therapy, whether it is a school, an adult mental health hospital, a prison, or a music therapist working independently, can colour the supervision. Similarly, the setting of the supervision and whether it takes place in the organisation itself, or externally, can influence the supervisory relationship. Driver (2008) noted that such factors as the type of organisation, the client group, and the way an organisation views the clinical work and supervision in terms of providing a secure frame for it to happen can all influence and affect the unconscious dynamics of the supervisory process.

To help think about the organisational effect, Ekstein and Wallerstein (1958) extended the idea of the supervisory triangle to include the administrator (an aspect of the organisational setting and function), and in doing so created the concept of the clinical rhombus, with its four points of patient, therapist, supervisor and administrator/organisation. Therefore, bringing the interface of the organisation and supervision into focus, where each element, with the exception of the supervisor and client, is interacting with another, creates a multiplicity of relationships, each bringing their own organisational history, unconscious process and defences, which permeate across the different parts of the rhombus. I would like to draw on a clinical vignette to demonstrate how the clinical rhombus can be a useful device for thinking about the supervisory process.

CLINICAL VIGNETTE

A newly qualified music therapist provided individual music therapy across several care homes. Clients brought to supervision were described as living with enduring mental health needs, hard to reach and difficult to engage. Some were living with dementia or deemed near to the end of their lives. Many of the clients lacked the capacity to make decisions about their lives. Decisions about their care were made for them, as part of a best interest process undertaken by professionals. This included being referred for music therapy. Information on a client's history was limited, communication was not always clear around reasons for referral, and care staff seemed to know little about each client's personal histories or family. Many had no family nor contact with living relatives. The supervisee often reflected on their struggle to establish a secure therapy room in each setting that was private and uninterruptable. Building relationships with senior staff and carers was challenging due to their different shift patterns. At times it seemed as if the organisation would attack or fail to take the therapy seriously by not respecting boundaries, nor providing a clinical space for effective therapy.

In sessions, the sense of the client being hard to reach was figural. The supervisee's attempts to engage and be with each client was often met with resistance, both passively and overtly. Clients would be described across a spectrum of seeming withdrawn, distant, forlorn, drowsy or confrontational and denying any need for emotional support. At times, a client's ambivalence to engage musically created a blurring of boundaries between words and music. The supervisee often found themselves working with words, and the term *imposter syndrome* was sometimes referred to by my supervisee, as they doubted their ability and skills to work therapeutically with this client group. Rejection, guilt and feeling devalued seemed very present in the material, along with a sense of uncertainty felt by the supervisee regarding the therapeutic value of their work. The question around whether the therapy was to help clients to work through their difficulties and promote personal change, or to provide a place for a meaningful connection and attachment and promote a better quality of life was often reflected on.

When we agreed to meet for supervision, my supervisee would sometimes arrive late and often give plausible reasons for their delayed arrival. On arriving my supervisee would appear uncertain around what or which clients to bring to supervision. Having started to reflect on one client, their narrative would frequently get enmeshed with another. There was a sense of forlornness in their presentation. While I would hold on to the feelings around their lateness to supervision, I would notice the enmeshed quality of their reporting.

As our supervision sessions continued and supervisory relationship developed, I noticed my curiosity around my supervisee's ability to connect to their authority. Navigating the therapeutic boundaries across the different clients and institutions seemed demanding and daunting. Steadily, as my supervisee continued to listen and trust their intuition to steer their way between these diverse boundaries, I was observing and witnessing a supervisee who was finding ways to establish, engage and recognize the differing needs of each client. For example, with client 'A', who was ambivalent about receiving music therapy, the supervisee patiently and thoughtfully engaged them and enabled the development of a therapeutic musical relationship. This slowly began with singing hymns and known songs together. As trust developed between them, the client was able to move away from the structured hymns and songs, and interactive improvisations were cautiously created. I heard my supervisee's narrative shift, from hearing a client who was isolated, withdrawn and fearful of change and intimacy, to one who felt noticed, listened to and showed a motivation and openness to relate, to make choices and find their own musical voice.

CLINICAL DISCUSSION

Thinking about this example in the context of each element of the rhombus, and the unconscious processes at work in the different relationships of client, supervisee, supervisor and organisation, a key theme seemed to permeate, which related to feelings around the lack of capacity to make decisions. Searles (2015) noted that the supervisor's emotion reflects an aspect of something going on in the therapist – patient relationship and is situated mainly in the client. It could be suggested that in this example, unconscious feelings of rejection, guilt, feeling devalued and an absence of self-agency associated with the client were permeating across the different points of the rhombus, to become symmetrically linked.

When my supervisee would arrive late, feeling devalued and not taken seriously were figural to my own feelings and thoughts. This seemed to mirror the supervisee's experience of the organisational settings. Here, the absence of client information and history, and staff challenging and not respecting the therapeutic frame and boundaries of the clinical work, seemed like a communication around not taking the therapy seriously or valuing it. These feelings were further intensified by the client's disengaged presentation in sessions, leaving my supervisee feeling rejected and deskilled. This, in turn, appeared to touch on their own anxiety of being a newly qualified music therapist, raising their self-doubt around whether they were 'getting it right'. This seemed to echo attributes of the client's experience and their anxiety about using the music. The undermining behaviour of the staff and organisation seemed to push my supervisee into a state of mind where it felt difficult to hold on to their sense of agency, their power and authority, and listen to their intuition – all of which can influence our decision-making capabilities. It was as if the relationship between my supervisee and the organisation reflected parts of the client's experience.

In my own reflections, I was reminded of my supervision training and being a recently qualified supervisor. I recalled the challenges of connecting with my benign authority as a supervisor, and now noticing a symmetry between our separate experiences. Obholzer (2019) postulated that taking up one's authority is often related to a state of mind connected to feelings of powerlessness. He comments that in order to connect with our authority, it can often involve an interaction between this state of mind and external resources, which can be used to reinforce one's power. With power comes authority and this implies having the permission to make decisions. Supporting my supervisee to connect with their authority seemed a containing factor in our initial work, as we established a space to reflect and think together. Through this process, it became noticeable that, as they were able to listen to their own intuition, and make their own choices around the clinical work, trusted therapeutic relationships with their clients evolved. As Obholzer (2019) suggests, when individuals are in a state of dejection and depression, effecting change can feel hindered by an undermining state of mind where power and authority are situated outside the self. Initially this seemed to be the case for my supervisee, and also for some for their clients. For client 'A', the therapeutic relationship facilitated changes in their state of mind which enabled them to connect with their sense of autonomy and agency, to find their own music, and to make decisions and choices in their areas of the life they could affect. The reflection process was functioning in two ways, from the therapy to the supervision and from the supervision to the therapy (Mattinson 1975).

A SEARCH FOR A MUSIC THERAPY SUPERVISION THEORETICAL FRAMEWORK

Drawing on the structure and logic of the unconscious, the reflection process and clinical rhombus concept has contributed to my understanding of the unconscious anxieties and dynamic relationships at work in the supervisory process. While this theoretical framework has furthered my perception of the client and offered clinical meaning, I am reminded of Stimmel (1995), who comments on the importance of rotating the clinical lens away from the client on to other contributors to the process, including the supervisor. Stimmel's remark not only raises awareness that my own unconscious potentially has a role in the supervisory task, but it also makes me reflect on the musical processes and the rich information these can offer to the supervisory encounter and unconscious communications. Whether this is the different qualities of music, with its rhythm and timbre, or the way a client uses and accesses the music, or the supervisee's and supervisor's responses to the music, they can all offer another way of listening to the unconscious and provide an alternative source of information relating to the client's emotional life, complementing words and other forms of symbolic communication.

During my supervision practice, I have experienced numerous occasions when as a supervisory couple we have felt stuck and unable to think together. Yet on listening to musical audio extracts from the therapeutic dyad, something shifts. It is as if the music and the feelings being expressed link our unconscious and conscious worlds. Experiences such as these ignite my curiosity as a supervisor in searching for ways to further understand the unconscious and musical dimensions of the supervisory situation. Given the multiplicity of relationships at work in this task, I am left reflecting on whose unconscious anxieties are being communicated through the music – is it the client, supervisee or the organisation – and whether as supervisor and supervisee we let the music speak for itself or together translate it into words? While part of me is searching for a theoretical framework which encapsulates the complex processes of words and music in music therapy supervision, I recall Hirsch's (1995) cautiousness in trying to make the information we become aware of fit the concept. In the meantime, I will continue holding the position of evenly suspended attention (Freud 1912) when listening to my supervisees and their clinical material, both musical and non-musical, as I connect with my own emotional experiences and support my supervisees in working with unconscious processes in the context of music therapy supervision.

REFERENCES

Berman, E. (2000) Psychoanalytic supervision: The intersubjective development. *International Journal of Psychoanalysis*, 81, pp.273–290.

Casement, P. (1985) *On Learning from the Patient*. London: Routledge.

Collens, P. & Van Hout, F. (2017) Learning in psychotherapy group supervision: Transcending complementarity and the generative potential of group conflict. *British Journal of Psychotherapy*, 33(2), pp.177–191.

Di Benedetto, A. (2001) *Before Words: Psychoanalytic Listening to the Unsaid through the Medium of Art*. London: Free Association Books.

Driver, C. (2008) Assessment in supervision: An analytic perspective. *British Journal of Psychotherapy*, 24(3), pp.328–342.

Ehrenzweig, A. (1953) *The Psychoanalysis of Artistic Vision and Hearing*. London: Shelton Press.

Ekstein, R. & Wallerstein, R. S. (1958) *The Teaching and Learning of Psychotherapy*. Madison, CT: International Universities Press.

Freud, S. ([1912] 1955) *Recommendations to Physicians Practicing Psychoanalysis*. In *The Standard Edition of the Complete Psychological Works of Sigmund Freud, Volume XII (1911–1913): The Case of Schreber, Papers on Technique and Other Works*, pp.109–120.

Freud, S. (1915) 'The Unconscious.' In S. Freud (1986) *The Essentials of Psychoanalysis: The Definitive Collection of Sigmund Freud's Writing*. London: Penguin Books.

Graf, M. (1910) *Die innere Werkstatt des Musikers* (The workshop of a musician's mind). Stuttgart: Verlag von Ferdinand Enke.

Hirsch, I. (1995) Supervision Amidst Abuse: The Supervisor's Perspective. Paper presented at the Fifteenth Annual Spring Meeting of Psychoanalysis (39), American Psychological Association, Santa Monica, CA, April.

John, D. (1992) Towards music psychotherapy. *British Journal of Music Therapy*, 6(1), pp.10–12.

Levinge, A. (2002) Supervision or double vision: An exploration of the task of music therapy supervision. *British Journal of Music Therapy*, 16(2), pp.83–89.

Matte-Blanco, I. (1959) Expression in symbolic logic of the characteristics of the System UCs or the logic of the System UCs. *International Journal of Psychoanalysis*, 40, pp.1–5.

Matte-Blanco, I. (1998) *Thinking, Feeling and Being: Clinical Reflections on the Fundamental Antinomy of Human Beings and World*. London: Routledge.

Martin, E., (2005) 'The Unconscious in Supervision.' In C. Driver & E. Martin (eds) *Supervision and the Analytic Attitude*. London: Whurr Publishers.

Mattinson, J. (1975) *The Reflection Process in Casework Supervision*. London: Institute of Marital Studies: The Tavistock Institute of Human Relations.

Nagel, J. (2008) Psychoanalytic perspectives on music: An intersection of the oral and aural road. *Psychoanalytic Quarterly*, 77(2), pp.507–530.

Obholzer, A. (2019) Authority, power and leadership Contributions from group relations training. In Obholzer, A. & Roberts, V. Z. (eds) (2019) *The Unconscious at Work: A Tavistock Approach to Making Sense of Organizational Life*. London: Brunner & Routledge

Odell-Miller, H. (2009) 'The History and Background of Supervision in Music Therapy.' In H. Odell-Miller & E. Richards (eds) *Supervision of Music Therapy*. London: Routledge.

Rayner, E. (1995) *Unconscious Logic: An Introduction to Matte-Blanco's Bi-Logic and Its Uses*. Hove: Routledge.

Richards, E. (2015) 'Music, Attachment and the Group: Mainly Theory.' In A. Davies, E. Richards & N. Barwick (eds) *Group Music Therapy: A Group Analytic Approach*. London: Routledge.

Searles, H. (2015) The informational value of the supervisor's emotional experiences. *Psychiatry*, 78(3), pp.199–211.

Stimmel, B. (1995) Resistance to awareness of the supervisor's transferences with special reference to the parallel process. *International Journal of Psychoanalysis*, 76, pp.609–618.

CHAPTER 13

Something Different

Exploring the Perspectives and Experience of a Palliative
Care Doctor Receiving Supervision from a Music Therapist

JANE LINGS

In my supervision practice I am particularly inspired and influenced by
Forinash's description of supervision as being an 'unfolding' process.
This is seen not as following a method but rather as a journey, or, as she
describes it, 'An odyssey of sorts', where both supervisor and supervisee develop and 'likely leave transformed in some way' (Forinash 2001,
p.I.). This chapter explores an interprofessional supervision relationship
based in the work context of palliative care.

The supervision relationship was between Olivia (not her real name),
a second-year registrar, working towards becoming a palliative care consultant, and myself, a music therapist who had just completed 15 years
working in a hospice.

We met for three years for a total of 31 sessions moving between
face-to-face and online sessions as distance and pandemic conditions
dictated. Our work together ended as planned, at the end of Olivia's first
year as a consultant in a large city hospital.

The chapter is based on a reflective conversation which took place
three months after our sessions ended. I transcribed the recording of
our online meeting, and Olivia read the transcript and clarified one
comment. She has read this chapter, provided feedback, and has given
full permission for what appears here.

BACKGROUND
Olivia

Olivia had already undergone seven years of uninterrupted medical training when we met. Her rigorous training included techniques for conducting medical conversations. She knew what she was looking for in order to diagnose, treat and prescribe effectively. She also knew who and where to turn to if she needed help with medical decisions. Managerial and evaluative supervision took place with a palliative care consultant in each one of the contexts she worked in during her training. As a registrar, she was deeply involved in the complex care of patients at the end of their lives, some of whom she met briefly, others for as long as a year, depending on the length of her post. As a palliative care consultant her direct role with patients lessened but her clinical responsibility and decision-making increased.

Olivia approached me for clinical supervision during her second year as a registrar and our monthly meetings continued during the rest of her training as she moved between three different hospice and hospital posts. Once she began her consultant post, Olivia delayed beginning the clinical supervision offered by the large city hospital for a year, until she felt more established in her new role. Oliva described herself as being *self-selected* to this specialism; it is one that draws some people and makes others want to flee. It is a role immersed in the care of patients and their families at the end of their lives, where suffering, grief and what is described as 'total pain' (Saunders & Clark 2006) are experienced vicariously, often on a daily basis.

Jane

My music therapy background includes working with many different client and age groups, teaching on a music therapy course and, in recent years, clinical supervision. During my own training, a guest lecturer came to talk about his palliative care work. It was a pivotal lecture, igniting in me an unexpected certainty that I wanted to work in this area. It took time for an opportunity to begin this work but eventually I spent 15 years in an adult hospice as part of a multi-professional team. Central to this work was liaising and working closely with professionals of other disciplines. Occasionally I would be in a patient's room when a doctor or consultant was at the bedside, delivering very difficult news. Every few months I would invite the latest new registrar to take part in a musical experience as a way of explaining my role as a music therapist.

These sessions provided an insight into some of the emotional, intellectual, spiritual, personal and professional challenges faced by these young doctors as they learned new aspects of their craft in a palliative care context.

My own experience as a supervisee, once I moved into hospice work, was mainly interprofessional. Relevant experience felt more essential than a shared clinical discipline. A transpersonal psychotherapist and different clinical psychologists all influenced and developed my practice and thinking, each providing different insights, perspectives and support.

Five years after qualification I registered as a clinical supervisor with the Association of Professional Music Therapists (APMT) and my supervision practice built up slowly, initially supervising colleagues and music therapy students. Several years later I had my first interprofessional supervision experience, when I was asked to supervise a group of experienced community nurses. This proved to be another significant experience for me. Now I'm in semi-retirement, where clinical supervision is the mainstay of my freelance practice; a considerable proportion of this is still interprofessional supervision.

THE DISCUSSION

The reflective discussion for this chapter took place three months after our final session. It took place online for pragmatic reasons as, by then, Olivia was living in another part of the country. I prepared a few questions to guide our discussion but hoped the conversation would flow as naturally as possible. There was laughter and a few surprises for both of us in what emerged as we talked. Her exact words appear throughout the text in italics. Olivia began with a disclaimer: *I have a very bad memory, Jane*. However, despite her concerns, a rich and thought-provoking conversation ensued.

WHY CLINICAL SUPERVISION?

Olivia had previously explained that for doctors in training there is no requirement for non-medical supervision. Although registrars are required to be self-reflective this a solitary activity, writing regular reflections on their work for scrutiny by an assessor. Tomlinson (2015), a doctor and researcher, critiques this process, suggesting that because these self-reflections are mandated and evaluated, what gets explored is not necessarily what is important. He argues that the process has the potential to be unsafe and Olivia described the complexity involved in writing these reflections. She felt that there was potential for mis-understanding and even that her career prospects could be affected if she wrote about the issues that were critical for her. In addition, she described being *much better at talking than writing things down*, as for her the verbal process had *much more meaning*.

But why, when management supervision was available from her consultant, and she had support from peers and other staff, was she prompted to ask for something else at this point in her career? In our conversation, Olivia articulated her need for something more...*just for me, where I could talk very openly...and maybe show vulnerabilities that I wouldn't necessarily show to those other people I was working with.*

Olivia explained what was underpinning this need:

> *I was in my second year as a registrar in training and was feeling very over-whelmed by everything that I was seeing and doing. My patients and the responsibility towards them, the difficult conversations. And there was stuff I felt I could do, I was good at, but it was still heavy, and I felt like I needed somewhere to put that... I also had hanging over me a difficult experience from my first year of training, which I think probably made me question myself and I guess those two things combining meant that I felt I needed something more than just the supervision I was getting from work.*

She identified the heavy emotional toll of her work as disturbing her equilibrium. As befitted this stage in her training, she was given more responsibility and expected to make clinical decisions with less consult-ant input. However, an experience during her first registrar post had undermined her confidence. In short, she was looking for *something more* that would give her a safe place to explore her work and the impact on her as a person.

John Launer, a doctor, educator, family therapist and advocate for supervision in the health professions, asks the question 'Why shouldn't we conceptualise supervision in medicine as primarily therapeutic in its purpose – not just for the supervisee, but also for the supervisor and hopefully for the patients?' (Launer 2008). It seemed to me that Olivia's thoughts on her supervision experience appeared to align with his argument.

Lots of people ask me, both colleagues in other specialities and friends – how do you do the job you do? How you deal with all the issues? And I often talk about supervision as part of that; I don't necessarily see it as 'counselling' or 'therapy' but there is a part of it that does have those qualities.

WHY SUPERVISION FROM A MUSIC THERAPIST?

Practitioners will often find their supervisors as the result of a personal recommendation. Olivia approached me via this route; however, she explained that it was *not the music bit that drew me in.* What she was saw as important was the following: *You had worked in the hospice setting. You were part of the team, but your role was very different…seeing the human side of our patients.*

She also expressed certainty that she was looking for something looser than the more structured, technique-orientated supervision that she imagined might be offered by a psychologist. Olivia described being attracted by the *something different* of music therapy, a profession she had not come across in her work. She imagined that it *might sometimes be a bit more creative* but, ultimately, it was about her *role with patients.*

DEFINING CLINICAL SUPERVISION

I asked Olivia how she now conceptualised the supervision, how she might define it. There was some laughter as she noted that it was usually my role to summarise.

It is very tricky, because to me it felt like a whole mix of different things. There would be all these different thoughts and issues going on and something about the space and time and bringing it all together to make a bit more sense of everything.

After some exploration Olivia did sum it up: *Maybe there's something about the relationship and the space and making sense of myself as a palliative care doctor in order to sustain me doing that job for many years.*

These two phrases appear to reflect what was at the heart of Olivia's experience of the supervision process. Supervision offered her a safe space, where her overwhelmed feelings about all that she was *seeing and doing* could be delved into and processed, a place where she could bring all the aspects of her job into the room: *My patients and the responsibility towards them, the difficult conversations...the different thoughts and issues.* This was a place to begin both to make sense of *everything* and to make sense of herself *as a palliative care doctor.*

In my work at the hospice, I occasionally met patients whose experience of medical professionals would leave me feeling angry. Compassion fatigue and burnout are well recognised in palliative care settings (Kearney *et al.* 2009) and the resulting lack of empathy or a dehumanising approach can, understandably, be traumatic for a patient already trying to come to terms with their impending death. During her training Olivia had already observed communication and behaviours that offended her sense of good practice, and she was determined to have in place the support that meant that she could *sustain doing that job (well) for many years.*

THE FIRST MEETING

For Olivia this was her first experience of *this type of thing*. We met for the first time in my work room at home which I use for supervision. It is quiet and undisturbed; two small armchairs on either side of the window look out on to a garden. There are lots of books, a guitar in the corner, artefacts on the windowsill. She remembered, *You made me a cup of tea; and it was nice to engage with someone and I felt we connected very easily.*

Olivia remembered that I asked her about the experience of being in the room and whether it felt somehow that she connected with it. I was surprised both to hear that I had asked that question, and, in the light of her opening statement, how clear the memory was. What I had remembered was my uncertainty about whether I could be 'good enough' for this soon-to-be consultant. It was important to me that she knew at the beginning that she had a clear get-out clause. *I guess you really laid the ground for me to escape almost – that this isn't right for me.*

In our discussion of this early memory Olivia was surprised to learn about my insecurities, but related it immediately to her own practice and the universality of this feeling: *I imagine it's the same when I go to see patients and families. It probably never even crosses their mind that there might be some kind of doubt or insecurity in me.*

In the very first session I recall little about setting up any sort of contract or explanation around the supervision. What my notes describe is that Olivia, rather than cautiously putting her toe in the water to test the temperature, dived in immediately. Her honesty, openness and vulnerability were evident from the very beginning. There were tears, as there were often in my own experience of being a supervisee. She graphically articulated and explored the *difficult experience* that was having a substantial impact on her sense of herself and her confidence in her clinical work.

TAKEAWAYS – THE KEY THINGS

During our discussion, Olivia mentioned things that were helpful: thoughts, ideas and approaches from this distinct perspective offered through interprofessional supervision that she would take away. Summarising these key things provided a framework for writing about Olivia's experience of supervision.

Space for and around supervision

When it was possible to meet face-to-face, the supervision was bookended by a 25-minute drive. Olivia noted that, at first, she resented the drive but then found unexpected value in the travel time. This *dead-space, headspace* allowed the time necessary for reflection on the content of the session and for considering how she could *apply* ideas that we had discussed. This led Olivia to either avoid squeezing supervision into a work day, or to make sure that she had protected time and was not going to be doing any clinical work, to provide time for ideas to be processed and integrated. Olivia highlighted that when we met online the same mental and physical space surrounding supervision was just as important: *One thing that I will definitely take away: the kind of space you are in when you do these sessions is really important.*

Olivia described a Zoom supervision in work time that had taken place in a room that was *all glass sides and so I felt really exposed...it didn't feel right at all.*

Creativity for herself

From the outset Olivia took the lead and set the pace in the supervision sessions. My approach chimed with those described in a research paper about interprofessional supervision: 'open questions and reflective listening ... challenge, attentive listening, paraphrasing, summarizing, affirmation, feedback, reframing' (Davys, Fouché & Beddoe 2021).

Alongside these more verbal approaches I also drew on the use of other creative media where that seemed helpful. I used a collection of evocative images that I had accrued over many years:

FIGURE 13.1: MAGAZINE PICTURES AND POSTCARDS OF FINE ART

FIGURE 13.2: A BOWL OF MOSTLY NATURAL SMALL OBJECTS
SUCH AS DISTINCTIVE PEBBLES, SHELLS AND SEA GLASS

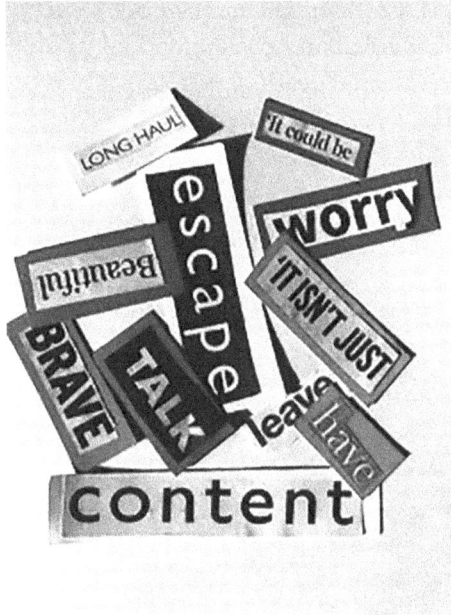

FIGURE 13.3: A SMALL BOX OF EVOCATIVE WORDS CUT OUT FROM
MAGAZINES AND SO ON, AND MOUNTED ONTO CARD

All these media could open expressiveness, creativity and a different type of thinking, seeing and feeling. It seemed to me that it was the space, time, the relationship and different perspective that all combined to make the supervision process helpful.

As issues arose, we were able to explore approaches and techniques that Olivia might be able to use for herself to increase self-awareness and process the impact of the work.

Olivia described that she had found it *really useful doing something a bit different*. This was particularly the case in earlier sessions, when she had felt overwhelmed and had not been so prepared for what to bring, when talking seemed less useful or we had already visited the issue often. She recalled an example:

> *Ooh, do you remember where you got out a load of pictures? And I can still see the picture that I chose. I don't know who the artist was, but there was this bridge so I think we used the picture to describe me and some of things that I, or maybe someone else, would see about me.*

Olivia had chosen a painting copy I had made of Claude Monet's

Waterlily Pond. As she described her response to the picture it became a metaphor for her role and how she wished to practise: the bridge spanning between life and death.

FIGURE 13.4: OLIVIA'S WATERLILY POND

There was a lot of practical advice things that you gave me over the years – again things that I can do with my patients but also things to do with myself and how I can look after myself. You talked to me about just writing for ten minutes, and not in the structured way that I would write a reflection. I had to just set a timer, write stuff, and get it all out on paper.

Olivia also remembered, *I had to write down some words and make a song or a poem out of it.* Some techniques were mentioned in passing, others returned to, some she developed for herself that I never knew about until our reflective conversation. As a coping strategy after a difficult death, she said, *I guess previously I had always seen myself as someone who was more into doing things. I think when I started coming to you, I would see myself as doing yoga or going for a run.* However, she realised that while those approaches were good for her wellbeing, she also needed that space and time to *properly think about it*.

In my own experience of supervision when working in palliative care, I would find myself unexpectedly overwhelmed and in tears regarding a patient. One of my supervisors was helpful in pointing out the need for ritual around the deaths of people I had a therapeutic relationship with. Although I was not a family member, there was a relationship and I too experienced loss and grief. Her suggestion was to do something symbolic, something like putting a flag in a tree. That idea did not resonate for me but led me to try different things that were personally helpful, including musical improvisation. I was moved to hear that Olivia had discovered her own ritual that allowed her to mark the dying process and subsequent loss of a patient.

> In the last year, what I have done is draw a picture. I'm not very good at drawing, but I quite like the process of doing something quite quick – 10–15 minutes. Sometimes it's a random picture that I end up drawing, sometimes it's associated and sometimes not, but I've often looked back and remembered 'that was for that person, and that was for that person'. It feels calm and okay, and it doesn't feel 'ooh that person died and that was awful' even if at the time it was awful. I feel a lot better if I have done that, rather than just boxing it away and forgetting about it.

As I reflect now in writing this chapter, I am struck that during our conversation Olivia only spoke in detail about one early session. That session entailed art and metaphor. She described the discovery that making art for herself was her own way to commemorate, remember and process the life of someone she had been involved with.

Communication and connection with patients

Olivia described the doctor – patient hierarchy as *one of the really key things* that supervision helped with. She said, *Traditionally there's this big divide between a doctor and their patient* and she was wanting to shift this dynamic, considering how sometimes it might be appropriate for her to establish more *normal human relationships* with patients. The process of supervision confirmed what she found she was doing naturally by *naming it more, making it feel okay, and maybe slightly pushing that boundary a bit more*. She talked of looking after a young patient whose mother she had known for over a year, reflecting that *coming to*

221

supervision really helped me feel comfortable with opening up a conversation that's very different from a medical conversation.

She described making use of being open about what was happening in the here and now when she was with a patient.

> *For example, when I had a patient who I was really struggling to get through to, maybe expressing to them how I was feeling in that relationship. Those were things that I hadn't really explored before in terms of being a doctor – how I might reflect on that doctor relationship with someone – and I found that very useful.*

Olivia was noticeably clear about the need for sensitivity: *I'd only use* [this kind of conversation] *for certain people; I don't think it's for everyone.* She described the usefulness of being able to bring patient stories, in particular *challenges around communicating with people* and the difficulties sometimes of establishing a rapport, *when people have perceived you in a negative light, partly because they are perceiving their disease, or the idea of palliative care in a negative light.*

She talked about the value of getting another *perspective on how to say things to patients, or how they might be perceiving things.*

Encouraging and supporting the team
Marie De Hennezel, a French psychologist working in a hospice, wrote:

> One actually is less exhausted by a total involvement of self – provided one knows how to replenish one's reserves – than by the attempt to barricade oneself behind one's defences. ... Those who give of themselves, however, also recharge themselves at the same time. (De Hennezel 1998, p.130)

It is well understood that palliative care contexts demand emotional labour from all involved. Olivia's role, particularly as a consultant, involved a great deal of leadership: *I have really noticed how people are not equipped to deal with this stuff and then they see the difficult deaths and they have no mechanisms or skills.*

In her second year as a registrar, Oliva talked of seeking supervision because she was *overwhelmed by what I was seeing and doing.* Now in her consultant role she discloses her strategies with other staff: *I tell them that I do something like that* [art]. She described how others assume that she is *not normal, I mean how can you deal with this type of stuff every day?* She shared:

> *I can only deal with this stuff every day partly because there is something probably about the type of person you are and being self-selected to do the job, but also being quite proactive about the way you process these difficult situations and the deaths that you see.*

Olivia was aware that *there's a way of finding the answer* for clinical conundrums, however:

> *It's the relationship stuff there isn't an answer to. It's the thing that clinicians are more afraid of, don't know what to do with, because we don't have very robust psychology training. Therefore, often my colleagues will come to me when it's the psychological things that are the deepest problems for a patient. So even when they come to me for expert pain advice, it's often been recognised that there's this big emotional issue going on for someone and everyone's just a bit scared about feeling a bit helpless in knowing what to do with it.*

Launer, in his paper 'Conversations inviting change' (2008), contrasts the difference between 'medical doctors and psychological therapists' and how therapists might assume that the 'acts of talking and listening' bring about change, whereas doctors and other professionals might have far lower expectations and assign far less value to those communications. For the case of music therapy, I would also add *musical interaction* to this list of therapeutic actions. In our conversation I suggested that Olivia had come, partly through supervision, to feel confident that she was 'enough' and to encourage others to recognise that what they are doing is psychological help. She responded:

> *People often think that just by talking to this person that's not enough. 'I need to do something more.' They feel like it needs to be a specific thing that they are giving them and are not actually recognising that the things that they say, the approach that they've taken, the support that they've given them, 'being there', are the psychology. Feeling confident in your expertise but also recognising what those things are and being okay naming them – 'That was psychological support I gave that person' – rather than thinking, 'Oh I'm not an expert in this, I'm not a psychologist and therefore I can't deliver that type of care.'*

Interpersonal relationships with colleagues and others

In supervision sessions Olivia concluded that *there's been a lot about relationships with colleagues and teams and the challenges that you can face there.* Often supervision would have a focus on:

> *some of the feelings and emotions that have come up in me over the years, like I would do something very differently or that it becomes obvious to me that is not how you would lead or speak to someone. Also getting angry, frustrated or disappointed and what to do with those feelings as well.*

Olivia was sometimes in positions where her own values and sense of what was acceptable clashed with work colleagues' attitudes and, particularly during the pandemic, with others whose behaviours and standards conflicted with hers. Being able to explore these issues in the supportive and safe place of supervision was needed.

When in supervision I used the term 'moral labour' for the first time, Olivia found this to be a helpful 'naming' of what she felt.

> *I feel like we spent quite a lot of the time talking about my values and my morals, but we never really named it as that. I think quite frequently what we would talk about is wanting to stand up or raise my hand when I felt something was wrong or something needed to change, and that is a key part of me. But we never really laid it down as 'these are my values'; that was never very explicit, but it was very much part of what we were talking about. I think over the years there has been a lot of emotional impact on me from those things and so working through that has also been extremely useful.*

NOT USEFUL

In transcribing Olivia's description of her experience of supervision I realised she had said almost nothing about what might not have worked for her and that this was unlikely to be a full picture of her supervision experience. Shohet, in his chapter 'Fear and Love in Supervision' (2008), recounts many examples where facing fears and being honest about difficulties can be transformative for supervisor, supervisee and client. Had I tried to protect myself by avoiding prompts in our discussion which would have allowed more problematic elements in supervision to surface?

In an email exchange that took place a few days after our conversation,

I asked Oliva to think back to what she might have liked less of or was unhelpful. I proffered that 'I sometimes talked too much, didn't listen enough, or offered suggestions instead of waiting for you to figure things out for yourself.'

Olivia disagreed with my analysis but said *sometimes I felt that we reflected back on my* [difficult] *experience a bit too much. But it was also one of the triggers to me seeking you out and formed the initial story of our meeting, and probably needed a lot of working through.*

On reflection I do remember her fleeting facial expressions, suggesting that we had visited the experience enough, but at the time had not paid them enough attention or brought the material into the supervision space.

CONCLUSION

It is a rare experience to be able to talk at length about supervision retrospectively with a supervisee. The discussion itself brought to the surface aspects and dimensions of the experience that we had not talked about and that were not previously fully known, perhaps by either of us.

When I first began hospice work, I swiftly realised I needed to approach my work in diverse ways to be helpful. Much of what I had learned in my training had to be stripped back or amplified and developed. I found myself drawing on a much wider range of techniques and approaches, some of which were shared in supervision. Mostly I needed to find the courage to be myself, to be fully 'human', not putting on or hiding behind a role. My own supervision experience often enabled me to conceptualise and frame how I was working with patients, giving me courage to go deeper and to be braver in the work.

Olivia always came to the supervision sessions with courage, determined to be real, honest, vulnerable. My hunch was that my different knowledge and perspective helped create the safe place she was looking for, where she could be supported to think about her life and work both now and for years to come. Olivia's exploration of her experience of supervision with someone whose therapeutic skills are not based in medication or physical examination seems to have allowed her to integrate parts of herself that had been eclipsed during her training.

Having now supervised many practitioners who are not therapists but who work with people in demanding situations, including prison and post-release contexts as well as palliative care, I am convinced that experienced music therapists can offer insights that are the result of our particular approach to practice and the tools that we become familiar with.

I have fallen into this work rather than actively seeking it. Maybe the profession of music therapy should recognise that there are many aspects of our training and practice that equip us to be helpful supervisors beyond our own profession.

POSTSCRIPT

My last email to Olivia ended with these words that signified my respect for her: 'I just wish you all the very best and hope that when my time comes, I will meet someone like you at my bedside.'

REFERENCES

Davys, A., Fouché, C. & Beddoe, L. (2021) Mapping effective interprofessional supervision practice. *Clinical Supervisor*, 40(2), pp.179–199.

De Hennezel, M. (1998) *Intimate Death: How the Dying Teach Us to Live*. London: Warner Books.

Forinash, M. (ed). (2001) *Music Therapy Supervision*. Gilsum, NH: Barcelona Publishers.

Kearney, M. K., Weininger, R. B., Vachon, M. L. S., Harrison, R. L. & Mount, B. M. (2009) Self-care of physicians caring for patients at the end of life: 'Being connected...a key to my survival.' *Journal of the American Medical Association*, 301(11), pp.1155–1164.

Launer, J. (2008) Conversations inviting change. *Postgraduate Medical Journal*, 84, pp.4–5.

Saunders, C. & Clark, D. (2006) *Cicely Saunders: Selected Writings 1958–2004*. Oxford: Oxford University Press.

Shohet, R. (2008) *Passionate Supervision*. London: Jessica Kingsley Publishers.

Tomlinson, J. (2015) Using clinical supervision to improve the quality of patient care: A response to Berwick and Francis. *BMC Medical Education*, 15, 103. Available at: https://bmcmededuc.biomedcentral.com/articles/10.1186/s12909-015-0324-3 (Accessed 6 January 2024).

CHAPTER 14

At the Still Point

JULIE SUTTON

Except for the point, the still point,
There would be no dance, and there is only the dance.
T. S. ELIOT

This chapter explores supervision as a constant around a still point throughout a therapist's working life, and how one's relationship to this constant will change across time. With the understanding that supervision is a joint undertaking, vignettes will illustrate supervisors' and supervisees' experiences occurring in different ways at different stages of their careers, including links with broader contexts alongside a clinician's unique needs and wants. This acknowledges how supervision is part of lifelong learning, is necessary for healthy practice, and recognises how we have potential to keep learning and growing throughout our professional life: we never know everything, we continually gain experience.

In his poem 'Burnt Norton', Thomas Stearns Eliot encouraged us to think about time not as an abstract concept, but as part of life. He wrote about being in the present moment, where we know the future is unknown, and how, however much we might want to, we cannot change the past. This links us to the work of psychotherapy and to how we experience time, when, like music, the present moment is in a state of becoming. The poem inspired me to reconsider supervision as a lifelong commitment to working as a therapist, and that we might come to understand supervision either as an abstract concept, or a way of being. Particular phrases from the poem resonated with me and they form the basis of some sections of the chapter.

I hope the following thoughts will activate the reader's own contemplation of their relationship with and to supervision across their professional lifespan. I have avoided references to the music therapy literature which other colleagues have incorporated, and to the history of supervision within the profession, details of which are already known. Rather, I make use of analytic and musician authors to broaden a space for thinking, as well as drawing on my four decades of experience. The literature referenced occurs across a wide timeline, because along with the new, sometimes old ideas remain relevant to today's contexts. Underpinning much of what is written is an integration of both musical and psychoanalytic theories, particularly those from improvisers (e.g. Bailey 1993; Cage 1967; Clifton 1976; Prévost 1995) and psychoanalysts (Ashton & Bloch 2010; Bion 2007; Freud 1914; Green 1999, 2009; Grier 2021; Harris Williams 2010; Nagel 2013; Odgen 1997; Rose 2004; Sabbadini 2006; Sandler 1976; Wilson 2018; Winnicott 1960, 1971).

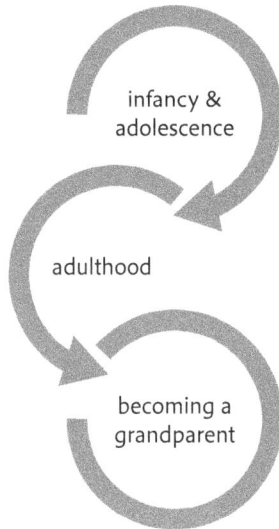

FIGURE I4.I: A DEVELOPMENTAL VIEW OF SUPERVISION

I propose that we bear in mind a generational metaphor when we think about supervision, and that lifelong development exists when we move across the generations professionally. As we age, our continuing reflective practice (with supervision at its core) also moves through developmental processes in various forms. Remembering the term is from a latin root *supervidere*, meaning to oversee and/or inspect, I suggest we reconsider the word *supervision* and include an additional concept along this developmental trajectory.

Figure 14.1 acts as a simple structure from which to think about a working life, beginning with training and a form of infancy and adolescence, leading to adulthood and emergence into the profession. Having matured into one's professional identity, at the end of this long trajectory is a change of emphasis and eventually a movement towards retirement. Not all music therapists follow this trajectory neatly, but it does underpin professional life and is a fruitful context from which to view supervision.

SUPERVISORY BEGINNINGS

In the UK, music therapy training takes place within a master's programme, usually across just over two full-time years or the part-time equivalent. This time is spent in the application of theory and the lived experience of working as a therapist within the apprenticeship model. I am using the term *apprentice* to indicate something that is not about a legal agreement with an employer but is closer to the Latin root *apprehendere*, to grasp, with the senses and/or mind, and to learn. This is initially via observing others' ways of working, and mimicking this to some extent in the service of taking in a lived experience of how others do the job. Over time (including post training), the apprentice appropriates their experiential knowledge and then incorporates it into an individual personality and style. This form of training includes a first experience of supervision, which is a true 'over-seeing' of an apprentice's work. It has a focus on core competencies, in terms of the foundation of future work as a therapist.

Depending on one's personal development and training setting, this first supervision can be experienced along a wide spectrum, from supportive to shaming; in other words, as constructive and creative, or something that feels more destructive. 'Over-seeing' has traces of an external, observing superego. Taking in a helpful, realistic stance alongside more unsettling experiences of supervision is also a process of potential growth. This is not without its challenges, because the transferences that occur in supervision can be difficult for both supervisee and supervisor (Ehrlich *et al.* 2017; Filho & Pires 2010). A key to understanding transference is in the term itself: something is being transferred onto the supervisor that has a bearing on the supervisee's needs, wishes and previous experiences and relationships. Supervisors should also bear in mind the possibility of projecting their own needs onto supervisees. For example, the dynamics that result from an apprentice's accelerated learning can include a positive idealising, or more negative transference reactions. The supervisor is placed into a role that is particular to the supervisee and often has some relationship to their parents. Supervision requires sensitivity to the kinds of dynamics incorporating the developmental shifts or glitches that come along, while remembering that our apprentices are adults, not children. For effective, boundaried supervisory parenting one should consider both aspects of a parenting couple: something that not only might nurture and support growth, but also challenge, and robustly face the important realities of the work. A supervisor will model a way of working via their presence and behaviour, in order to safeguard, encourage and help maintain their supervisees' healthy practice.

Stepping out into the profession after training is when music therapists begin to practise their craft and further develop as therapists and musicians. It is a significant shift from the more protected, structured environment of training. Supervision at this stage calls for a supervisor to be attentive to what therapists might be searching for, to have awareness of (but not necessarily work with) the relational supervisory dynamic being set up, to safely hold the space in which experiences can be explored and thought about, and maintain a clarity about what is realistic in the supervisee's external and internal contexts. A post-qualification supervisee who has felt bruised by training experiences may feel anxious, while someone with a more positive encounter will tend to be less worried and expecting support rather than judgement. For others, an idealising transference can recruit the supervisor into particular aspects of a parental role, where they might sense the pressure to only reassure, rather than open up discussion of where the challenges in the work are. They may feel flattered to be viewed as the root of all knowledge; or feel sole responsibility for clients, sensing the supervisee's more vulnerable forms of dependence, where independent thought becomes an essential, careful focus of future work.

If a negative transference develops during supervision, a supervisor will have to navigate a delicate area between their therapist's understanding and the role of a supervisor. One should also be attentive to being drawn into enactments or collusions, where the supervisor's own difficult areas are activated. Just as in psychotherapy, it is not easy to bring to light the more difficult aspects of a negative transference within supervision. The supervisee may not be aware of their more hostile feelings, or of how these feelings are repeating something else in their history. As past experiences bubble up during supervisory meetings, these feelings are transferred onto the supervisor. It is not the work of supervision to engage in personal therapy, but some aspects might be worked on by focusing on the parallel process between the supervisee and their client, or by considering the institutional dynamics. If all goes well, the supervisee will find their way into personal therapy and work through this. Sometimes, supervisees are looking for therapeutic rather than supervisory support; one might need to directly approach the topic of further personal work as a duty of care for a supervisee who is genuinely struggling. These are delicate threads, and if not taken seriously and with humanity, there is a danger that a supervisee may then wish to escape all supervision and not engage with this essential aspect of lifelong learning.

There are other reasons why a therapist will not avail themselves of supervision. While the UK profession is more than 60 years old, many music therapists continue to be pioneers. They work alone and are often isolated from colleagues. This makes accessing supervision problematic. Therapists work hard to establish their practice and are often self-employed, with no supervisory provision or expectation in their workplace, apart from managerial supervision. With supervision having to take place outside working hours, it places additional pressure on valuable free time, money and family commitments, and often there are young children to consider. Considerable geographical distances may need to be navigated to meet with colleagues. There may be only one supervisor available, or none at all. The therapist may have had a difficult previous supervisory relationship within training or have taken on board others' views of a particular supervisor without discovering their own impressions. For these kinds of reasons, supervision may become haphazard or actively avoided. There is also no 'one size fits all', making the choice of a supervisor a significant and crucial one. It may be that one benefit of the pandemic is the increased availability of online supervision, enabling contact with colleagues from further afield. While this does not replace being in the same room, it has become an effective, helpful way of working and can run productively alongside occasional face-to-face meetings.

Coming out of training, therapists might wish to retain their connection with their theoretical home and to continue exploring their work from this base. If the only supervisor is from another tradition, this could be confusing and difficult to engage with. With a colleague wanting someone to talk to for general support, a supervisor must be sensitive to holding the supervisory exploration without imposing their own style, or getting caught up in quick fixes, which is not easy when the supervisee may be asking directly: what do I do? It is also a time when unfinished business from training can bubble up, such as questions that were not asked, the impact of any challenges or protests that were not made at the time, and the detritus of unresolved experiences of the training and its institution. As noted earlier, this may also create a negative supervisory transference, presenting technical issues for a supervisor, or pull the supervisor into a more therapeutic role. The lines between supervisor and therapist can be challenged at such an important time in a therapist's career, as in the following vignette.

VIGNETTE 1

Music therapist (Yolanda) has approached the only supervisor (Tom) in her area. Yolanda is six months post qualification, with one day of work but wanting to expand to more days. Yolanda and Tom think about what she is looking for in supervision. She asks for support but does not seem to be too clear about what she wants. She is nervous about bringing video material from sessions, but seems to settle when Tom explains this is for both of them to experience and observe the client collaboratively from a helpful distance. She then makes an appointment to discuss some of her work with Tom in supervision. Tom is aware that Yolanda trained in a different programme to his original training, but he has had experience of working with colleagues across a wide spectrum of approaches, including past and existing supervisees. Within this first supervision session, while he senses he and Yolanda can work together, as the conversation continues, he is not sure Yolanda feels the same.

As their discussion moves on, Tom feels pressure to reassure, rather than explore, Yolanda's work with her. It is difficult for Yolanda to think beyond her experience of her client and the workplace generally. Her music seems stilted and somewhat muted. Tom suggests Yolanda improvise with him for a few minutes as her client had played, and he will play a version of what she had played. He asks Yolanda to show him what she'd played, which she does. They begin playing and Tom soon notices he is being drawn away from Yolanda's style of playing, into a more containing role. After playing, Yolanda finds it difficult to put into words her experience, but she takes some cues from Tom where he opens up the conversation about how he sometimes thinks in colours, temperatures or textures. This helps Yolanda begin to speak about her experience of her client and she is surprised how sensitive they were to her music, which she'd felt had had little impact.

Tom draws the meeting to a close, saying his impression is of Yolanda possibly looking for the right mix, how he would be happy to meet with her again, but he is also wondering how Yolanda herself wants to proceed. Perhaps she wants to link up with somebody from her original training, for example, as many do. Yolanda does not take this up, arranges another meeting but does not turn up. After Tom has contacted her, Yolanda says she forgot and is apologetic. Tom offers Yolanda another meeting, but this time suggests it might be used to support and think about where Yolanda goes from here. Yolanda attends the meeting and the conversation that follows helps unearth her ambivalence towards supervision, underneath which Tom senses is a wish not to claim a supervisor, but to be claimed as a supervisee. It transpires that Yolanda has been struggling a great deal, with old experiences from childhood resurfacing alongside her training and personal therapy ending. Tom helps her think about the support she might get from personal therapy first and foremost, as it seems there is potential for further discoveries. He says he is happy to meet with her again to think about her work with her when things have settled. A few weeks later, having reconnected with her therapist, Yolanda contacts him to re-establish supervision.

What is clear from this example is how music therapists in the period immediately post qualification might experience significant pressure and a sense of being cut adrift. This is particularly pertinent to those working in parts of the world where they are the only music therapist, isolated and at some distance from any other colleagues. One has a sense of the way this experienced supervisor works, and of their sensitivity to and awareness of the line between supervision and therapy. The way they listened to their supervisee was also multi-layered and attentive, with aspects of a quiet, patient parental holding, offering space and time for the supervisee to work their way through what was necessary for them, in their own way.

Solnit (1970, p.360) once wrote, 'supervision is more than teaching and less than treatment'. These words encompass what supervisors might grapple with during the course of an early supervisory relationship: holding the line between the working-through of the process towards a form of understanding, and the work of being a therapist at the same time one is a supervisor, where the supervisee may have consciously or otherwise also come looking for therapy. On other occasions, supervisors are approached by a therapist near to or in crisis, when part of the supervisory role is to advise best safe practice, checking out what support the therapist already has, and/or opening up a direct discussion about seeking personal therapy if necessary.

It is a mistake to assume that we know what it is like in the room with the client, or to think we know what the client's or supervisee's experience is. As we mature as therapists, we are more able to sit with this important unknown, something that has the benefit of hours of being in a room with those we work with. We develop a particular kind of curiosity about the experiences of others, with less of a wish to know, and more of a focus on finding spaces where understanding and insight might occur. We have to believe that a supervisor might know something we don't yet know, but in reality, it is the discoveries we make ourselves within supervision that stay with us. The space between knowing and not knowing is the space where something new might happen, which supervisors and supervisees are interested in, and from which both will learn.

MID-LIFE CRISIS: THE UNHEARD MUSIC HIDDEN IN THE SHRUBBERY

Once one has many years of experience and has established a way of working, supervision takes on another role and meaning. Some therapists want to explore a way of working outside the profession or expand their knowledge beyond their original training. Others want to continue to develop along the lines they already practise, or expand their work in other ways. This is when therapists might seek out somebody whose work they have admired, or who writes in a way they feel drawn to, or whose work they resonate with. Others find someone whose personal qualities they warm to, or who they feel comfortable with. Supervision may or may not be with a music therapist.

Professional middle age can be a time of further stretching of one's wings, in new ways of working, or of finding a new focus or energy. We are more aware of our blind spots, our strengths, and the areas we thrive less comfortably in. We feel more at ease with work situations because of the experiences we have gathered across time. We become more adept at saying no and knowing where to concentrate our energy. Yet, it has been my experience that therapists with an established practice across many years can experience a defining moment, wondering anew what their therapeutic identity is. This can feel like a crisis of confidence, but it is a developmental aspect of one's career and growth, and one that therapists might well consult about with their peers or a senior colleague. The following two vignettes explore some of these threads.

VIGNETTE 2

A supervisor (Susan) is working with a colleague (Fred) who is well known and established in his work. While having qualified a decade after Susan, Fred has many kinds of expertise, including one area of work Susan is less experienced in. They have been meeting for several years. One day Susan notices how Fred is unusually reticent to talk or bring any work to discuss. Fred looks more dishevelled than Susan has remembered.

As the meeting progresses, Susan says she has an impression that something is bothering Fred but that it may or may not be something he wants to bring to their meeting today. Fred blurts out that he has been struggling for months with a lack of his usual excitement about his work, and he is uncharacteristically unsure about where to go from here professionally. He says, 'I'm not even sure who I am any more as a music therapist.' Susan hears the panic and agitation in Fred's voice but has another context from which to understand what is happening: that this might be a form of crisis of confidence linked to recent developments in the profession that may have caused Fred to feel left behind. Susan has this thought based on knowing there are no incidences of personal or family issues in Fred's life, and drawing on their supervisory work to date. An exploratory discussion takes place that results in Fred identifying a number of new aims, including passing on some responsibilities to a less experienced colleague, to make space for work on a publication. Fred feels permission to navigate this decision with the understanding that he is making space not just for himself, but also for a colleague to gain more experience. The work of succession has begun.

VIGNETTE 3

A long supervisory relationship is marked by mutual respect and openness. Ben (supervisor) and Derek have been meeting for many years and Ben has shared Derek's ongoing development across more than a decade. One day, Derek comes for supervision and says he is going to retrain as a psychotherapist, wanting to use words rather than music. Having entered twice-weekly personal therapy, Derek has become more focused on psychodynamic theory, and has been reading the literature in relation to psychoanalytic concepts. He intends to apply to train as a psychotherapist and use this training to open up his work with verbal music therapy clients.

Ben is aware that the training Derek wishes to undertake is a different method from music therapy, and how integration of the two methods either may not be possible, or take some time to fully grasp. Rather than discuss this, Ben waits for Derek to complete his training. Ben silently tracks how Derek finds his way to this conclusion himself.

Another thread that emerges at the same time is Derek's wish to develop his supervisory practice, something Ben has suggested he considers for some years. This is navigated with Ben's silent wondering in what ways Derek may privately identify him, for example as someone to measure up to, or envy, or idealise, or be inspired by. Understanding this to be the work of psychotherapy, again Ben remains quietly aware of this thread during these discussions. Eventually, Derek is able to speak about his mixed feelings of both envy and respect that were worked through in his psychotherapy, which culminated in a sense of gratitude and a wish to pay forward the fruits of the supervisory work. This is a constructive identification enabling movement forward and professional growth.

In these two contexts, rather than think of super-vision, a consideration of the term *consultation* is helpful. This is a term that can capture the kinds of enquiry and exploration that established therapists might do. *Super*vision (over-seeing) might belong earlier in one's professional life, before one feels fully confident of and at ease with one's therapeutic identity, valuing the checking-in and benign over-seeing of one's work. Consultation has a less hierarchical aspect and indicates how one is conferring with peers or senior colleagues. Many may use the term *supervision* interchangeably with this concept, but the question is, as the vignettes show, how does the term affect experienced practitioners?

Professional middle age (or maturity) can be thought of as a time when one's identifications occur across a broad canvas, including all the ages one ever was. As Odgen (2022, p.2) recently wrote, '[g]rowing up is hard-won at every stage of life, but in adulthood, advances in becoming more fully oneself become less easily measured than in an earlier period of life'. When working with both younger colleagues and those of the same chronological age who more recently qualified, one is reminded, consciously and unconsciously, of one's own experiences of these times. This brings us alongside an original idea and vision of what working life would entail – wishes that may or may not have been fulfilled. All these experiences can usefully be drawn on but may also touch our heart strings and remind us of past missed opportunities, mistakes and regrets. It is a time when one is put in touch with the kinds of losses that naturally occur as one ages. The profession is always evolving, new people come to the fore, and changes in society itself have an impact. The lockdowns caused by the pandemic are an example: therapists had to adopt new ways of practice that their training did not prepare them for. The profession had to reinvent music therapy in unusual, previously unthought-of ways, during a time of great anxiety and loss.

Considering supervision during analytic training, Ahktar (2013) observed more than one way a supervisor (training analyst) will listen. He listens like an analyst, which provides insights into the trainee's 'work ego, besides of course the analytic process between him and the patient' (Ahktar 2013, p.146). He may have thoughts about the way the trainee appropriates their own characterological qualities or quirks but cannot work with this as he might in an analytic session – he is not the trainee's analyst. However, the supervisor can identify 'blind spots' (p.147) and any sense of resistance he notes transferentially during a supervision session. He may then bring these to light in terms of their impact on the progress of the analytic work the trainee is doing. There are striking parallels between these kinds of layered listening and what music therapists do with musical ears that can pick up details, textures and layers.

An overview of some of these developmental aspects of supervisory work is given in Figure 14.2. The figure is a starting point, that the reader may wish to consider as a basis for their own thoughts, and to use as a springboard for their own developmental view.

While all the above aspects remain pertinent, some belong to particular stages in a music therapist's professional life. For example, increasingly less teaching is required from a supervisor as time goes on. More threads weave in and out of an experienced therapist's lifelong learning, both as a supervisee/consultee and as a supervisor/consultant. There is greater integration of professional development up to this point and one's therapist identity is usually clearer and more easily identified.

As one's supervisory practice increases, there is also more likelihood of increasing negative capability, in the sense of a grounded capacity to sit with not knowing. The wisdom of a mature therapist includes both knowing when to intervene, and when to wait.

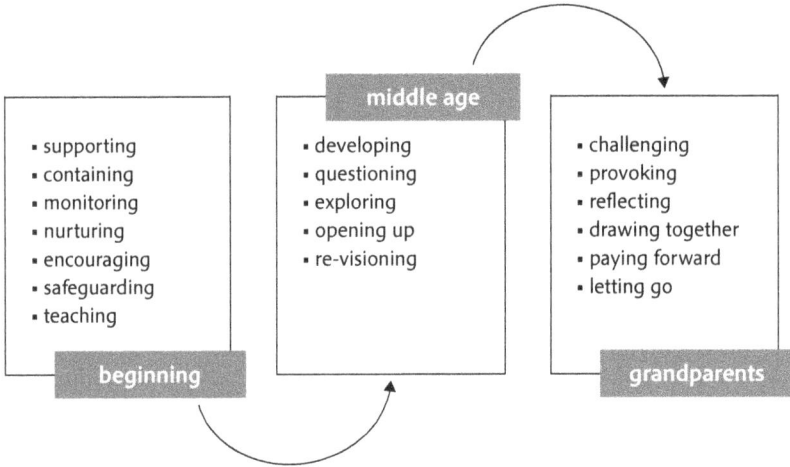

middle age

beginning		grandparents
• supporting	• developing	• challenging
• containing	• questioning	• provoking
• monitoring	• exploring	• reflecting
• nurturing	• opening up	• drawing together
• encouraging	• re-visioning	• paying forward
• safeguarding		• letting go
• teaching		

FIGURE 14.2: DEVELOPMENT THROUGH SUPERVISION
ACROSS A PROFESSIONAL LIFETIME

GRANDPARENT MUSIC THERAPISTS
– KNOWING THE STILL POINT

> Change always involves giving up the old as well as bringing us into contact with the anxiety of the new, and it is often the case that letting go of what is familiar is the more difficult part of the task. (Steiner 2011, pp.149–150)

When becoming a professional grandparent, lifelong learning has a different quality and timeline. One's professional identity and way of working has the benefit of many years' practice and life experience generally. Some therapists are already grandparents in their personal lives, or in the process of becoming grandparents, or coming to terms with this not happening. It is also a time where we are put in touch with loss in a different context, including retiring from what may well have been a deeply meaningful vocation. We have also been deeply sensitised to loss in the context of the pandemic, which has changed the world and affected our past freedoms. Climate change is another aspect of a necessity to take stock of how we live our lives, what we give back, and what we have to lose along the way. Additionally, working with a supervisee who is in the throes of changing supervisors will also bring up aspects of loss for both, something that may resonate with losses along our personal timeline.

Grandparent music therapists have a qualitatively different awareness of the generations and of inter-generational relationships, both personally and professionally, often looking back more than turning forward professionally. Priorities change, our sense of time changes and we are more likely to inhabit still spaces: being rather than doing. The therapeutic presence of an experienced therapist will also be qualitatively different from someone nearer the beginning of their career, and the same is true of supervisors. At this stage of a career, there is less to prove to oneself or others, and those who still have much to offer in terms of energy will continue to work and learn. There can be a still point one returns to increasingly more regularly as one's professional life goes on.

When a therapist is actively planning retirement, and giving up various aspects of their work, supervisees will be told their supervisor is no longer available. This can repeat previous losses for the supervisee, particularly if the supervisor has had a significant or meaningful role in their professional lives. Moving on to another supervisor or finding a new person to consult with is an opportunity for further expanding one's practice but comes at a price and depends on the supervisee moving from the loss to being able to miss the supervisor as that part of their working life draws to a close. Something that could be experienced as exciting might become filled with resentment and a sense of abandonment. Mixed feelings are not unusual, but can be navigated maturely, even if experiencing more infantile states of mind. Discovering gratitude for what one had, and a willingness to pass on what was learned from the retiring supervision, is the gift at the end of this process.

As the world turns, we tend to forget the long experiences gathered by our professional grandparents, and once they become less active professionally in terms of presenting or publishing, or give up public office, out of sight can become out of mind. Some are gone but not forgotten via their publications, or are sought out to consult with, or to provide specialist teaching input. It is our profession's grandparents who sit quietly by, watching the younger members revisit a phase they already went through earlier in their career, with the understanding this is necessary to reintegrate it anew in current times. Ideally, a profession that encompasses all generations is a healthy one, signs of which may be seen in the new mentoring posts established by the British Association for Music Therapy during 2022. We might even welcome professional great-grandparents, as well as remember those who are no longer with us. They have influenced the development in and developing of music therapy across many decades. We continue to learn from them via their publications, or those they supervised or trained – the work of succession. Yet I believe it is the music therapists quietly getting on with work who will truly take our profession forward.

CODA: SUPERVISORY LISTENING TO LISTENING – LISTENING WITH A MUSICAL EAR

Like the work of therapy, supervising and consulting are underpinned with listening. In the past I encouraged music therapists to claim their inherent listening skills as fully as possible: to listen not only the sounds we and our clients make, but to our silences. This is a layered listening to the textures in any musical exchange, textures that run both horizontally and vertically (Sutton 2018, 2020, 2023). Silences both communicate and hide possible meanings: they are at least as important as sounds. The same is true of working in a supervisory or consulting capacity, where we will also be listening for collective silences, including those we get caught up in without realising, and which create blind spots in the work. There are also silences that we can leave as they are, as in the final vignette.

VIGNETTE 4

George is nearing the end of his career and is in the process of negotiating delegating and passing on various aspects of his job to colleagues, including being part of a process of employing a new therapist within a department he has worked in for two decades. He brings some work to Teresa, a psychoanalyst with whom George has consulted for the last eight years. The work is with an elderly man with dementia, who is near the end of his life. As George and Teresa view the video recording of a recent session, Teresa's eyes start to fill with tears. It is a small thing, and George seems not to notice. Teresa reflects on the loss of George from the profession, and wonders if the profession will notice this. She is also moved by the work, and by how the elderly gentleman is making small, but expressively full movements and sounds. Teresa and George continue to discuss the work presented in a similar way to their usual conversations. They watch the end of the session, not knowing it is the last session with the elderly man, who dies soon after. Although not unexpected, the news of this has not yet reached George.

George then comments that he had seen Teresa's eyes become watery, and says he realises he has had a dull ache in his chest through-out the video recording, and then remembers having this sensation after the session had ended. At the time he was quite puzzled by this, and it passed quickly, but in this moment with Teresa, George says, 'I'm going to miss these moments with that old man', and his own eyes fill with tears. He then realises he is also talking about the conversations with Teresa, and his move into retirement. He says, 'I'm sad to be retiring; it is a genuine loss after so many years of work, but I think these tears are also gratitude, not just for what my job has given me, but more for what I've learned and how it has grown these aspects of me. I have just real-ised that I have been enjoying passing this on to the next generations, and it is theirs now.'

Anne Alvarez once wrote how 'listening is nevertheless a complex art' (Alvarez 2012, p.163), bringing with her words an awareness of different registers of listening and experiencing ourselves and others being an essential underpinning of a therapist's work. Supervisory listening must include all these aspects and a further perspective, that of the privileged eavesdropper who has precious insight – the one allowed into what happens in a therapy session that has already taken place, but who is also not there. An observer from a distance who will recreate in their mind something close by. Audio and video recordings of sessions allow us to gather impressions of the inside from the outside, check them out with the therapist concerned, and also to jump time and rewind sections to more fully understand the processes involved. It incorporates listening to clients who cannot listen, and/or to therapists struggling with listening. Listening to what is there and what is not there. It truly is a complicated art.

A word about hesitation, which is a form of waiting, and linked with a style one might gather across time; for example, when to bring up certain threads in a supervision/consultation, and when to wait to see what happens, to push a therapist too quickly into an area they are already beginning to explore, or to introduce something too soon can rob them of their own discovery. This will turn supervision into something false or jarring in an unhelpful way. The supervisor's 'knowing' becomes paramount, rather than wondering, or thinking or questioning to open up space for the yet to be known to emerge. Moving across professional generations, we became more acutely aware of past mistakes, and continually tweak our approaches to more of an open enquiry where questions may remain unanswered, and perhaps provoke new questions. An oscillation between forms of knowing and staying with the unknown becomes increasingly more important – a fundamental form of musical thinking.

Music constantly asks of us a curiosity about life. It both calms and stirs up our equilibrium. Music provides no clear answers, yet it is deeply meaningful. It encompasses in-between states, that are sounded, and occur in silences between sounds, between or before words, between different aspects of life, between experience and meaning, and between what we know and do not know. It is, as Riek (1953, p12) noted, 'The intangible that is invisible as well as untouchable can still be audible. It can announce its presence and effect in tunes, faintly heard inside you.'

To this I add two closing thoughts. The first, that what is faintly heard may well be imperceptible, but it is worth opening our ears to. Second, that the ineffable aspects of music are close to the ineffable aspects of a therapeutic process, and that perhaps, as Zigaran suggested, 'language does more to negate the musical experience than assist it' (Zigaran 2008, p76). If true, this does not prevent us from being curious about the challenge of how we communicate music therapy experiences, and how supervision is a fertile ground for that exploration. It is an integral part of supervision and consultation. The intergenerational history of the profession has much to offer our lifelong learning about our continuing development as individuals and as a profession as a whole, and I think it can be a still point that should be visited and revisited as often as possible.

A part of all art is to make silence speak.

The things left out in painting, the not withheld in music, the void in architecture – all are as necessary and as active as the utterance itself. (Stark 2014)

REFERENCES

Akhtar, S. (2013) *Psychoanalytic Listening: Methods, Limits and Innovations*. London: Karnac Books.

Alvarez, A. (2012) *The Thinking Heart: Three Levels of Psychoanalytic Therapy with Disturbed Children*. Hove & New York, NY: Routledge.

Ashton, P. W. & Bloch, S. (2010) *Music & Psyche: Contemporary Psychoanalytic Explorations*. New Orleans, LA: Spring Journal Books.

Bailey, D. (1993) *Improvisation: Its Nature and Practice in Music*. New York, NY: Da Capo Press.

Bion, W. R. (2007) *Second Thoughts* (second edition). London and New York, NY: Karnac Books.

Cage, J. (1967) *Silence*. Cambridge, MA: MIT Press.

Clifton, T. (1976) The poetics of musical silence. *Musical Quarterly*, 62(2), pp.163-181.

Ehrlich, L. T., Kulish, N. M., Fitzpatrick Hanly, M. A., Robinson, M. & Rothstein, A. (2017) Supervisory countertransferences and impingements in evaluating readiness for graduation: Always present, routinely under-recognized. *International Journal of Psychoanalysis*, 98, pp.491-516.

Eliott, T. S. ([1944] 1983) *Four Quartets*. London: Faber & Faber.

Filho, G. V. & Pires, A. C. J. (2010) Benign and disruptive disturbances of the supervisory field. *International Journal of Psychoanalysis*, 91, pp.896-913.

Freud, S. (1914) 'Remembering, Repeating and Working Through.' *The Standard Edition of the Complete Psychological Works of Sigmund Freud* (pp.145-156). London: Hogarth.

Green, A. (1999) *The Work of the Negative*. London: Free Association Books.

Green. A. (2009) *Time in Psychoanalysis: Some Contradictory Aspects*. London & New York, NY: Free Association Books.

Grier, F. (2021) The music of the drives, and the music of perversion: Reflections on a dream of jealous theft. *International Journal of Psychoanalysis*, 102(3), pp.448-463.

Harris Williams, M. (2010) *The Aesthetic Development: The Poetic Spirit of Psychoanalysis*. London & New York, NY: Karnac Books.

Nagel, J. J. (2013) *Melodies of the Mind. Connections Between Psychoanalysis and Music*. London & New York, NY: Routledge.

Ogden, T. H. (1997) *Reverie and Interpretation: Sensing Something Human*. Northvale, NJ: Jason Aronson.

Ogden, T. H. (2022) *Coming to Life in the Consulting Room: Towards a New Analytic Sensibility*. Abingdon & New York, NY: Routledge.

Prévost, E. (1995) *No Sound is Innocent*. Harlow, Essex: Copula.

Riek, T. (1953) *The Haunting Melody: Psychoanalytic Experiences in Life and Music*. New York, NY: Farrar, Straus & Young.

Rose, G. J. (2004) *Between Couch and Piano: Psychoanalysis, Music, Art and Neuroscience*. Hove and New York, NY: Brunner-Routledge.

Sabbadini, A. (2006) On sounds, children, identity and a 'quite unmusical' man. *British Journal of Psychotherapy*, 14(2), pp.189-196.

Sandler, J. (1976) Countertransference and role-responsiveness. *International Journal of Psychoanalysis*, 3, pp.43-47.

Solnit, A. J. (1970) Learning from psychoanalytic supervision. *International Journal of Psychoanalysis*, 51, pp.359-362.

Stark, F. (2014) 'On Silence.' In *The Zodiac Arch* (p.193). London: I. B. Tauris.

Steiner, J. (2011) *Seeing and Being Seen: Emerging from a Psychic Retreat*. Hove & New York, NY: Routledge.

Sutton, J. (2018) The invisible handshake: A context for improvisation in music therapy. *British Journal of Music Therapy*, 32(2), pp.86-95.

Sutton, J. (2020) 'As Time Goes By…Music Psychotherapy and Trauma.' In A. Chesner & S. Lykou (eds) *Trauma in the Creative and Embodied Therapies* (pp.45–56). Abingdon: Routledge Mental Health.

Sutton, J. (2023) Silences on the edge of dreams. *British Journal of Music Therapy*, 37(2). Available at: https://doi.org/10.1177/13594575231165212 (Accessed 6 January 2024).

Wilson, S. (2018) (ed.) *Music – Psychoanalysis – Musicology*. Abingdon & New York, NY: Routledge.

Winnicott, D. W. (1960) The theory of the parent-infant relationship. *International Journal of Psychoanalysis*, 41, pp.585–595.

Winnicott, D. W. (1971) *Playing and Reality*. London: Tavistock Publications.

Zigaran, M. (2008) *Powers of Music: A Psychoanalytic Investigation about Music and Meaning*. Saarbrücken: VDM.

Contributors

Gabriela Santos Silva de Almeida was First Secretary of the São Paulo Association of Students and Music Therapists in 2022. She is a clinical supervisor, responsible for teaching supervision-based classes on topics related to clinical practices in Music Therapy and the application of Music Therapy within ABA science.

Luke Annesley worked in the NHS for Oxleas Music Therapy Service after training at the Guildhall School of Music & Drama in 2006–08. He has been a senior lecturer in music therapy at the University of the West of England, Bristol, since 2018 and produces and presents the BAMT podcast *Music Therapy Conversations*. He is also a jazz and improvising saxophone player, most recently heard on tour with John Wilson's Sinfonia of London and in his own projects such as the band Moonscape with trumpet player Jim Howard.

Mandy Carr, previously senior lecturer in dramatherapy at Anglia Ruskin University, is a freelance dramatherapist, creative arts supervisor and educator. Her passion for widening inclusion led to convening the British Association of Dramatherapists' Equality and Diversity Sub-Committee from 2007 to 2018. Having worked with vulnerable children and young people in urban areas, she is now in private practice. Relevant publications include 'An Exploration of Supervision in Education' in *Supervision of Dramatherapy* (2009) for Routledge, and with Amelia Oldfield she edited *Collaborations Within and Between Dramatherapy and Music Therapy* (2018) for Jessica Kingsley Publishers. In 2023, she completed a professional doctorate exploring the implications for dramatherapists and their clients of religious, spiritual and belief identities.

Michaela de Cruz is a music therapist, professional musician and recording artist from Singapore. As a relatively new member of the UK music therapy profession, Michaela has already left an imprint through antiracist activism, writing and ongoing community engagement. Michaela was a key member of the BAMT Racial Inequality Panel in 2021, leading to the co-founding of an independent global network for music therapists of colour. She runs a private practice working primarily with adults facing a range of mental health needs and offers a lecture series on Antiracism and Cultural Humility in Music Therapy for training programs in the UK.

Gustavo Schulz Gattino is a music therapist and associate professor in the Department of Communication and Psychology at Aalborg University, Denmark, where he teaches in the bachelor's, master's and doctoral programmes in music therapy and is accredited as a music therapist by the Portuguese Music Therapy Association. He is the North region coordinator and Denmark's country representative in the European Music Therapy Confederation, chair of the publication's commission of the World Federation of Music Therapy and a member of the International Music Therapy Assessment Consortium. Gustavo is a guest lecturer in music therapy at University Pablo Olavide (Spain), University of Barcelona (Spain), Music, Art and Process Institute (Spain) and Codarts University (Netherlands).

Nicky Haire has worked as a musician, educator and music therapist in a wide variety of contexts over 20 years. She is a lecturer at Queen Margaret University, Edinburgh. Her areas of practice include work with persons living with dementia, adults who have acquired brain injury and children and young people who are living with disabilities and mental health issues. She has led skill-sharing music projects in collaboration with local partners who are working with children living with disabilities in post-conflict communities in East and Central Africa and has coordinated the BAMT Scotland area group, and the BAMT Improvisation Network. Her doctoral study focuses on relational experiences and perceptions of humour in music therapy, specifically with persons living with dementia, and embraces arts-based critical reflexivity and thinking through improvisation.

Tatiana Harumi Komi graduated in music therapy from the Faculdades Metropolitanas Unidas, has a postgraduate qualification in autism spectrum disorder at Faculdade Unina (São Braz) in Curitiba, Brazil and is a postgraduate student in applied behavioural analysis intervention for autism and intellectual disabilities at the CBI of Miami, Brazil. Since 2018, she has worked with babies and children with atypical development, providing parental guidance and clinical supervision with a behavioural focus.

Sarah Caroline Jeronimo da Silva has an honours degree in music therapy from the University Centre of Faculdades Metropolitanas Unidas, Brazil. She is a specialist in applied music therapy from development to ageing at Santa Marcelina College and a postgraduate student in existential analysis and Franklian Logotherapy at the Ítalo Brasileiro University Centre.

Adam Kishtainy is currently a senior lecturer and clinic lead at the University of the West of England, also working as a music psychotherapist and clinical supervisor in private practice. He is an accredited Balint leader, working with trainee doctors in the NHS and also applying the Balint model to other professions, including music therapists, healthcare professionals, social prescribers and church leaders. Previously he has worked as a music psychotherapist on acute inpatient psychiatric wards, in a combined music therapist/chaplain role in a children's hospice and in areas including prisons, dementia and looked-after children. He is an improvising multi-instrumentalist who is particularly drawn to anything that can be plucked. Adam leads the Christians in Arts Therapy network, has a particular interest in the role of spirituality in therapeutic practice and is lead pastor of a church in Bristol.

Andy Lale is a music therapist who specialises in music psychotherapy as an effective mental health tool. Following his qualification in music therapy from Roehampton University in 1998, Andy went on to study an MA in psychoanalytic psychotherapy at the Tavistock Institute, London. His clinical focus has always been on the process of projective identification within the transference field, and how to use this intelligently as a clinical tool. After 25 years with the NHS, Andy now works independently, supervising and maintaining a small cohort of private cases.

Jane Lings has wide range of clinical experience, which includes 15 years working in palliative care. In semi-retirement, she has a multi-professional private supervision practice and works in a women's prison leading choirs and facilitating a small song-writing project for mothers. Jane has previously combined work as a clinician in an adult hospice with a senior lecturer role at the University of the West of England. Multi-professional supervision began at the hospice when she was asked to supervise nurses. She supervises other professionals in palliative care and justice system contexts. She regularly presents at conferences and has previously been published in palliative care, bereavement and songwriting contexts.

Anna Macken is a music therapist in the UK, working with children and young people in specialist educational settings which support people with challenging behaviours and social, emotional and mental health issues, and adults in the community who have been marginalised by society and are facing issues relating to previously unprocessed adverse childhood experiences and trauma. She is the fundraising lead for music therapy charity Waves Music Therapy and is passionate about the work she undertakes on behalf of Waves, sharing the ethos that there should be no barriers (financial, social or physical) to accessing clinical music therapy or meaningful musical engagement.

Hilary Moss is Professor of Music Therapy at the University of Limerick, Ireland, and previously the director of the National Centre for Arts and Health, Dublin. She has over 25 years of research and practice experience as a music therapist and manager in mental health, older age and adult medical environments, as well as supervising numerous music therapists. She has published widely on music therapy and music and health topics, and her book *Music and Creativity in Healthcare Settings* was published by Routledge in 2021.

Júlio Ramon Oliveira is a music therapist working with autistic people since 2016 and is the first music therapist in Brazil to work for Amil, which is part of the United Health Group based in the USA. She currently specialises in neurology at Albert Einstein Israelite Hospital in São Paulo and is a lecturer on music therapy postgraduate courses. She also works in applied behavioural analysis clinics implementing music therapy.

Sally Pestell is a freelance music therapist and a member of the Cornwall Music Service Trust therapy team, working with adults and children in various settings. Her focus is working with people who have advanced dementia, and she has presented this work at various conferences in the UK. Recently, Sally has returned to work in both primary and secondary schools as a music therapist, supporting young people with emotional and mental health issues. She is also an Advanced Level Guided Imagery and Music trainee.

Simon Procter is Director of Music Services responsible for oversight of education, research and public affairs activities for Nordoff and Robbins in London. He has worked in a wide range of settings, most recently within adult mental health services. As a trainer, he emphasises the importance of developing acute musical-personal awareness coupled with practical musical means of actively and imaginatively helping people to flourish, and as an ethnographic researcher he is interested in the craft skills required of music therapists so that their work can be as useful as possible.

Maria Radoje undertook the first clinical supervision training for music therapists at the University of the West of England in 2016, and has a private practice that incorporates supervision, music therapy and Guided Imagery and Music (GIM). She is an experienced music therapist who has worked in dementia care and adult mental health, as well as leading music therapy teams in learning disability services. Maria is passionate about using GIM with arts therapy trainees, as well as her work with the British Association for Performing Arts Medicine, with performers, musicians and actors, addressing a range of mental health issues. Maria has also lectured at the University of South Wales and the Academy of Contemporary Music and has several publications.

Joyce Ribeiro graduated in transverse flute from the São Paulo State School of Music, graduated in music therapy from Faculdades Metropolitanas Unidas and is a postgraduate student in applied behaviour analysis at the Metropolitan University in São Paulo. She has worked as a music educator and in early childhood education for nine years and is currently a clinical music therapist in neurodevelopmental rehabilitation institutions.

Joy Rickwood is a music therapist and supervisor with a special interest in supervision and arts therapies with people with a learning disability. She trained at the University of Roehampton. Joy is professional lead for arts therapies and lead arts therapist for learning disabilities for Aneurin Bevan University Health Board. The team there are exploring and developing outcome measures and evaluation with co-productive colleagues. Joy loves to sing and has run a rural community choir since 2012.

Sophie Riga de Spinoza originally trained as an integrative psychotherapist, then qualified as a music therapist from the University of Roehampton. Much of her work has been in the education sector, specialising in children with learning disabilities, as well as sibling and family work. She has a special interest in bereavement, using music as part of a wider creative arts method of support. Recently, Sophie has joined the Apricot Centre in Suffolk as part of their Wellbeing Service, to work with children who are adopted, fostered or under special guardianship, and their families. She is a creative arts supervisor, and as part of her private practice provides individual and group supervision in the arts, education, arts therapies and charity sectors as well as presenting on supervision at conferences. She has previously been a guest lecturer on the Creative Arts Supervision Training Diploma, based at the Royal Central School of Speech and Drama.

Jemima Rodrigues has an honours degree in music therapy from the Faculdades Metropolitanas Unidas, Brazil, and a postgraduate degree in applied behavioural analysis for autism and intellectual disabilities from the CBI of Miami. Her MBA from the Business Behavior Institute of Chicago focused on burnout syndrome. She currently works with autistic people but has also worked with adolescents, adults and the ageing population. She facilitates drum circles and has volunteered in Portugal and Spain.

Ann Sloboda has been Head of Music Therapy at the Guildhall School of Music & Drama since 2005. She is a qualified psychoanalyst and a member of the British Psychoanalytical Society and is a tutor in infant observation to trainee psychoanalysts. After qualifying from the Guildhall Music Therapy training in 1985 she worked as a music therapist in the NHS for over 20 years. A past chair of the Association of Professional Music Therapists, she was Head of Arts Therapies at West London Mental Health Trust for ten years where she developed art, drama and music therapy provision in medium and low secure forensic services. She has worked in the fields of adult learning disability, eating disorders, general and forensic mental health and post-traumatic stress disorder. She currently divides her time between the role at Guildhall, her psychoanalytic practice, supervision of trainee and qualified music therapists and playing the piano.

Hilary Storer studied the oboe at the Royal College of Music and pursued a career as an orchestral oboist, becoming a member of the BBC Philharmonic and playing with many orchestras throughout the country. Later in life she returned to studying and completed her music therapy training at the University of the West of England, later gaining fellowships in neurologic music therapy and the Bonny Method of Guided Imagery and Music. She has since worked predominantly in the field of neuro-disability and rehabilitation. She also has experience of working with people with dementia in care settings and has a special interest in music therapy for adults with cancer using the Bonny Method of Guided Imagery and Music.

Dr Julie Sutton is a psychoanalyst working in private practice. During 2020 she retired after almost four decades of music therapy work, during which she specialised in therapeutic and musical processes, and psychological trauma. She was a past Head of Training for Nordoff and Robbins London and was editor-in-chief of the *British Journal of Music Therapy*. She published and presented widely about music therapy and was active in roles within different areas of Europe. She continues as an author and researcher and is registered with the International Psychoanalytical Association and the British Psychoanalytic Council, and is a full member of the Northern Ireland Psychoanalytic Society. She is a member of the European Psychoanalytical Confederation.

Davina Vencatasamy is a music therapist and supervisor, and a PhD student at Lesley University, USA. Her music therapy practice in the UK has spanned 19 years across a wide range of fields, specialising in children with learning disabilities in special educational needs settings. She has worked in a therapeutic community prison and is currently working in a specialist child and adolescent mental health

NHS setting. She is a qualified eye movement desensitization and reprocessing (EMDR) therapist. Davina has provided supervision for a range of professionals and is currently a mentor for newly qualified music therapists as part of the Newly Qualified Music Therapist BAMT programme. She is on the board of directors for a small arts organisation and is conductor for their orchestra, set up to address issues of race and diversity in music.

Catherine Warner is a musician and music therapist based in Bristol, UK. Catherine was programme leader of the MA in music therapy and a senior lecturer at the University of the West of England. She also oversees the supervision training for music therapists at UWE, is the chair of the BAMT Training and Education Committee and chairs the education working group for the European Consortium of Arts Therapies Trainers. Her doctoral research was based on using music therapy groups as participatory action research with people with learning disabilities, and her research interests cover music therapy training experiences, and music therapy for early trauma. She regularly engages in discussions at a national level relating to equity and diversity in training.

Abigail Williams is a music therapist and supervisor who has a special interest working in the adoption community and with people with a learning disability. Abby graduated from the University of the West of England in 2012 and completed the Supervision of Music Therapists training at the same institution in 2019. Abby was a music therapist and senior arts therapist at National Star College in Cheltenham for ten years. There she developed an in-house supervision service for the team of music therapists, dramatherapists and dance and movement psychotherapists, which included individual and mixed-modality group supervision. Abby is currently a music therapist for the learning disabilities service within the Aneurin Bevan University Health Board. She runs a local community choir and plays in a samba band.

Robin Wiltshire is a music therapist and supervisor and is a group analytic psychotherapist. His music therapy practice has spanned over 20 years across a range of services, including adult learning disabilities, adult/older people's mental health and adult palliative care. This has involved providing individual and group music therapy. He is a trained clinical supervisor in psychodynamic supervision and has a small supervision practice. Robin is regularly with The Golden Thread Playback Theatre Company as their musician, performing and working with communities across Wales and the South west of England.

Oksana Zharinova-Sanderson trained as a pianist in Ukraine and as a music therapist at Nordoff and Robbins, London. Her experience as a music therapist covers work with traumatised refugees and torture survivors (Germany), neurological rehabilitation, oncology and mental health (UK). She is currently one of the directors of music services at Nordoff and Robbins UK, chief practitioner of the charity and one of the directors of the Nordoff and Robbins International Trust. Utilising her experience as educator and supervisor, she teaches on the Nordoff and Robbins master's programme, supervises music therapists and runs a mentoring programme for supervisors.

Index